Wearing Chinese Glasses

How **not** to Go Broke in Chinese Asia

Gregory A. Bissky

Book Design by Greg Bissky
Cover Design by Victor Crapnell

Note for Librarians: A cataloguing record for this book is available from Library and Archives Canada at www.collectionscanada.ca/amicus/index-e.html
ISBN 1-4251-1186-6

PUBLISHING™

Offices in Canada, USA, Ireland and UK

Book sales for North America and international:
Trafford Publishing, 6E–2333 Government St.,
Victoria, BC V8T 4P4 CANADA
phone 250 383 6864 (toll-free 1 888 232 4444)
fax 250 383 6804; email to orders@trafford.com
Book sales in Europe:
Trafford Publishing (UK) Limited, 9 Park End Street, 2nd Floor
Oxford, UK OX1 1HH UNITED KINGDOM
phone +44 (0)1865 722 113 (local rate 0845 230 9601)
facsimile +44 (0)1865 722 868; info.uk@trafford.com
Order online at:
trafford.com/06-2945

10 9 8 7 6 5 4 3 2

To

three generations of women in my life,
Elsie May, Carol and Katya May,
mother, wife and daughter.

It wouldn't have been as much fun without you.

Thanks ladies.

About The Author

Greg Bissky arrived in Chinese Asia in early 1985, planning to stay for 18 months then to return to Canada for a Ph.D. His plan changed, and, to his surprise, he returned home fourteen years later, bringing Chinese wife, young daughter and list of Chinese clients with him. He now lives in Canada but works in Chinese Asia, traveling often and living in the Chinese time zone.

Greg knows the Chinese like few others. Business owner as well as consultant, he negotiates and implements contracts, leading region-wide productivity-improvement projects (reengineering, performance management and balanced scorecard). He is as comfortable on the factory floor as in the boardroom, and as familiar setting region-wide strategy as he is implementing it at the lowest levels. Greg has been there and done that.

An accomplished teacher, since 1988 he has taught Chinese his 3-day *Logical Thinking and Communication* workshop. Teaching logic gives him a unique view into Chinese thinking and communication. Greg also teaches cross-culture to Chinese and Westerners, teaching Westerners how to overcome Chinese complaints and Chinese how to deal with Western complaints. Working both sides of the street is a virtuous circle: the more he teaches one side the more he learns about the other.

Greg is an optimist, and believes that working with the Chinese is not as mysterious as many think. If you know how to make a marriage work or how to make a best friend in your hometown, you already know how to succeed in Chinese Asia. The key is the ability to *see* things as Chinese see them. A cultural optometrist, he wrote this book to give you a pair of Chinese glasses. Don't wear them and you do business in China blind, and that is never good.

Greg never did the Ph.D., attaining instead an MBA (Masters of Business in Asia).

Contents

Section 2: Using Chinese Glasses (Applying the Rules)

Maps, Diagrams, Tables, Case Studies and Tips

It is only the wisest
and the most stupid
who cannot change

Confucius

For Those Who Just Want Things To Work

Friends, clients and family pushed me for years to write this book. My standard excuse was I never had time. A shift in career focus a few years back changed that. For my 50th birthday present to myself I stopped leading projects in Chinese Asia and returned to my first love, cross-culture.

Leading projects is game for youngsters, especially when you live 15 times zones from your team. No more working Chinese hours and two-hour conference calls at 3AM, no more trying to cope with outrageous policies, decisions and deadlines made in a HQ office 5000 comfortable miles away from the Chinese front lines, no more struggling to get Chinese from different departments, locations and countries to work together, or work period. Held responsible for results with nothing but the power of persuasion to force action is … tiring. A job best left to the young.

I had time on my side, finally a 9-5 job, comfy in my home office. I had time to write. Sure I did. I discovered old clients don't give up easily, and *no* projects became *few* projects. But I still had time, loads of it. Where to start, what to write? Easy I thought. Just go to my "ideas" file, scribbles made on scraps of paper over the years, ideas I'd had in airport lounges, dinners-for-one or boring meeting. What I found were strange drawings and cryptic sentences that no doubt were brilliant when I'd made them but now were just so many lines and words. They just added to my confusion. Where to start?

This took the better part of a year, puttering, stuck in neutral. Then a brainstorm: why not write like a teacher, not a writer. Ah.

Something I knew how to do. My focus on teaching explains the book. I have treated the pages as minutes, parts of an all-day class I am teaching. I have looked at the book exactly as I look at a room full of people—I may never see them (you) again, and this is my one chance to pass on what I know.

I dislike jargon. In Graduate school we students were asked what we planned to do with our degree. Trembling, we said pollster, organizer, aide, teacher, even lawyer, all respectable, predictable *Political Science* (my department) professions. My turn: "I'd like to write a magazine on international politics sold beside the tabloids in supermarket lineups. I can explain international politics using backyard politics as examples, a neighbor's tree on your property, fixing a common fence, loud music at night. The principles are the same." Professors were not amused. I have followed that approach, using everyday examples to explain complicated subjects, in everything I have done since, including this book.

Every day airplanes land in Chinese Asian airports full of Westerners who just want to make a buck. Every day the internet hums with emails from back office staff who just want to make sense of the latest message from their Chinese partner, supplier or vendor. Every day Western managers of Western companies in Chinese Asia just want to figure out how to manage and motivate their Chinese organization. This book is for them, the Westerners who just want to make what they are doing **work**.

Putting my 'teach, not write' focus and my everyday examples and language together explains the conversational tone I hope I have managed throughout the book. As one kind friend put it, "It is just like you are standing there in front of me speaking the book." That familiarity is certainly what I have tried to achieve: instead of just 'reading' the book, I have tried to make it as if you and I are just talking about things Chinese. To paraphrase Martha Stewart, I hope you consider that a Good Thing … especially when I ask questions.

Finally, I am the first to recognize that I repeat myself, explaining the same key points in different ways in different chapters. Blame the teacher in me, my desire to make sure that you leave the class (er, book) with a pair of Chinese glasses of your own. This is a book on the fundamentals, Chinese 101, and your understanding of certain themes is far more important than wading through a long list of specific techniques, strategies or dos and don'ts. My hope is that after this book, after you've put on your Chinese glasses, you will be better able to benefit from learning advanced techniques, the dos and don'ts. I certainly was.

Greg Bissky
Room 901, Hotel Royal, Hsin Chu, Taiwan
November 1, 2005

CHAPTER ONE

My First Pair Of Chinese Glasses

The plane rolled to a stop at Chiang Kai-Shek[1] airport in Taiwan and the fasten seatbelt light went off. People surged out of their seats, opening overhead bins, hoisting luggage and struggling to be first off the plane. I sat, nervous and unsure of what to do next. It was just before midnight on January 10, 1985, and here I was, my first time to Asia. Alone. I did not know one person, could not speak Chinese and had no idea what to do next, how to get to Taipei or even where to stay that night. Making things worse, I had bought a one-way ticket across the Pacific. I did have money in my pocket, but not enough to buy a ticket home. I was not nervous. I was scared.

Chinese friends and professors at my universities[2] had told me not to worry, that the Chinese[3] were very friendly and that it was easy to find work and to make friends. They were right. Phew. I was teaching English three days after arrival. After three weeks I was living with a Chinese family and had made two groups of Chinese friends. I started to relax. Life was good. It did not last.

In the sixth week I deeply offended the family and one group of friends, and had no idea why or how I had done it. I was embarrassed but even more I was confused. What had just happened? Answering that question changed my life and is the real start of this book, and my career. Not knowing what happened bothered me for two years; it took me that long to figure it out. By then I was hooked on trying to understand the Chinese-Western divide.

My original plan was to stay one year in Taiwan then six months in China to learn the language, then to return to the West to do a Ph.D. in modern Chinese politics. Like all plans it changed, and I ended up living in Chinese Asia[4] for 14 years. Why? Within six months I realized what I had learned in books about the Chinese was … not quite right. The deeper I got into life in Chinese Asia the more I realized that life on the Chinese street was different from life described in books about the Chinese. Not wrong exactly, just not quite right.

An Unexpected Fourteen Years in Chinese Asia

I decided as my goal was to learn how the Chinese *really were* then to act as bridge between West and East, the smarter thing to do was to learn about the Chinese by living with them, not by returning to the West and learning from books. I gave up the Ph.D. idea and plunged into life in Taiwan. I married a Chinese woman then divorced her. I started my own company and built it to 25 people then went spectacularly bankrupt. I started over with nothing in a new career as a management consultant/trainer, and built a successful niche firm that has led to travel and work throughout Chinese Asia, Europe and North America. I married another Chinese woman and had a daughter. In 1998 I moved our little family back to Canada but kept working in Chinese Asia, traveling frequently and working the Chinese time zone. Now past the 20-year mark, I look back and smile at that scared young man on the airplane, wondering what would happen once he got the courage to get off the plane. Life ended up good.

It was not always good. During my years in Chinese Asia I had incredible highs but even more incredible lows. I made almost every mistake imaginable, found myself in difficult, often bizarre situations. A client sued me and, alone and in Chinese, I defended myself (successfully) from a charge of criminal fraud.[5] I ran afoul of Chinese gangsters over money borrowed to keep my first company afloat. For a friend I organized an all-day outdoor rock festival, one of the first ever in Taiwan. I hired the bands, arranged MTV to cover the event, begged (and bribed) various levels of government to let us use a municipal stadium, worked with artists and PR types to design the posters, logos and bus ads, planned and made proposals to potential corporate sponsors then baby-sat them once signed, and hired and managed the security and event staff. A huge effort, the concert finally went ahead, only to be *ty-phooned* by Tim. As concerts should, it ended with a bang, just one band early. The grand finale was Typhoon Tim flying the stage decorations up in the air then crashing them down on top of the drummer. Spectacular.

There are more tales to tell but you get the picture. I can't say I did it all, no one can, but I did do a lot in my years in Chinese Asia. I learned from each experience, often the type of lessons that money can't buy (but you sure can pay for!). Each lesson, each mistake (and each success) added to my understanding of how Chinese think, work and communicate, what motivates them and what turns them off, what works and what doesn't. I still don't have 20:20 vision wearing Chinese glasses, but each lesson helped me see a little bit more clearly. What I saw through my Chinese glasses helped me understand *why* things happened as they did; without understanding that I surely would have burnt out early as most Westerners do. Without Chinese glasses, I never would have stayed as long as I did.

Getting My First Chinese Glasses

How I got my first pair of Chinese glasses is a story in itself. I had been in Taiwan about two years and had just started my first business. I was in a taxi heading to a meeting. As usual, the taxi driver was auditioning for Death Race 2000 and I was cowering in the backseat (my plea to drive slower only made him drive faster). He ran a red light and … I saw the car coming and … my life flashed in front of my eyes, certain I was going to die. Somehow, he avoided an accident. As my heart raced and I caught my breath, a thought popped into my head, that 'Chinese have their own rules for doing things, for acting and for communicating, and that these rules are different than my (Western) rules.' It sounds simple, but that thought changed my life. In retrospect, I should have tipped the taxi driver.

'Hmm,' I thought, 'if Chinese have their own way of thinking, of looking at things, then in order to understand them I need to learn how Chinese see things.' There they were, my first pair of Chinese glasses. Once I put them on I began to see things in a new way, began to understand why this had happened, why that hadn't worked and why I had made so many mistakes. It was an amazing if also humbling experience. Best of all, I began to understand how I had offended my Chinese family and friends way back at the beginning, and was finally able to remove the pebble in my shoe that had been bothering me for two years. Figuring out what had happened changed my feelings towards the Chinese and put me on a new path, a path I still travel. I start every workshop, speech or discussion, for Chinese and for Westerners, with this example, the story of three invitations to dinner.

Accepting Three Invitations To Dinner

I was in Taiwan for six weeks, living with a Chinese family and with two groups of Chinese friends. All conversations below happened in English; after only six weeks of Chinese lessons all I could say that Chinese understood was, "I don't understand." Chinese New Years (CNY) was coming soon. I knew it was important, the most important Chinese cultural holiday of the year.

CNY dominated the conversations, them explaining New Year's traditions and me comparing their traditions to Western Christmas traditions. There are an amazing amount of similarities, like special foods and music, decorating the house and gift giving. Each conversation followed the same pattern, with my friends or the father of my Chinese family; during each I asked similar questions and received similar answers.

Sometime during each conversation the subject of CNY Eve came up. I was told New Year's Eve was the most important night of the (14-day) holiday, that this was the night when the family **had** to be together for dinner. Each group told me that there were no stores open on New Year's Eve, no restaurants open, nowhere for me to eat dinner, a situation that would last for 3-4 days.[6] Intrigued and eager to make friends, I hoped one of the groups or the Chinese father would invite me for dinner.

Before I go on, a question. Say I am in your hometown during Christmas, alone in a hotel. Being nice, you think no one should be alone at Christmas, so you decide to invite me to join your family for Christmas dinner. How would you invite me? Not would you phone or ask me face to face, but what words would you say to invite me?

Being polite, you would probably start by asking if I was doing anything that night. Discovering I was free you would likely say something like, "Well Greg, no one should be alone at Christmas. Would you like to join my family for Christmas dinner?" This is a yes/no question, a question with only three possible answers: 'yes, I'd love to,' 'no, I can't,' or 'I am not sure right now; I will call you tomorrow and let you know.' Every Western invitation uses a yes/no question format, includes a 'would you like to?' type of sentence. It's black and white: without a yes/no question there is no invitation, period. Westerners can hint about an invitation, sure, but the invitation itself must use a direct yes/no question. No yes/no question, no invitation, no exceptions.

What is a Westerner?

By Westerner I mean people born and educated in Europe, Canada, USA, Australia and New Zealand. It has nothing to do with skin color or ethnic background. Anyone can become a Westerner.

Where is Chinese Asia?

Chinese Asia includes the four Chinas, China, Taiwan, Hong Kong and Singapore, and, as far as communication and most values, beliefs and actions are concerned, Korea and Japan as well.

Are there differences between Americans, English, French and Dutch, or between China, Singapore and Taiwan Chinese, or between Chinese, Japanese and Korean? Yes, of course. Nevertheless, on the subjects in this book, especially communication, these groups are far more similar than different.

Table 1: What is a Westerner? Where is Chinese Asia?

Back to the story. After each group told me there were no restaurants or stores open on New Year's Eve, each then asked if I was doing anything that night. Expectant that an invitation would soon follow I eagerly answered no, that I was free that night. Each group then told me something about what would happen at their homes that night, how much fun CNY Eve would be. By now I was on the edge of my chair, waiting for the question, 'Would you like to …?' Waiting to hear it, jump up and say Yes! But the question never came. No one, not friend nor father, asked anything like 'Would you like to ….' I was never able to jump up and say Yes.

I was confused. It was almost like the Chinese were *playing* with me, getting me all excited about an invitation … then not inviting me. I knew I still had a lot to learn though, and decided maybe there was some tradition that said only family could join for New Year's dinner, that my friends were just being polite to me, something like that. Whatever, the morning of Chinese New Year's Eve I woke up with nowhere to eat dinner that night. I figured I would just buy some chips and beer and eat alone in my room. (Pre- 7/11 Chinese convenience stores are another tale.)

The telephone rang at 11:00am. It was my Group A friends (to make things clear I call them my Group A and Group B friends). The conversation went, "Greg we will pick you up for dinner at 6:00 tonight." Their meaning was not, 'Dinner is at 6:00. Can you come?' It was, '[Greg, we've already invited you, you've already said yes] we are now confirming the pickup time.'

I was both surprised and confused, but kept both to myself. I answered, "6:00. Great." I put the phone down, lit a *Long Life*[7] cigarette and thought, 'When did they invite me? When did I say yes?' I was happy I had somewhere to eat dinner that night, but, still, when did they invite me? When did I say yes? I thought over all of our conversations but with no success: I could not recall any invitation, or where I had said Yes to anything. 'Oh well,' I thought, 'I must have missed something. No big deal. At least I have somewhere to eat dinner tonight!' I finished the cigarette and put it out happy, thinking about going out and buying some flowers. You can't go to dinner without a gift.

I stayed happy for 30 minutes, until the telephone rang again. It was my Group B friends. "Greg we will pick you up for dinner at 6:30 tonight." Huh? Group B's call was not to invite me. Like Group A, both their invitation and my acceptance seemed (to them) to be a done deal. This call was just to set a time and place for pick up. Huh?

I had to say something; I now was going somewhere else so I had to speak up, plus I was confused. "James, I'm sorry, I can't go with you tonight; I'm going somewhere else."

"But we invited you Greg and you said yes." Huh?!? Just when were these invitations happening?!? When was I saying yes?

A few more words and I hung up, more than embarrassed. I knew all about the Chinese opinion that Westerners are impolite, the 'ugly Westerner,' and was determined never to be ugly. Yet here I was, being the ugliest of Westerners possible, accepting an invitation *to the most important night of the year* and then, at the absolute last moment, saying, 'oh yeah, sorry, I have decided to go somewhere else instead.' A long way from home, lonely and desperate to make friends, I had just done something unlikely to gain new friends[8]. I lit another Long Life cigarette, sat back and tried to puzzle it out. *What* had happened? *How* had it happened?

I went over every conversation with both groups. I had beers with both, but used to play rugby and I knew how to drink. There was no way that I was so drunk I missed an invitation, not one I had been fishing for. Certainly not twice! It was not a language problem; sure, they spoke 'Chinglish' (Chinese English) but it was good Chinglish and I understood every word.[9] I was 100% sure that no one had invited me to dinner, absolutely certain there was never a chance to say 'Yes.' I sat there in the living room, chain smoking, trying to figure it out. A bad situation, right? It was about to get worse.

The father of my Chinese family had good English, and had listened to my side of both telephone conversations. As I sat chain smoking and scratching my thinning hair he came up to me and, with a real long face, said, "But Greg, you said you were having dinner with us tonight." Huh?!? What!?!

Not once, not twice, but **three** times I had been invited to the most important dinner of the year. All three times the Chinese thought I had understood the invitation and had clearly said Yes. In all three times not only did I not know I had been invited, *I had no idea I had said Yes!* How did that happen? Why did that happen? These questions plagued me for two years. Not until I put on my first pair of Chinese glasses did I even begin to answer them.

So, what happened? I pose this question to my Chinese and Western workshop students. Westerners usually look up with a blank expression; most have no idea. Those with the most wrinkles on their China hands sometimes suggest it happened because of culture and Chinese being polite, but that's as far as they go. The question and the example puzzle Westerners. Interesting though, when I ask if anyone has a similar type of experience in

Chinese Asia a few always raise their hands. Chinese are a little more forthcoming but still dance around the subject, offering the same 'because of culture' suggestions. The best answer, that I had not say no. "True," I replied, "but how could I say No when there was no invitation, no yes/no question to say No to?" No answer.

A Common Language Is Not Enough

I answer the 'what happened' question in detail later in the book;[10] for now let me just stress once again that it was not a language problem, i.e., not a grammar, pronunciation or vocabulary problem. It was a 'way language is used' problem. This is a crucial distinction.

People think all that you need for successful cross-culture communication is a language in common. Any language works, as long as both parties understand it. Without a language in common (or a translator, another subject covered later in the book) you can't do business. While body language can work for a bar-type conversation, it is impossible to negotiate the terms and conditions of a contract without spoken/written language.

When cross-culture communication problems happen—like Smith-Chen in the next chapter—both Westerners and Chinese tend to think it is because their language skills are not enough.[11] Language skills are important, true, and poor skills often do cause communication problems, but most cross-culture communication problems come from using language the wrong way, not bad speling, grammar or pronunciation.

Every culture has unique Rules of Communication, a set of Rules on proper language use. We learn these Rules as children from parents and teachers, learn how to be polite when communicating. Once out in the real world the Rules determine how we communicate with coworkers, bosses, friends and family. The best way to introduce the Rules of Communication concept to you is to examine the difference between Chinese and Western Rules about an everyday issue, what to do when you don't know something.

The Western Rules of Communication in this case is 'ask questions if you don't understand,' the Chinese Rule is 'don't let people know you don't understand something.' I see the effects of this Rule every time I teach a class or lead a meeting. Westerners raise their hands often, usually not embarrassed to ask questions in front of others. Chinese tend not to raise their hands, even when I ask if there are any questions. Instead, Chinese wait until a break and then, alone with me, ask a question.

This Rule has a dramatic effect on how Westerners manage meetings in Chinese Asia (and many other areas as well). The Westerner (usually the boss) makes a point or outlines a policy and asks if there are any questions. If no one asks a question she assumes that everyone understands and/or agrees, so moves on to the next point. After the meeting the Chinese attendees meet and ask each other, "What do you think she meant by that? What do you think she wants us to do?" If the Westerner is lucky, and creates the opportunity by making herself available, the Chinese will come by themselves to ask a question in private. If unlucky, say she leaves right away and doesn't create an opportunity for Chinese to speak in private, the Chinese will not ask a question. This creates two ways to lose: the Chinese will be unsure what to do (so may do the wrong things) and the Westerner will think the Chinese know what to do (so will not think to offer help or further explanations).

This is the start of a 'going broke' relationship. What will likely happen when the Western boss discovers the Chinese are not doing the right thing … as they *agreed* to do (silence means Yes in the West)? The boss will ask why. The Chinese answer, 'I didn't understand what to do,' will not be very satisfying. Their answer to the next question, 'Why didn't you ask me,' likely an embarrassed silence or a sheepish 'I don't know,' will be less satisfying. Relationships need trust to succeed, and the Western boss might start to wonder if she could trust Chinese staff to ask questions if they did not understand something. If the Westerner forces the issue, say making a big fuss about asking questions and such, especially (as usually happens) in a group situation so that everyone gets embarrassed, Chinese might in turn start not to trust the Westerner as 'she doesn't respect our feelings.'

I examine how to deal—as best you can—with this situation in a later chapter. For now I just want you to notice that this 'no questions' problem has nothing to do with language skills. Both sides understood the words said, they just had different ideas about how   to use language to deal with asking and answering questions. The Westerner thought questions should be asked openly, Chinese thought questions should be asked in private. Neither side was wrong, they just used their own Rules to communicate, not the other sides' Rules. They wore their own glasses, not the other culture's.

This small example illustrates the key problem in West-East communication. Unaware of the Chinese way of using language, of the Chinese Rules of Communication, Westerners listen to spoken words with Western ears, read written messages with Western eyes and supply meaning to words by applying Western Rules of how language is used. Chinese do the same, only with Chinese ears, eyes and thinking. Both sides use only their own glasses. Still confused? Here is another example, another mistake of mine. Sigh.

Disagreeing Without Disagreeing

After about two years in Taiwan I was ready (so I thought) to start my own business, offering high-end, professional business English, management training and management consulting. A management consultant only really needs two things to be successful, a tie and a briefcase. The client has everything else; the consultant just takes the client's information, repackages it then sells it back to the client. The ties and briefcase are needed for appearances: you make a wrong first impression walking into the client's office in a T-shirt with your papers in a plastic, supermarket bag. I already had a tie. This is the story of buying my first briefcase.

First, let me ask you question. Say you and your wife (or husband) were shopping. You choose a briefcase to buy and ask her opinion. She *totally disagrees* with your choice, and wants to *make sure* you *don't* buy it. How does she tell you not to buy it? Does she simply hint the 'don't buy' message, hoping you figure out what she means, or does she come right out and say some type of a clear, "I don't think you should buy it" direct sentence?

Most Westerners say their (Western) wife or husband would disagree openly, using some type of a direct sentence. It might start out being quite polite, maybe some hints about not to buy it. If the hints were not understood though, direct words would follow. If it is important to them that you don't buy it, your spouse will eventually be clear and direct with disagreement. Why?

In the West more important than being polite is being clear: results matter more than form or style. The spouse will judge communication success by whether you understand the message—did you buy the briefcase or not—not by how polite the message was. The stronger your spouse disagrees the clearer disagreement will be. No matter the final words used, one thing is sure: before finished, you will know your spouse thinks you should not buy the briefcase. Disagreement would be clear.

On with the story. It was a momentous time for me, about to start my first business and just recently married. My Chinese wife[12] was a graduate of Taiwan Normal University, English Department, and was a High School English teacher. You would think this meant her English was good, but … let me just say her knowledge of grammar was better than her spoken English (a common combination). To help her improve her spoken English (to talk to my family and friends) we normally spoke English to each other, as we did in this story.

My wife and I went to a local leather-goods store. While I looked at briefcases, she examined the purses. Finding what I liked I called her over, showed her my choice and asked, "What do you think?" She looked at the price tag, then at the price tags on other briefcases, and replied, "It's more expensive than the other ones, isn't it?"

"Yes, but I don't think that is most important." I explained why, that it was only a little bit more expensive than the others but was better quality and would last longer, thus a better value. I added that it was also a successful-looking briefcase, important in creating that key first impression. After I finished explaining, I asked her what she thought now. "It's pretty small isn't it?"

"Yes, that is one reason I want it." I said that no matter the size you always fill your briefcase (or purse), making a large briefcase a heavy briefcase, which I didn't want. Adding some humor, I then explained another point in favor of a small briefcase, that, tends to be true, the higher your position in a company the smaller your briefcase. A big boss does not carry a briefcase; he is followed by assistants who carry his briefcase. As I was Boss of my new company (delivery boy too) I wanted a small, boss-size briefcase. I finished my explanation of why small was good, turned and asked, "What do you think?" She was silent. I thought that meant she agreed. I bought it. A big mistake.

Three steps out of the store she turned to me and, angrier than I had ever seen, yelled, "Why did you buy that briefcase? I *told* you not to!" Surprised, my immediate response was, "No you didn't." "Yes I did." *No you didn't! Yes I did!!* **Didn't! Did!** We argued about it for three days. So much for the honeymoon.

In a formal or ideal Western sense, did she tell me, *Don't Buy It?* I don't think so. My wife maybe hinted at disagreement, but certainly did not make her disagreement clear. Viewed through Western glasses all she did was raise two objections: maybe it was too expensive and maybe it was too small. I dealt with each objection in turn.

I first explained that I thought better value was more important than the slightly higher price, and then asked what she thought. That gave my wife two choices. If my 'better value' argument did not convince her (did not satisfy her objection), she could move from objection to disagreement, words like, "Well, I still think it's too expensive. Don't buy it." Her other choice was to signal agreement (I had satisfied her objection) by being silent or by changing the subject. She changed the subject.

We then repeated the process. I asked her was she thought, then tried to satisfy her 'too small?' objection with my 'small is good' argument. That gave her the same two choices: go from objection to disagreement, or to express agreement by agreeing, changing the subject or being silent. She was silent. I took her silence to mean she agreed, to mean I had satisfied her objections. Not once did I think she disagreed (my side of our marathon argument). Since then others have told me I could have been more sensitive to her—I agree—but most Westerners still say my wife never clearly *disagreed*.

Chinese students think otherwise. When I say the 'price' part of this example women in my Chinese classes start to smile; when I tell the 'too small' part the men start to smile: when I ask if my wife 'disagreed' with me, almost all Chinese say she did. Clearly disagreed too. Huh?

Objection vs. Disagreement

An objection is actually a request for more information before you can make a decision. Let's say I propose a course of action in a meeting and ask if there any questions. A person asks if I could offer more information about X. I do, and wait: if my explanation satisfies him about X he says so or is silent; if it doesn't he tells me so, and thus will move from raising an objection to disagreement, maybe by saying, "Well, I still am not convinced about X so I can't agree." Objections are fluid, disagreements are final.

Sure, office politics can be so bad that people won't disagree openly when asked their opinion, and then later disagree behind the scenes. Most Westerns think behind-the-back disagreement is bad manners (or worse).

Another Western Rule of Communication is "state your opinion, even if you disagree." This Rule is why Westerners consider silence to mean agreement.

Table 2: Objection vs. Disagreement

My wife thought she had clearly disagreed with my buying that briefcase, and I had refused to listen to her, that I *defied* her! This was why she was so angry. I did not understand (then) how she could say that, especially as I thought I had included her in the decision, each time asking, "What do you think honey?" This was why I argued back so strenuously: How could she accuse me of defying her when she had never told me she disagreed, and I had been so nice? This argument was the start of our relationship moving to the 'going broke' stage: she began to think that I would not listen to her and I thought she was accusing me of doing something I knew I had not done. Eight stormy months later we separated, and divorced soon after.

Who was wrong? What happened? How could my wife (and my Chinese students) think she clearly disagreed? The problem was the glasses we wore. While we used English words, my wife followed the Chinese way of using language to communicate disagreement. Unaware of this, I listened to her words with Western ears, analyzed the meaning of her message with the Western way of using language. I never heard the disagreement she tried so hard to express. A sidebar to the story, she disagreed because she wanted me to wait until next payday to buy it, that's all. Nothing about size or price! If she would have just told me that I would not have bought it and, who knows, maybe we would still be married.

Still confused? Welcome to life in Chinese Asia. In the following sections I explain how Chinese use objections as a way to disagree, just one of the many ways Chinese say no without saying 'no.' Here I want to make the point, again, that communicating with Chinese, or across any two cultures, depends upon more than simply having a language in common. Without also having a way of using language in common, a way of thinking about language in common, communication success is difficult.

Themes and Lessons

People worry about the wrong things when they come to Chinese Asia, about whether they can use chopsticks properly or pass a business card with two hands. While it is nice to know Chinese methods, habits, traditions and such, most problems happen because of innocent communication mistakes. Westerners don't realize Chinese have a different way of using language than Westerns do. This difference has nothing to do with vocabulary, grammar, pronunciation or other language skills, but is caused by each culture using their unique Rules of Communication.

1. It is easy to give offense without realizing it. In most cases you can recover though, as long as you are willing to ask questions and apologize for what you did. Being able to laugh at yourself helps a LOT.
2. All cultures have unique ways of using language, called Rules of Communication.
3. Every culture uses language in different ways to achieve identical goals.
4. Chinese don't need to use a direct, yes/no question (Would you like to? Do you want to?) to extend an invitation.
5. Chinese don't need to use clear 'disagree words' (don't) in order to communicate disagreement.
6. Successful West-Chinese (all cross-culture communication) depends on two things: both sides having a language in common and a way of using language in common.
7. You must pay close attention at all times to what is being said and what the Chinese message might be rather than to what those words would mean to a Westerner. You must listen to Chinese talking with Chinese ears.

CHAPTER TWO

It's All About How You See

Smith (a Westerner) and Chen (a Chinese) work together. A key customer has a problem, so Smith and Chen meet to discuss it. Speaking English, they talk talk talk, and reach agreement. Discussion over, they leave, happy to have solved the problem. Is it solved though? Too often the answer is no, it isn't.

What often happens is Smith walks away thinking, 'Good, I explained why we **must** do X,' while Chen walks away thinking, 'Good, I explained why we **cannot** do X.' Both heard the same words, yes, but from those same words each received a different message.

This is bad. What happens a day, week or month later when Smith discovers that Chen is not doing X *as he agreed* to do? Smith gets on the telephone or writes an email and, one hopes politely, asks Chen why he is not doing X. In Smith's mind Chen has made a mistake or broken the agreement, and seems to be guilty of saying one thing while doing another. As he makes the call, Smith starts to wonder if Chen is a person who can be trusted.

Chen is surprised at Smith's question, and tries to explain that he is just doing what *he and Smith agreed on* (to not do X). When Smith expresses surprise at this answer, and says something like, 'Wait a minute, we agreed to do X; why are you changing the agreement?' Chen gets confused: what is Smith talking about? How can Smith be angry? Chen is doing exactly what he and Smith agreed to do! Chen now starts to wonder about Smith, and the longer the discussion goes on the more Chen thinks Smith is two-faced, a person not to be trusted. Smith thinks the same about Chen.

Going Broke Relationships

Smith and Chen now have the start of what I call a 'going broke' relationship, one characterized by suspicion and mutual distrust. Neither side thinks they are wrong; fault belongs totally on the other side. Each will now try to protect themselves and their side, the opposite of trying to find win-win, mutually beneficial solutions and actions. The Smith-Chen relationship now depends upon a contract and not on trust, a worrisome situation even in the West but far more dangerous in Chinese Asia. If you depend upon contract to make a relationship work in Chinese Asia you will go broke. It is that simple.

This pattern of Westerners and Chinese getting different meanings from hearing the same words occurs in every Chinese Asian city, from Seoul to Tokyo, Shanghai to Singapore, Hong Kong to Taipei. It may be the most common cause of problems between Westerners and Chinese; it certainly is one of the most dangerous. A business relationship in Chinese Asia without trust is … a relationship destined to go broke.

Is this problem inevitable? No. Why did it happen? Simple: each side used their culture's way of using language to determine what the actual words meant. Smith looked through Western glasses (used Western ears); Chen wore Chinese glasses (used Chinese ears). What you see depends upon what glasses you wear; each used their own culture's glasses, thus each only saw (heard) things one way, their way. Can you overcome this problem? Yes. You just need to wear Chinese glasses. (Chinese also need Western glasses of course, but they get their own book.)

Just Like Satisfying Customers

If you want to be successful in Chinese Asia, you must learn to see things the way Chinese do. You need Chinese glasses. You already know this, even if you don't know you know. You already do it, everyday. It's called satisfying customers.

Every day you pay attention to what your customers[13] want and how they want it. No matter what industry or agency you work with, no matter whether you sell a product, service or nothing at all, you strive to understand the people you work with, your customers: you try to understand their needs, wants and expectations, then you struggle to match what you sell and how you sell it to customer needs and wants. This includes understanding their preferred way of communicating then tailoring your messages, both what you say and how you say it, to match customer preferences. We change every day for customers.

It is easy (or easier) to change when we are in the West. We have more than just a language in common: our customers have the same basic mindset as we do. We also have well-developed methods of discovering customer needs, focus groups, surveys and such. From these methods we learn how to 'see' the world as our customers do, allowing us to know where and what we must change. We naturally and comfortably wear 'customer glasses.'

Wearing customer glasses to do business in the West is exactly the same principle as wearing Chinese glasses to do business in Chinese Asia. You must learn what Chinese want and how they want it, in service type, product specifications or communication style. You must be able to 'see' things the way Chinese do. This is just common sense.

"Okay," I hear you say, "I agree. That makes sense. How do I do it? There are no well-developed methods to discover what Chinese think, no focus groups or surveys. Chinese are so different from me. How do I learn to wear Chinese glasses?"

Good News

I have good news. If you asked that question then you have already taken the all-important first step: realizing that you need Chinese glasses. If you don't realize or admit that you need to change, or at minimum to learn to 'see' in a different way, a Chinese way, you will find yourself in one 'going broke' relationship after another. So be happy: you have already taken the first step.

The good news continues. I believe you already know how to be successful in Chinese Asia, you just don't know that you know. If you have a best friend in your home country (same culture as you), if you know how to make a marriage work, you already know the most important rules to success in building business relationships in Chinese Asia. Chinese base business relationships on the rules of friendship and marriage, not on the rules of law and contract. If you know how to make a best friend or a happy marriage, you know how to do business in Chinese Asia.

I hear questions already, "Can it really be that simple? There must be more to it." Of course there is more to it, but the 'more' does not include special tips and strategies, learning Chinese language or pithy Chinese sayings like 'white face, black face.' Success depends upon how you look at the problem, upon your feelings and your willingness to try to see things as Chinese see them.

Chinese Are Not Mysterious, Not A Puzzle

You must start by changing how you look at Chinese. If you look at Chinese as a puzzle to solve, a mystery to figure out, **you will fail**! Why? Because if you start out looking at the Chinese as a mystery you will find what you are looking for, a mystery, and the more you try to solve the Chinese mystery the more mysterious the Chinese will become. You must instead start by looking at Chinese as *just people*, just like you and me. Sure Chinese do things differently than you do, often very differently, but they are just people who want the same things you do. The key to success is just that simple, looking at Chinese as people, not as mysteries or puzzles. Chinese are different from Westerners, sure, but then your wife or husband is different from you and you made that relationship work. Western men and women are as different from each other as Chinese and Westerners are. Or almost as different.

I like and respect the Chinese, but after 20+ years studying Chinese culture, living and working in Chinese Asia, speaking the language and marrying two Chinese women[14] I am no longer *romantic* about the Chinese. I am *practical* about the Chinese, and view them no differently than I view other types of people, engineers, Europeans or children say. Every group of people, every person, has good and bad points, and a unique way of looking at things. To succeed I must see things as they see them, must wear their glasses and adjust my actions to meet their expectations.

The book that follows explores the following themes in detail. That the main cause of problems between West and East is miscommunication and misunderstandings, not intent. That culture determines how we think communication *should* be and what we think are polite and appropriate actions. That success depends upon applying commonly-understood principles about how to achieve customer satisfaction, which in turn depends upon understanding how Chinese customers or partners see the world, then adjusting to that view. That the Chinese are not mysterious or "inscrutable," but are just people who do things in a unique way (albeit in a way different than most Westerners are used to). Lastly, that if you know how to make a best friend in your hometown or how to make a marriage work then you already know the most important rules to making a Chinese-Western relationship work.

I divide the book into two sections, *Getting Chinese Glasses* (learning the rules) and *Using Chinese Glasses* (applying the rules). Getting Glasses is just what it implies; it gives you the background needed to see things as Chinese do. I include some theories about communication in general and about how culture affects how we communicate, see and judge the world. One chapter looks at Chinese and Western history and culture, and how each affects our daily actions and beliefs. One truism about culture is the best way to understand your culture is to leave it, so to see it from a distance. As this book can't magically transport you to China I instead contrast a typical Chinese view to a typical Western view, an exercise I call 'understanding them by understanding us.'

Putting on a pair of Chinese glasses is just the start; you must learn how to use what you see to change how you think, communicate and act. Section Two, Using Chinese Glasses, includes small cases studies with related tips and suggestions about how to use your new sight in daily life. Some chapters focus on issues for those who live in Chinese Asia and manage Chinese directly, some for those who manage long-distance contract relationships (traders and such), some for those who just want to communicate with Chinese. Finally, while the book emphasizes business, it should also interest and help anyone who wants to develop relationships of any sort in or with Chinese Asia.

You can skip any section or chapter and go directly to what interests you most, but I don't recommend it. Especially dangerous is skipping theory parts. The best compliments I receive during my workshops[15] are from those with the most experience and wrinkles on their China hands, frequently hearing things like, "Oh, now I understand why such and such happened" and "I wish I would have met you 20 years ago." (It is very gratifying.) The point is that even though these China Hands have years of practical experience and often are serious China scholars in their own right, they have learned 'what' works but not 'why' it works, i.e., they have learned that when [x] happens doing [w] tends to work and doing [t] tends not work. This is learning from experience, the Holy Grail of training. Problem is, they don't know why [w] tends to work, and [t] doesn't.

A Word About Learning

Learning from experience is wonderful and necessary, I agree, but it actually means *learning from making mistakes*, frequently an expensive proposition in international business. It also is a very limited way to learn, as all one learns is to do [w], not [t], when situation [x] happens. A good thing to know whenever situation [x] happens, true, but essentially useless when a new situation, call it situation [r], happens. Then the process of learning what to do by making mistakes repeats itself.

Learning theory means you learn not just 'what' works but also 'why' it works, *why* doing [w] and not [t] when [x] happens tends to work. Once you understand the reasons why certain types of actions tend to work and why others tend not to, why Chinese tend to react in certain ways to certain types of actions and events, you begin to gain predictive ability. Now, when faced with new situation [r], you have more than a 'learn from mistakes' way to learn what to do; before reacting you can think, 'Hmm, Chinese tend to want things done this way and not that, so maybe I should try reacting to [r] in that (Chinese friendly) way first.' You now can predict which actions are *likely* to work, thus saving you from expensive lessons about what doesn't work. It creates a virtuous circle: the more you learn the more practical experience you have, thus the better you can predict how best to act and communicate with Chinese. You can then add your own experiences to the structure and examples I use and thus gain an ever-deeper understanding, all without making more mistakes.

Learning from experience, from making mistakes, certainly does work, but there is a better and cheaper way to learn. How? By learning from someone else's mistakes, not your own. In my 20+ years working and living with Chinese I have made almost every mistake there is (a lot of mistakes anyway). My hope is that by reading my book you can learn from my mistakes and can skip making your own, a learning process a heck of a lot cheaper and easier for you.

I hope you read the chapter on Chinese history (3), on communication (4) and culture (5). You may have already read books on Chinese history and/or on how to work and communicate with the Chinese, so feel you already know the subject. Other books have no doubt helped you, but … I have also read many such books, and, truth be told, find many of them lacking in practical applications. Not because the history is wrong or the tips and suggestions are incorrect, but because most authors don't draw the proper lessons from the history and/or don't explain why the tips and suggestions (tend to) work.

Need More Than Tips

It is not enough to say, "History is important to the Chinese." You need to know why history is important and how it shapes modern day actions, values and beliefs. If asked to change how *you* do things, you need to know *why*—why Chinese do, act and think as they do. For example, there is that classic piece of advice, to 'be polite' with the Chinese. Great, but what does it mean? Most books don't go on to explain that 'Chinese polite' is very different than 'Western polite,' and don't explain that the more you are 'Western polite' the more impolite the Chinese will think you are. You need more detail, not just *what* to do but *why* to do it.

Then there are the tips and suggestions that fill many 'How To' books about working with the Chinese. My experience is that unless people understand *why* doing a certain thing (the tip) is important, *why* it works, most people will either not do it or do it in a half-hearted way. They think, 'Hmm, this is so different than what I am used to; it's a lot of trouble to do; it can't be that important' … thus they don't do it consistently, or at all. Tips are useful only when put into the context of why the tip works.

One last word about tips and suggestions. Many books include a list of Chinese techniques and strategies, often from ancient times and with fascinating titles, things like *Buy The Casket And Return The Pearl* or *Kill A Chicken To Warn The Monkeys*. Are these techniques important to know? Yes, and no. Yes, because you should be aware of what is happening around you and because learning techniques and strategies give insights into Chinese thinking; no, because you don't understand the context in which they can and can't be used, meaning it is easy use them incorrectly. In the last chapters I do explain a few of these well-worded techniques and strategies, but you will only really understand them and how they should and should not be used if you have read the first sections on theory, history and culture.

Don't Try To Be Chinese

You can't 'out Chinese the Chinese,' that is, use Chinese techniques to get what you want. The Chinese are the home team, and the home team always has the advantage. No matter how many Chinese techniques you know, or even how well you speak Chinese, you will always be part of the visiting team. The more you try to play by Chinese rules the more the Chinese will have the advantage. You may know 100 strategies but the Chinese will know 500, and more important, will know how to counteract the strategies you use. Don't try to be Chinese. Be a Westerner, a respectful Westerner.

The tips and suggestions in the final chapters are written for Westerners, and based on principles, actions and attitudes Westerners commonly use and are comfortable with. Perhaps the wisest comment I've received during a workshop is from a manager from 3M, "Greg, your advice is not just good for Chinese. Your suggestions are just as useful in the West; you are just describing how to be a good manager." Exactly. Or how to be a good friend, good spouse, partner or teammate. As I wrote above, you already know how to be successful in Chinese Asia, you just don't know that you know. My hope is that this book will show you that you do know how to succeed, and that success in Chinese Asia isn't as difficult as you think, or fear. Heck, if I can do it so can you.

There is no magic formula, no piece of advice that is always true, no course of action that always works. Chinese are just people after all, and people are complicated. The best you can hope for is to be more often right than wrong, to learn and do what will *likely* work. This is why I use the caveat 'tends to' throughout this book. Generalizations are always dangerous but absolutely necessary when learning how to deal with other cultures. You will meet Chinese that don't act or communicate the way I describe such in this book, I guarantee it. Nevertheless, I stand behind my argument that Chinese 'tend to' act and communicate in certain ways. You should use my suggestions as a starting point, and be ready to adjust your actions as needed.

The best advice I can give you is to be patient, learn the rules of Chinese communication, actions and politeness, and keep your Chinese glasses on. Wearing Chinese glasses is uncomfortable at first, and while your sight will improve the more you wear them, you will never have perfect, 20:20 vision. You will always be somewhat uncertain about what you are seeing. But not wearing Chinese glasses means you build relationships and do business blind, and that is never good. So, don't worry if what you see through your Chinese glasses is not quite clear; blurry vision is better than not seeing anything at all! And it will get better.

Themes and Lessons

Most problems Westerners have in Chinese Asia have a simple root cause: Westerners don't know how Chinese 'see' the world, or how they use language. Most Westerners can succeed with the Chinese. Westerners need to learn to wear Chinese glasses.

1. Simple misunderstandings can have HUGE consequences. One common outcome is that Chinese and Westerners don't know if they should trust each other.

2. The most common reason for misunderstandings is both sides listen with their own culture's way of using language, not the other culture's.

3. To succeed in Chinese Asia, Westerners must learn to *see* things the way Chinese do; they need Chinese glasses.

4. Wearing Chinese glasses means using the same principles and techniques used in marketing in the West: understanding customer needs and wants then adapting your product and service to meet these needs.

5. Chinese are not a puzzle to figure out; they are just people who want the same things you do, just in different ways than you do.

6. If you can make a marriage work in the West, can make a best friend in your hometown, you can be successful in Chinese Asia.

7. Don't be romantic about the Chinese: be practical.

8. Learning from experience is not enough. You need to understand 'why' things happen because if you new situations require you to learn by making mistakes, once again. This is also true about following tips: you need to know why they work.

9. Don't try to become a Chinese. Instead try to become a respectful Westerner.

Desire to have things
done quickly
prevents their being
done thoroughly.

Confucius

CHAPTER THREE

In Chinese Asia, History Is Now

Have you been to Rome and seen the Coliseum? It is magnificent. How about the pyramids outside Cairo? The great pyramids have to be seen to be believed, and even then are hard to grasp. The 2004 Summer Olympics in Athens introduced a new generation of travelers to the Acropolis and the Parthenon, testaments to the Golden Age of Greece. Three destinations, each with historical treasures and one more thing (at least) in common: none of the cultures and societies that built these treasures exists today.

The taxi driver that speeds around the Coliseum today has nothing to do with ancient Rome. Roman culture and society disappeared a long time ago. Modern Italians don't keep slaves, make sacrifices to Jupiter or go to stadiums to watch gladiators fight or lions dine on Christians. The tour guide leading you on the back of a camel around the pyramids has nothing to do with the civilization of the pharaohs: he doesn't read hieroglyphics or worship the sun. The same is true of bus driver taking you to the Acropolis; he can't read ancient Greek and doesn't go to Delphi to listen to the Oracle. These three ancient civilizations have disappeared, the languages spoken, the social and economic systems used, religious figures worshipped and beliefs held, all gone.

Have you ever been to the Great Wall of China? It is truly impressive, no matter if viewed from outside Beijing or from any number of other vantage points. Snaking over hillside and mountaintop, the Wall can not be described by words. Like the great pyramid, you need to see it really to grasp its size and grandeur.

Unlike at the pyramids though, the hawkers selling tourist baubles beside the Wall are the direct descendents of the people who built it. Unlike ancient Rome, Greece or Egypt, the civilization that built the Great Wall still exists, the tour guide still speaks and reads the language used by the architects who designed it, prays to the same Gods and learns the same basic social rules.

Am I guilty here of over-simplification? Yes and no. Modern Chinese Asia has of course changed from the ancient China of emperors, harems and foot binding. But in many important ways China has not changed much at all since the Wall was built. While each of the Chinas uses some form of modern (Western actually) politico-economic systems, communism, capitalism, democracy and such, all modern Chinas are still built upon a Confucian structure, still use the Chinese pictographic language, still venerate age as wisdom and value humility over self-promotion. The food is the same too: a modern time traveler would not find pizza in ancient Rome but the barbeque duck and fried rice found in a modern Beijing hotel are the same as they were a millennia ago.

How far back can you trace a Western family? 500 years? 1000 years? I am no genealogical expert, but I would be suspicious if you said you were the direct lineal descendent of Charlemagne (AD 742-814). Too far back: how would you prove it? The same is true if you said you were related to Leonardo da Vinci, who lived a mere 500 or so years ago (AD 1452-1517). Same reason: how would you prove it? Sure, there must be Western families that can trace their roots back 500 years, or even a few hundred years more, but such cases are rare and most people would wonder at such a claim. Western civilization has gone through too many changes, too many upheavals, for families to claim such ancient relatives with a straight face.

Not so in Chinese Asia. In Taipei today is man who claims to be the direct lineal descendent of Confucius. Wow! That is roughly the same as a Westerner saying he is a direct lineal descendent of Plato, a near-contemporary of the Chinese sage. How long ago is that? Confucius lived 551-479 BC (Plato, 427-347 BC), 2,500 years ago! At a generous 20 years a generation, that would make the Taipei relative the great sage's 125th great grandson. Imagine the family reunion.

Anyone can 'claim' such a lineage, sure, and to be honest I find the great *great* grandson's claim hard to believe. What I believe is not important though; what is important is people in Chinese Asia believe his claim, believe that a Chinese family can have such deep, ancient roots. The Italian taxi driver may be proud of ancient Roman greatness, but even the most fervent Italian would not try to claim Virgil or Marc Anthony as his grandfather. To modern day Italians, ancient Rome is history, something learned from books. Not so the Chinese; for them, history still exists and they view themselves as just the latest in a long, unbroken line of descendents of the Yellow Emperor.

Chinese history is not important for who was emperor when, what dynasty followed what dynasty or what the Chinese invented (though how Chinese inventions failed to shape Chinese history is a prime example of the power of Chinese beliefs about themselves[16]). Chinese history is fabulously rich and full of stories and characters tailor-made for movie plots and bestsellers but, at least for the purposes of this book, what is important is not *what* happened but *why*, and how ancient (and not-so-ancient) Chinese history continues to shape modern Chinese attitudes and actions.

China Is Unique

All cultures are unique, true, but China's is more unique than others. Not just today either: China's uniqueness dates back to pre-history. There truly is no other great ancient civilization like old China. The overriding reason is geography. Put yourself back before airplanes and trains and look at China on a map (see next page). China is isolated from the rest of the world, to the east by the world's largest ocean, to the south and southwest by the world's tallest mountain range and incredibly dense jungle, and to the west and northwest by immense deserts.

Unlike all other great ancient civilizations, China developed on its own. The other ancient civilizations[17] learned from, borrowed from and built upon the preceding civilizations. The Egyptians learned from the Sumerians, the Phoenicians from the Egyptians, the Greeks from the Phoenicians and the Romans from the Greeks. Alexander the Great carried Western civilization across the mountains into ancient India and returned with Indian ideas and inventions. While each civilization made great contributions

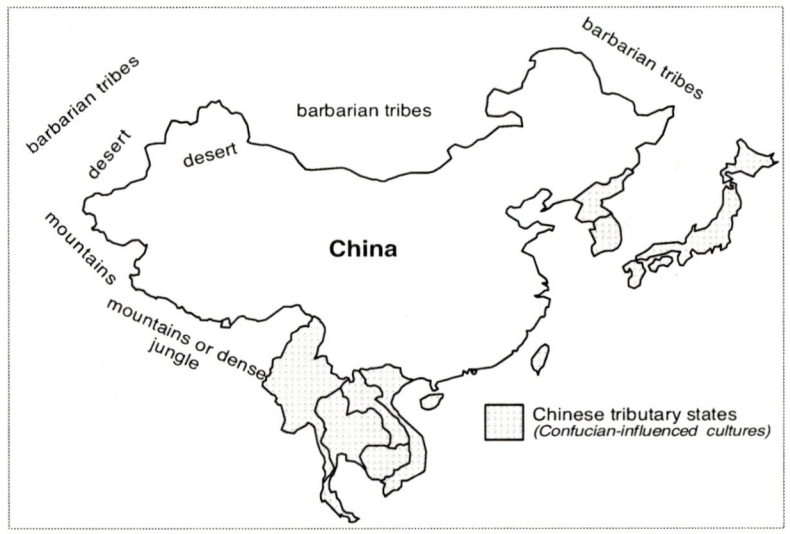

Map 1. China's Isolation

of its own, each also stood on the shoulders of the ones that came before, each benefited from ideas and inventions developed elsewhere.

China developed on its own. Yes, to anticipate a question, I know about the Silk Road, the great caravan routes across the western deserts that joined China to the West. The Silk Road had far more effect upon the West than it did upon China though; trade was mostly in goods, not ideas, and few Chinese were involved in the trade. In fact in China's long history there is only one good example of old China borrowing a key idea from outside, that of borrowing Buddhism from India during the Tang Dynasty (500-700AD), and even then it was a typical Chinese borrowing, not a straight transfer. It was changed. Made Chinese.[18]

Am I over-simplifying? I don't think so. There of course was some contact between the West and China, and there are no doubt examples of West-to-China knowledge transfers. Yet not only are these examples rare, none affected the course of Chinese history or social development to any significant degree. China was unique, and did develop independently.

Think about what that means. While it's hard to call Romans 'humble,' they were aware of and influenced by, say, Egypt of the pharos and the ideas of the Greeks. Even when astride the known world as a colossus, the Romans knew they were not unique. Best perhaps, but not unique.

Not so ancient China. The little that was known of the outside world was considered fanciful fable, and only really served to highlight how unique the Chinese were (so they thought). Developing on their own had a dramatic effect on how the Chinese viewed themselves; with no one to compare to, no one to learn some cultural humility from, the Chinese thought of themselves as the true, the only, founders of civilization.

The China Effect

Students ask, "But what about Japan or Korea? Didn't they affect Chinese development?" The short answer is no, they didn't. In fact the opposite happened; they were affected by the Chinese. To tempt oversimplification again, one could say that most key parts of Japanese and Korean culture came from China. Why? Because China came first, by a long way.

Chinese history is long. While Chinese say they descend from the Xia Dynasty, no real records or artifacts exist from the period—a key determinate of history—and most Western scholars consider the Xia dynasty to be mythical. Chinese history is considered to begin with the Shang Dynasty, 1,600-1,100BC. This is when Chinese writing first appears, symbols scratched upon animal bones then thrown into the fire, with the subsequent cracks used for divination. Written records start from the late Shang, and continue (and become far more detailed) in the Zhou Dynasty that followed. Long before Confucius, ancient China had all the trappings of a mature civilization, laws, government and taxes, bronze casting, arts and writing. While how and from whom such trappings entered Chinese society is lost in the mists of time, by any standards China was clearly an advanced society at a very early time.

Much earlier than Japan or Korea. For example, rice farming in Japan is thought to begin during the Yayoi Period, or around 100BC, at least a thousand years later than in China. Korean culture is similarly late, and similarly dependent upon borrowing ideas, methods and systems from China. This pattern of cultural borrowing holds true for all countries or cultures that surrounded China, Mongolia and all S.E. Asia. To each, also cut off from the ancient Mediterranean cultures, China was the Centre of the Known World.

Be it language, religion, traditions, philosophies, theories of communal instead of individualistic society and government, the peripheral cultures borrowed large parts of their culture from the Chinese. If imitation is the sincerest form of flattery, China had good reason to feel flattered: everyone they knew copied them. Even the barbarian tribes from beyond the Great Wall learned and borrowed from China.

Not since the Sumerians at the dawn of civilization in the Fertile Crescent did another ancient (or even modern) civilization ever had it so good. Even while building the pyramids, the Sphinx or the various temples with their huge columns and even-larger statues, the Egyptians were aware of, and fought on equal terms with, surrounding peoples. The Greeks not only had to compare themselves with each other, Athenian democracy vs. Spartan organization for example, they had both Persians and pyramids to keep themselves somewhat humble. Even the all-conquering Romans knew of, and learned from, various other cultures and traditions. The Chinese had no other such people to look up to or learn from, no reason ever to learn humility. The Chinese were superior, and knew it.

The Superior Chinese

The factual superiority of Chinese culture and society was matched by equal Chinese feelings and thoughts of being superior. I don't know which is tail and which is dog, whether everyone copying them made the Chinese feel superior or whether Chinese feelings of being superior made everyone copy them: probably some of both. No matter: what is important is Chinese did feel superior and all the other cultures orbiting the Chinese sun accepted Chinese superiority (even if they did not like it).

Think about what the view from China must have been like back then. Cultures and peoples in every direction were less advanced and very interested in learning from the Chinese. Nowhere could the Chinese see a culture, people or society they could learn from. It would be hard not to feel superior in such a situation.

Their view of the outside world and their place in it also matched the view of the Chinese when they looked inwards. Starting sometime early in the Han Dynasty (begins in 206 BC) Confucian scholars created a philosophical justification for Chinese superiority, the Mandate of Heaven. To these scholars China's ascendant position was only natural as China and the Chinese were, in essence, the bridge between Heaven (the Gods) and the barbarians (non-Chinese). China's superior position was thus not simply a matter of having a more advanced system but was also 'as it should be,' a moral superiority.

Chinese characters often show a lot about Chinese thinking, in this case about how they look at themselves and their position vis-à-vis the rest of the world. The word "China" is made up of two characters, first 中 (zhong), literally "center," second 國 (guo), literally "kingdom" or "country."[19] Put them together and voilà, you have "Central Kingdom," China. The Chinese were the people, culture and society in the centre between Heaven and the rest, the non-Chinese, the barbarians. You and me. If you are not Chinese you are a barbarian.[20]

Diagram 1: Chinese World View

The Mandate of Heaven involves much more than how Chinese view themselves though; it describes the way Chinese rulers legitimized their rule over China. Whenever a dynasty changed, Sui to Tang for example, the Chinese saw it as the current ruling family losing the Mandate and the new ruling family (or dynasty) assuming it. The right to rule was a moral issue; a change of rulers meant the Gods had judged the existing family to no longer be worthy (for example because their poor leadership had led to wanton corruption, over-taxation, famine and wide-scale suffering) to rule.

This is a potent brew, actual superiority combined with a belief in moral superiority. As the centuries rolled on and no other country or culture rose to threaten actual Chinese superiority, the Chinese belief in moral supremacy strengthened. Even while turmoil roiled inside China, dynasties rose and fell and brutal civil wars fought, nothing happened to change the Chinese belief that China and the 'Chinese way' were everlasting. The Chinese were right, for a few thousand years anyway.

Everlasting China

In one generation, 221 to 206BC, China changed dramatically, twice. Since 741BC China had become increasingly fragmented, a restless, warring pool of small states that vied for power during the Spring and Autumn, then the Warring States period. One state, Qin, gradually became stronger and stronger, absorbing rival states through diplomacy and war. In 221BC the war between states was over; Qin won, and a new dynasty, aptly named the Qin[21] Dynasty, was formed.

The war between rival states may have been over but the ascendancy of the Qin marked the start of a war inside China, a war over culture, systems and beliefs. The new Qin emperor, the self-styled Shi Huang Di (literally 'The First Emperor'), set out to remake China. Power was stripped from feudal landowners and regional powers and given to a new, centralized bureaucracy controlled by the emperor. Weights and measures were standardized, as were the Chinese characters. For the first time uniform laws and taxation were applied across all of China. Using a manpower surplus created by the changes, the Qin emperor added to and improved the series of smaller walls started by past rulers, marking the start of what eventually became the Great Wall.[22] In just 15 years China became a nation, not just a people. The feudal past was dead; in its place was a centralized monarchy that was to last millennia.

Behind the change was a radical philosophy, Legalism. Its author unknown, Legalism is the concept that clear laws and strict punishments can regulate all actions, and that all laws (and all people) should serve the interests of, and help support, central authority, the emperor. Almost overnight China became a police state. Worried about competing philosophies and threats to the throne, the authorities tried to remake China. Incredibly draconian laws and practices were applied, including confiscation and burning of all books of philosophy and the human condition, and, if that was not enough, scholars who resisted were executed; if reports can be believed, some were buried alive.

Resistance grew among the displaced scholars and aristocracy, and within a few years revolts broke out in central China. Bandit-turned-General Liu Bang defeated the Qin armies in 206BC and took the throne, forming the Han Dynasty. The Han then ruled China for the next four centuries.

Liu Bang consolidated his rule by embracing Confucianism and the many Confucian scholars opposed to the Qin regime. Originally only one of many competing philosophers of the age[23], Confucius' philosophy and ideals had gained more and more followers in the two centuries since his death. Liu Bang's decision made Confucianism the official government philosophy, a place it retained for the next two millennia. Based on the idea that morality mattered in all things, and that harmony and stable government and society—Confucius' overriding goals—depended upon individuals knowing their place in the hierarchy, following rules based on that position and acting with humility and moderation in all things, Confucianism[24] was perfectly suited to the Chinese character and to maintaining the *status quo ante*. It worked. Once established, Confucianism was never seriously challenged.

Over the next two millennia dynasties formed and fell, civil wars raged and foreign barbarians invaded and controlled China, yet Confucius and the Confucian system introduced by the Han endured. More than endured, it conquered. Based as it was on the idea that the past had all the answers, China looked backwards, not forwards, trying always to regain the glorious past (from the Zhou Dynasty) it had lost. For nearly two thousand years China didn't change! Not the language, not the religion (except for the introduction of Buddhism, and even that had been rewritten to match Confucian ideals) and not the system of government. China *was* everlasting.

Think about that for a moment. No change for almost two thousand years. Unbelievable! There is no similar success story in all of world history, a system that went unchanged for two thousand years. Without a doubt Confucian China was the most successful system the world has ever seen, or is likely ever to see. Making this achievement even more remarkable was the fact that China endured even in the face of serious challenges from barbarians from beyond the Great Wall.

Twice barbarians invaded and conquered China. First was the Mongols, with Kublai Khan (grandson of Genghis Khan) defeating the Song armies and forming the Yuan Dynasty (1280-1368). Next was the Manchurians (Jürchen tribes) from the northeast, who defeated the Ming and conquered China in 1644, forming the Qing (Ching) Dynasty (1644-1911). In both cases the barbarian rulers did little to change China, and instead worked hard to translate Chinese texts and ideas into their languages and systems, eventually becoming more Chinese that the Chinese (especially the Qing). Both had the might of arms to prevail on the battlefield but nowhere near the intellectual or organizational might to impose their ways upon China. Chinese armies lost the battles but Chinese civilization won the wars. China was truly everlasting.

Westerners And The End Of Everlasting China

Imagine for a moment the Emperor's view of the world in 1793, and the Chinese place in it. Proud of China's homegrown accomplishments in art, science, literature and government, and aware that *every* surrounding culture looked to China for ideas and inspiration, it must have been a heady feeling. No other culture could compete with the Chinese in any way, in art or arms, and every culture the Chinese knew and had met over the millennia wanted to be like the Chinese, wanted to learn from the Chinese.[25]

Not so the Western actors about to enter the Chinese stage, and there tells the tale. For the first time in its long history China met people who did not want to learn from the Chinese; they wanted to change China. How they wanted to change China and why, and how the Chinese tried to deal with these new challenges to China's superior position, sets the stage for the next act, the start of the end of everlasting China.

Three different types of Westerners came to change China, missionaries wanting China to convert to Christianity, traders wanting China to allow free and unfettered trade, and diplomats wanting China to conform to the rules of international diplomacy. Each of these three desires flew in the face of longstanding Chinese ideas of how barbarians should act towards China. China tried to control these Western desires using their tried-and-true methods, an approach that seemed to work only to fail spectacularly in the end under the force of Western cannon and industrial might.

Missionaries

The first missionaries, Jesuits, arrived in the late 15th, early 16th centuries. Unlike other areas controlled by 'heathens' though, South America and Africa for example, China was an advanced and wealthy country, thus missionaries were forced to adopt new methods. Instead of their normal, 'our way is right, your way is wrong, you have to stop believing your way' chorus, the Jesuits had to fit conversion to Christianity into the Chinese reality, had to adapt Christianity to fit Chinese ideas.

Adapt Christianity: What does that mean? There were various ways. One was to be very, ah, *creative* in translating Christian texts. For example, the Jesuits translated "God" as "Deity" or "Lord of Heaven," terms Chinese were familiar with … as they were commonly used to describe the Emperor! Another change was in dress and habit; Jesuits dressed as Chinese, studied Chinese classics and followed Chinese manners, and tried to convert top-down rather than their normal appeal to the masses. While these changes helped and early Jesuits did have some limited successes, their standing in China was due far more to practical earthly skills than metaphysical, life-after-death arguments.

As the "Lord of Heaven" the emperor was responsible for the calendar and predicting the change of seasons, crucial tasks in an agrarian culture. While the Chinese were in total far more advanced than European cultures at this time, the West was ahead in astronomy, proven a number of times by the Jesuits successfully predicting eclipses. In competitions between Chinese, Mohammedan and Jesuit astronomers, Jesuit skills prevailed. Being useful, Jesuits could reside in Beijing (an unheard of honor at the time), but were more tolerated than followed, with their influence directly related to how their practical skills helped the Chinese.

Other Catholic missionaries, Dominicans and Franciscans, were not willing to play so fast and loose with Christian theology though, even though their tried-and-true "your way is wrong" message and methods were not working. Perhaps driven by jealousy, perhaps by conviction, the non-Jesuits complained to Europe about what the Jesuits were doing, claiming a debasing of Christianity, strong words in the time of the Inquisition. At the same time many Chinese officials were becoming more suspicious and jealous of Jesuit influence, unhappy both about the very idea that Chinese had to reply on barbarians and that Jesuits had the ear of the emperor. These widely divergent foreign and native forces soon caught the Jesuits in a vice.

The perfect storm hit the Jesuits in 1706 when a papal delegation sent to investigate the criticisms met with the Kang Xi emperor to discuss theology. The papal delegation was horrified with the Jesuit's creative translations and semantic arguments. An example of the latter was that ancestor worship and public homage to Confucius were 'civil' and not 'religious,' therefore Christian Chinese could still practice the Chinese rites. The delegation quickly issued an edict forbidding Catholic missionaries from letting Chinese converts use this ruse. Hearing this, Kang Xi in turn gave missionaries a choice, sign a certificate agreeing with the Jesuit (and his) civil/religious position or be expelled from China. Some Jesuits signed but most did not: within a few decades Christian influence and presence in China was minimal. When Kang Xi's son took power a few years later persecution (and worse) of Christians, Chinese or otherwise, was officially condoned, over the years adding to growing anti-Chinese feelings in the West.

Traders

Traders are next in the troika of Westerners coming to change China. Marco Polo returned to Venice in 1295, and even though his tales of a fabulous, rich and advanced China made many skeptical (his book was eventually known as *Il Milione*, the Million Lies) it became one of the most celebrated books of the era. China became more dream than destination, its wealth tantalizingly just out of reach but never out of mind. China had entered the Western imagination.

Overland trade would not work though. The Silk Road was good only for camel-size loads only, plus trade was intermittent and impossible to control. Real trade had to wait until the Age of Exploration, when Europeans manned small[26] wooden boats and mapped the world.

The Portuguese were the first Europeans to come to China's southern shores, arriving in the late 1500s. The Chinese demanded that all trading and indeed all Western presence be confined to Macao (near Hong Kong), and be done following strict Chinese rules.[27] Based on the long-standing Tributary System China developed for dealing with neighboring cultures, if the Portuguese wanted to trade they had to do it the Chinese way, no exceptions, and only if they showed proper respect and acknowledged Chinese superiority. It worked at first, but didn't last. Chinese superiority was about to be put to the test by the British demand for the hot new drink from China, tea.

Formed in 1600, the British East India Company was Britain's response to the rush among European powers of the day, the Portuguese, French and Spanish, to secure trade goods, routes and rights in the quickly-opening East, India and S.E. Asia, the Spice Islands. The first British ships began to arrive in China in 1635. Perhaps because the British did not demand formal relations with the Qing court (as the Portuguese and Dutch had done) the British were soon allowed to operate out of Canton (now Guangzhou) and a few other ports, not just Macao as was the case for the rest. Good sense and some appreciation for Chinese feelings gave the British a leg up on their competitors, an advantage they used well.

China removed some of its restrictive policies in the late 1700s, not because they wanted to facilitate trade but because they wanted the taxes from the increased trade and a better way to control prices. An easier trade system made tax collection and price manipulation easier as well. In 1720 Chinese merchants in Canton (watched closely by officials) formed a monopoly guild to deal with Western traders, the *Cohong*, soon called just the 'hong' by Westerners. Trade had to go through one of the twelve hong merchants, and each foreign trader had to be 'guaranteed' (think bonded) by a hong member. By 1760 all Western trade was restricted to Canton, even Britain's.

The new system worked well at first. Though taxes were often excessive and arbitrary, the tea trade provided huge profits to both British and Chinese. Demand for tea grew in England, and with it also grew the demand for expanded trade rights among traders, as did their call for a fairer system. The way the Cohong system worked, the hong merchants were the only people the Western traders could talk to let alone trade with. Westerner traders were also forbidden to live in Canton year-round, only during the trade season (October to March). Western grievances at their treatment and the overly-sharp hong trading practices had to be put in writing to the hong merchants, in the hope they would pass on such to the court in Beijing. As you can imagine with such a fox-guarding-the-chickens-system though, not many hong merchants passed on complaints about themselves. British (and European) displeasure about the system grew, exacerbated by economics and other examples of poor Chinese treatment of Westerners.

Two examples of poor Chinese treatment became widely known in Europe. In 1741 a British naval ship in the area to attack Spanish shipping was damaged in a South China sea gale. The captain pulled the ship into Canton for repairs, thinking the Chinese would follow the then-current European law of the sea and treat the ship as a neutral. It did not happen. Chinese officials refused to answer (or even acknowledge) messages for weeks at a time, charged huge prices for supplies that turned out to be garbage and spoiled food, and refused to let the captain carry out needed repairs.

In 1759 the British East India Company tried to go around the Canton hong and to appeal directly to the emperor for changes. Captain Flint, an old China hand and fluent in Chinese, using guile and a good-size budget for bribes sailed his ship to Tianjin, the port nearest to Beijing. At first his effort seemed successful, and the emperor seemed sympathetic to his requests. The audience over, Flint tried to return to Canton overland (a good thing as his ship sank on its return voyage). On his trip Flint was arrested, charged and convicted to three years in jail. His crimes? Terrible: he was convicted of sailing to a restricted port, improperly petitioning the emperor and *learning Chinese* (a crime at this time in China)! Both stories were widely reported in Europe, and added to a growing anti-Chinese sentiment.

The economic argument was more prosaic: inflation. The British wanted tea (and porcelain, silk and other exotic goods) but what did the Chinese want in return? The British offered items like British manufactures, raw cotton and woolen goods, but the Chinese were not impressed (see below for more on this subject). Chinese only wanted one thing in return for their tea, they wanted silver. This outpouring of silver led to a drain on British reserves and to creeping inflation. No matter what the British tried to offer instead of silver the Chinese remained adamant: it was silver or nothing.

Enter the trade good everyone thinks of, opium. Contrary to what Chinese think, British did not invent opium smoking in China. Smoking opium probably began in the early 1700s, brought to China from Taiwan, and by the 1770s there was widespread literature in China on how to smoke it. Opium smoking appealed to groups under stress or just plain bored, eunuchs, wealthy women, court officials with no real jobs, students studying for exams and soldiers off to battle. China's population increased in the ensuing years and growing corruption made life more and more a struggle just to survive, so the number of smokers steadily increased. The British did not invent opium smoking, but it was British (mainly) merchants who made cheap opium widely available.

Grown in India, opium seemed the answer to British prayers, a win-win solution to their problems. Not only did trading opium for Chinese tea relieve pressures on Britain's silver reserves, traders could now make money on all legs of the voyage. This was the famous triangle trade: English manufactures to India, opium from India to China and tea from China back to England. As British demand for tea exploded so did British shipments of opium to China. Understandably, this concerned the Chinese.

Opium was initially legal in China and traded by government-approved traders. This changed in 1813. Opium was declared illegal, and caught smokers treated to 100 blows of a bamboo cane and a wooden collar to wear. The hong merchants forbade traders from importing opium, but to little effect. British (and French and, after 1794, American) traders simply anchored their ships at small ports up and down the long Chinese coast and sold their opium to adventurous—and unofficial—Chinese who then smuggled the opium into China.

While Chinese officials were concerned for opium addicts, perhaps another byproduct of opium smuggling bothered them more: inflation. Chinese smugglers paid for opium with silver, leading to a huge and growing drain on China's silver reserves. The inflation shoe was now on the other foot; it hurt and the Chinese vowed to stop the opium trade. Unable to control the coastal smugglers the Chinese went to the source, Canton and the British and French traders.

Diplomats

Before continuing the story I must introduce the final group of Westerners wanting to change China, the diplomats. While latest on the scene, the diplomats carried the most weight, control of naval cannon and army guns.

During the first few hundred years of Western contact with China the diplomats were absent. Missionaries and traders acted mostly on their own during this period: they had no representation in China and no one at home telling them what to do. Official disinterest in China began to change in the mid-1700s, especially concerning trade. Tea put China on the diplomat's table.

Europe was also changing. In 1776 Adam Smith coined the term 'mercantilism,' the economic theory that dominated the

European view of the era of foreign trade and economic expansion. Mercantilism held that as there are only a fixed number of goods in the world, a nation's health depended upon controlling trade and raw materials, hence the rush to establish colonies and to take over colonies started by rivals. European cultures started to act more like modern countries, complete with a growing system of international laws and conventions.

British officials worried about the growing amount of English silver that flowed to China as more and more Chinese tea flowed into English cups. And, as trade itself was now more important to the nation, British officials began to be concerned at how Chinese treated British traders. Initial attempts to discuss trade with China were met with Chinese silence. China was just not interested in talking to British officials, a point that came to bother the status-conscious British more and more: *How dare they?*

Now we move to 1793. As previously written, the view from the emperor's palace was glorious, China ascendant in every way. But a disturbance was coming, Lord Macartney from England. Sent (at the urging of the British East India Company) by George III as an official ambassador to the Qian Long Emperor, Lord Macartney had great difficulty even getting an audience with the emperor: a barbarian meeting the emperor was unheard of to the Chinese. Using the ruse of celebrating the emperor's 80th birthday to gain the much-sought audience, Macartney then refused to kowtow (prostrate yourself full-length on the ground, forehead knocking on the floor), an unbelievable breach of decorum. The Lord instead bowed on one knee, European fashion.

Perhaps oblivious of his less-than-spectacular beginning, Macartney pressed on, asking for a shopping list of actions: right to establish an embassy in Beijing, ending the Canton 'hong' trading system, opening up of more Chinese ports for trade and fixing of fair, equitable and open tariffs and taxes. Polite but stubborn, the emperor refused all requests, flat. Going further he gave Macartney an official edict from himself to the British King. An amazing and revealing document, it begins:

> You, O King, live beyond the confines of many seas, nevertheless,
> impelled by your humble desire to partake of the benefits of our

civilization, you have dispatched a mission respectfully bearing
your memorial.

Quite a beginning, it gets better:

> *As to your entreaty to send one of your nationals to be accredited*
> *to my Celestial Court ... this request is contrary to the usage of*
> *my dynasty and can not possibly be entertained ... How can our*
> *dynasty alter its whole procedures and regulations ... in order to*
> *meet your individual views?*

Not content just to dash British hopes of an embassy on lack of
precedent, the emperor thought of another logical reason for an
embassy—to learn from the Chinese—and to dash it as well:

> *If you assert that your reverence for our Celestial Dynasty fills*
> *you with a desire to acquire our civilization, our ceremonies and*
> *code of laws differ so completely from your own that, even if your*
> *Envoy were able to acquire the rudiments of our civilization, you*
> *could not possibly transplant our manners and customs to your*
> *alien soil. Therefore, however adept the Envoy might become,*
> *nothing would be gained thereby.*

Turning to Macartney's argument that China would surely benefit
from all that England could offer, the Emperor he wrote:

> *Our dynasty's majestic virtue has penetrated unto every country*
> *under Heaven, and Kings of all nations have offered their costly*
> *tribute by land and sea. As your Ambassador can see for himself,*
> *we possess all things. I set no value on objects strange or ingen-*
> *ious, and have no use for your country's manufactures.*

But perhaps Macartney's impoliteness could be explained by the
fact he was acting alone, without the blessings of his King, or
maybe the King just didn't know any better, thus:

> *It may be, O King, that the above proposals [Macartney's requests]*
> *have been wantonly made by your Ambassador on his own re-*
> *sponsibility, or peradventure you yourself are ignorant of our dy-*
> *nastic regulations and had no intention of transgressing them*
> *when you expressed these wild ideas and hopes. I have ever shown*
> *the greatest condescension to the tribute missions of all States*
> *which sincerely yearn after the blessings of civilization, to mani-*
> *fest my kindly indulgence.*

After a summary of all the points made, the emperor ended with a warning:

> *Should your vessels touch shore, your merchants will assuredly never be permitted to land or reside there, but will be subject to instant expulsion. In that event your barbarian merchants will have a long journey for nothing. Don't say that you were not warned in time! Tremblingly obey and show no negligence!*

One does not need a time machine to imagine Lord Macartney's reaction to the emperor's edict: 'How Dare They?' Nothing could be done about it though; Macartney had no force with him to make the Chinese change. Besides contributing to the hardening of Western feelings towards China all we have are Macartney's prescient comments about China and meeting the emperor:

> *The Empire of China is an old, crazy, first rate man-o-war, which a fortunate succession of able and vigilant officers has contrived to keep afloat these past 150 years, and to overawe neighbors merely by her bulk and appearance.*

Maybe Macartney did have a time machine able to peek into the future as his comments then included an accurate prediction of what was to come, saying that once it did not have such able leaders China would "… be dashed to pieces on the shore."

Chinese officials met future appeals for diplomatic representation, application of international laws and conventions and "proper" opening of China to foreign trade with stubborn silence and rejection. Or with insults, for example when Lord Napier tried in 1834 to communicate with the Canton Governor and was told that "the great Ministers of the Celestial Empire are not permitted to have private intercourse by letter with outside barbarians."

"Outside barbarians?" The industrial revolution was blossoming, a time when Westerners were sure of the superiority of Western civilization and the deficiencies of 'native' cultures. There was no room for compromise; neither the West nor China had any appreciation of or respect for the other side's point of view. A clash of cultures was inevitable.

The missionaries wanted better access to China's poor and suffering, especially the large numbers of Protestant missionaries who came to China in the early 1800s. The traders wanted free access to China's markets and an end to being controlled by arbitrary laws and corrupt officials. The diplomats wanted diplomatic representation and for China to act within the confines of international standards. All China wanted was to be left alone. Only one side could win. Opium was the excuse that turned the smoldering clash of competing desires into the open flame of warfare.

Cultures Clash

Opium imports into China increased dramatically, from 600 chests in 1750 to 4,570 in 1800 to 23,750 in 1832.[28] In 1838, the emperor called for the end of opium in China and sent Commissioner Lin to Canton and stamp it out. Lin's first attempts dealt with the demand side, including public declarations on the evils of opium based on Confucian values, appeals to education officials to teach students about the evils of opium, and new penalties for opium sellers and users. This worked, at least in part: thousands of Chinese arrested and large quantities of opium and pipes confiscated.

Lin then went to work on the supply side, the traders. He implored the Cohong merchants to stop helping known opium smugglers[29] ply their trade. He demanded, politely as his navy was no match for the Western fleets, that British and French traders turn over their opium and cease the opium trade (but did not offer any compensation). Lin tried to reason with the traders, explaining that if they knew how much suffering opium was causing they would stop for humanitarian reasons. He even went so far as to write an impassioned, moralistic letter to Queen Victoria, telling her of the evils the opium trade and asking her help to stamp it out. One wonders if she was amused.

The Western traders were not amused, and gave up only a token 1,000 chests of opium. Lin upped the ante by trying to arrest a British trader, who fled and was hidden by the other Westerners. Lin ordered all Chinese out of Canton's Western quarter then blockaded it, trapping hundreds of Westerners. Six weeks later the Westerners gave in and agreed to turn over 20,000 chests. Lin destroyed the opium in a public ceremony, washing around 3 million pounds (!) of raw opium into the sea. Thinking he had won, Lin wrote the emperor, that the Westerners "don't dare show any disrespect, and indeed I would judge from their attitudes that they have the decency to feel heartily ashamed."[30] Not for the last time did a Chinese misunderstand Western attitudes and body language.

Once the news reached England passions flared. The West was not going to stand for illegal Chinese acts against honest traders. Troops were mobilized and a fleet dispatched to deal with the Chinese. It arrived in Canton in June 1840.

The British blockaded Canton harbor but had bigger fish to fry than dealing with Commissioner Lin. Sailing north they blockaded the mouth of the Yangtse River then sailed to Tainjin (the port closest to Beijing) and blockaded it. The Chinese sued for peace, agreeing to pay a huge indemnity for the opium; to allow diplomats to establish direct contacts with the Qing court in Beijing; to give up Hong Kong to the British; and to open up Canton … if the British fleet would only leave Tainjin. It appeared to be a great victory, yet once the British Government discovered what they'd gained they were furious at such paltry gains. The Chinese were equally unhappy, with the Chinese negotiator first sentenced to death, then banishment.

Once London's displeasure was known, the British fleet pressed on. The initial blockades were not lifted and the fleet sailed up the Yangtse, first seizing Shanghai then Nanking, the old imperial capital, and halting shipping on the lower Yangtse. Traffic on the Grand Canal was blocked, stopping southern rice from reaching northern China cities. Too much for the Chinese, they again they sued for peace.

The Treaty of Nanking ended the first Opium War, a humiliating defeat for China. Just some of the conditions show why: Hong Kong was ceded to Britain in perpetuity; Westerners were to be judged by Western, not Chinese laws; five more ports (including Shanghai, the prize) were opened and traders were allowed to trade with anyone. Most galling of all, China had no choice but to grant Most Favored Nation (MFN) status to all countries, ending any chance of playing one off against the others, the traditional Chinese strategy of dealing with barbarians. Finally, China was not allowed to use terms like "inferior barbarians" when communicating with Westerners.

China was now open, traders and missionaries flooded to and throughout China. Not satisfied though, the Western powers (England and France) kept asking for more. Occasional clashes between Chinese and Westerners made Westerners more determined, leading in 1856 to open hostilities. Once again the Western fleet sailed to Tianjin, except this time marines came ashore and fought their way to Beijing. When twenty Westerners were captured while under a flag of truce the Western commander ordered the Summer Palace destroyed. At this the Chinese gave in, totally. Besides agreeing to existing demands and an even higher indemnity, Chinese allowed Western ambassadors to live in Beijing *as equals* and allowed missionaries to own land. China was losing control of its territory, and in danger of ending up just another Western colony.

China Is Too Successful To Change

It didn't happen. China did not become a British, French or other Western colony, but it was close. Instead of creating colonies Western nations carved China up into "spheres of influence," areas where their nationals were given exclusive trading privileges. China was big enough to share; no one wanted to fight over getting an even-larger piece. This land rush was not restricted to large European powers either. Besides England and France other countries, Austria, Germany, Italy and Russia among them, all received their piece of China. Even Japan, long just a minor planet orbiting the Chinese sun, also got a part of China to control.

What did the Chinese do to prevent this? Not enough. Unlike Japan, China did not accept that the world had changed and that they had to change with it (see table below). The Chinese court and vast majority of officials and gentry turned backwards, seeking answers from past glories to the problems now facing China. There was a revival of Confucian teaching, with stress on China's moral superiority and its application to practical affairs. Edicts from Beijing reinforced notions like the health and preservation of Chinese society depended upon a strict hierarchical organization with all following the proper rules and procedures for their position. While egalitarianism was sweeping the world, China stressed elitism. The ideal was static harmony, not dynamic growth.

Not all Chinese accepted this conservative vision of how China should react to Western encroaching on Chinese sovereignty. A small group of important scholars/gentry/generals began to argue China was weak not because of moral bankruptcy or because it lacked men of ability, but because it refused to change its institutions, especially the education system. These agitators believed Chinese officials must learn more from the West (a radical departure from 1000s of years of Chinese practice), in practical areas like mathematics, military science, technology, science and geography.

Yet even these forward-looking Chinese strongly believed in the basic superiority of Chinese culture. A popular slogan of the time sums up their attitude: "Chinese learning for essence, Western learning for practice." The agitators believed China did not need to make any basic changes, just learn Western techniques then graft them on to the Chinese system. Such a belief severely hampered their efforts, leading to cases like chemistry explained as stemming from the Chinese ancient belief in the 'five elements.' Everything new had to fit into old Chinese beliefs, and could not upset Chinese values. China sent 120 students to the US for study, but when Chinese officials saw they were adapting successfully to Western life and education, they said the students were becoming too "Westernized" and sent them back to China. The emphasis was always on changing the absolute minimum amount.

Nevertheless, from this group sprang China's first capitalists, investing in railways, shipping, textiles and mining. These efforts withered though, in large part because of a lack of support from Beijing and the ruling class. The conservative majority thought such modern or Western things like railroads or steamboats would hurt the peoples' livelihood, a good albeit short-term economic argument. In one classic example China's first railroad was bought by a conservative official, who then tore it up.

Japan and China: Two Routes to Modernization

The differing paths China and Japan took to modernization and dealing with the new Western world powers highlights key differences between these two very similar ancient cultures. In many ways these differences are true today.

From 1635 to 1854 Japan was isolated from the outside world; all contact, including with China and other Asian cultures, was restricted to one city, Nagasaki. During these centuries Japan looked inward, totally. In 1853 the American Commodore Perry sailed into Tokyo bay with his black ships, so named as they were coal-fired steamships belching clouds of black smoke. This show of power so overawed the Japanese that Japan quickly signed treaties with America (and soon other countries) that opened Japan after two hundred years of isolation. In 1868 Japan's long-standing power structure changed; power was transferred from the Shogun to the Emperor. At the urging of the new Meiji Emperor Japan actively looked outwards, sending delegations and students to the West to learn the secrets of science, government and military arts. Japan was transformed, almost overnight. The samurai ruling class was encouraged to replace swords with briefcases, becoming Japan's leading capitalists. Industrialization was quick and dramatic. In 1895 Japan defeated China, in 1905 defeated Russia, by World War I Japan was an industrial and military force to be reckoned with.

Why was Japan able to change and China unable? Starting from a near-identical base—conservative Confucian culture, desire to be left alone, belief in superiority of values and morality and a culture that had not changed for hundreds of years—what was it that made such a huge difference between Japan's and China's reaction to the coming of the West? A complicated question, below are the key elements:

China	Japan
• history of cultural superiority	• history of cultural borrowing
• motivators were small group of not-senior officials: no top-down pressure for change	• motivators were senior officials, emperor & samurai: top down pressure for change
• non-Chinese leaders were considered illegitimate	• Japanese leaders were considered legitimate
• loosely controlled society	• tightly controlled society
• top officials wouldn't be businessmen	• top officials became businessmen
• industrialization was resisted	• industrialization was embraced
• education and learning from outside actively discouraged	• education and learning from outside actively encouraged
• change was resisted and China lost control over change	• change was embraced and Japan kept control over change

It's the difference between inheriting and acquiring. China was like old money mostly gone, so sure of their rightful position—inheritors of the glory and position of the Middle Kingdom—they were unwilling even to consider change. Japan had only bought the Confucian mindset from foreigners so was ready to look at the new model for sale, the West and all its baggage, industry, capitalism, impartial laws and, gasp, democracy. The results speak for themselves. Perhaps the best way to end this analysis is to say China's response proved that there is such a thing as being too successful.

Table 3: Japan and China: Two Routes To Modernization

To add to China's woes, from the 1870s Ci Xi, the Empress Dowager, ruled China. Described as very cunning and strong-willed, the Empress was extremely conservative, totally ignorant of the West and totally confident of China's moral superiority. By manipulating the succession Ci Xi was able to remain regent and in control. China stagnated under the Empress' rule, looking inward and at the past rather than outward and to the future.

China had one last, best chance to change itself. In 1895 a young (37) Confucian scholar, Kang You Wei, presented a long memorial outlining where, why and how China had to change. Even though based on Confucius—using a clever interpretation of Confucius, Kang showed where the great sage actually supported his reforms—the proposed reforms were the real deal, calling for changes to the education system, wholesale adoption of Western techniques and reforms to crucial areas like banking and taxation. Nothing happened for three years, until the Guang Xu emperor, a supporter of Kang, went against his aunt Ci Xi and issued an extraordinary series of official edicts.

Called the 'Hundred Days Reform,' in three short months Guang Xu called for abolition of the Confucian education system (in place since the Tang Dynasty over a thousand years earlier), replacing knowledge of poetry and calligraphy with Western technical and scientific subjects, replacing essays on ancient texts with practical questions about the issues then facing China. Equally radical reforms were called for in agriculture, military affairs, bureaucracy and industrialization. China now had what it needed and had lacked since the coming of the West, top down pressure for reform. The top down pressure did not last.

Worried about the effects of such reforms on the ruling class and her imperial prerogatives, Ci Xi stepped in and took back power. Guang Xu was placed under house arrest, where he remained for the rest of his life (dying in 1908 in suspicious circumstances one day before Ci Xi died). His closest supporters at court were also arrested and executed. Kang You Wei escaped the purge, fleeing to Hong Kong (on a British navy ship). To the dismay of Chinese reformers and Westerners in China, reform was dead and the old conservative clique back in power. The last, best chance for the old regime to reform China and stay in power was over; China's misfortunes were not.

China Unravels

China's situation continued to unravel throughout the latter half of the 19th century. One disaster followed another. During the Sino-French war of 1883-85 the French destroyed large parts of China's modern navy and China lost control of Vietnam. To ensure this humiliation would not be repeated China undertook a huge 10-year naval buildup, but to no avail. In 1895 China and Japan fought over control of Korea. China's navy was decisively defeated, and China lost control of Korea and Formosa (Taiwan). Why didn't the Chinese naval investment pay off? It was the same old problems: Chinese spent money on hardware and not software, on ships and guns but not on training sailors; massive corruption led to naval shells with no gunpowder; and funds meant for navy ships were diverted to rebuilding the Summer Palace (destroyed by Westerners), including a marble boat for Empress Ci Xi to command.

In response to these humiliations and worsening economic conditions, the Boxer Rebellion erupted in 1900. The Boxers (Righteous Fists) were a superstitious peasant movement who believed that proper exercise and conditioning would make them invulnerable, even to bullets. Anti-Christian and initially anti-Qing, the Empress supported the Boxers and turned their furies from against her to against foreigners. When the Boxers surrounded the foreign missions in Beijing the West mounted an army to rescue them. China responded by declaring war on the West. After a short 3-month war the Western army fought its way into Beijing. Wearing a disguise Ci Xi escaped the city by cart while Western soldiers looted the city.

More concessions, more payments to barbarians and less control of key areas inside China: as most actions tried since the West arrived at China's shores, the Boxer Rebellion ended badly for China. The Chinese court tried to mollify growing internal demands for change with new reforms—replacing the Confucian examination system with Western-style schools the most important—but it was too little, too late. Chinese were now learning from abroad, especially from Japan (the new Asia hero after defeating Russia in 1905) and agitating for real changes in China.

My story ends here. I leave out the end of the Qing Dynasty in 1911, the rise of the warlords, Sun Yat-sen and the Republic of China, the Long March, Japanese aggression and World War II, civil war between Mao Zedong's Communists and Chiang Kai-shek's Nationalists, China divided. To explain such an eventful and calamitous century would take 20 pages, and, while fascinating, would not add much more to the themes already described.

Themes and Lessons

While it took longer than I thought—Chinese history is *long*—this actually very brief look at Chinese history shows how history has shaped Chinese thinking and attitudes, even to today. Here are the major themes and lessons I hope you draw from it:

1. China is truly unlike any other major civilization. It developed on its own, and because of that developed a belief that China was the true, the only center of civilization. Such a belief was quite natural: until the coming of the West every culture China encountered wanted to learn from China.

2. China is the only ancient civilization that still exists today. Amazingly stable, the Confucian system remained unchanged for over 2000 years, and still strongly echoes through Chinese culture today.

3. Chinese see themselves as the inheritors of the glory of imperial China, and see what happened in the past less as dry history in books than as colorful stories of their extended family.

4. China produced the most successful culture the world has ever seen. If the West had not arrived, China would not have changed. This is what Chinese learn in schools today. It probably is true.

5. China had no experience learning from the outside; the few lessons they did import were changed to fit Chinese prior beliefs before they were accepted or used.

6. Westerners that arrived came to change China, not learn from it. Other than the Jesuits, Westerners neither respected Chinese ways nor tried to fit Western ideas into Chinese cultural environment. This continues today.

7. China only changed when forced to change, then changed the absolute minimum amount necessary to solve the current crisis. The Chinese never developed a proactive policy towards change. This continues today.

I ask readers to remember the above points while reading further chapters. Westerners still ask China to change—WTO, copyright protection, following contracts—and, too often, still don't pay attention to China's unique situation. China has problems with change but Westerners don't, the cause of the biggest lesson Westerners should learn: instead of insisting Chinese do things "your" way, look at how you can adapt your ways to meet Chinese sensibilities. As explained in a later chapter, Westerners are result-oriented people, not process-oriented. Success in Chinese Asia comes from focusing on the result, not the process, a mistake Westerners make all too often.

The final lesson I hope you take from this brief examination of Chinese history is respect for what China was and sympathy for the position Chinese Asia is in now. Change was forced upon the Chinese, changes they were unprepared for. Changes are still being forced on the Chinese, and while one could argue that they could and should have done better in the last hundred years to prepare citizens for such changes, the truth is that they have not.

CHAPTER FOUR

Should You Market or Sell Messages?

Who is more important to overall communication success, the speaker or the audience? You or the person you are talking to? Not just when talking to Chinese, but to anyone. A good question, my answer is impolite, as it starts with another question: Do you know what I will write next?

No, you don't know what I will write next. *I* know what I will write next though; like all speakers (writers) I already have the message 100% clear and complete in my head. I know what I want to say, and what messages I want you to receive.

How do I judge communication success? Unless my goal is to talk to myself, I have to look to you (the audience) to judge communication success. My communication success or failure is measured in only one place, inside the reader's (audience's) head. If the audience understands my message 100% clearly and completely I succeed, if not, I fail. When I communicate, my goal is the audience receiving and understanding my entire message. If you agree with this so far—just common sense I think—then it seems to prove that you are more important than I am, that the reader (audience) is more important than the writer (speaker).

The Audience Is Important Than the Speaker

I know the message. You don't know the message. The only way I can succeed is if you receive my message clearly and completely. That makes you more important than me. I think the logic is simple, and leads to a crucial conclusion: your job as speaker or writer is to do everything possible to make it easy for your audience to understand your message! To emphasize this point during workshops I often make it while kneeling on the ground and banging my head on the floor, doing the *kow tow*[31] to my students to show that they are the boss of the class, not me.

I mean it: my students truly are my bosses. Think about it. I already know the material I teach. The only way I measure teaching success is how much of my material is transferred to between the ears of my students. What I have to do to accomplish that it irrelevant; the only important thing is that the transfer happens. Who cares if I have to act like a clown—it does happen—or like a serious, glued-to-the-lectern professor to achieve my goal? I am not important, students are, and their understanding determines my communication success, period. This gives us the first three communication principles:

Communication Principles

1. the goal of communication is complete and clear transfer of message from the sender to the receiver

2. the audience is more important than the speaker

3. communication success is measured by how much of the speaker's message is transferred clearly and completely to the audience

---

Usually about now someone, usually a salesperson, puts up a hand and asks, "But isn't the goal of communication that people agree with you?"

"No," I say, "agreement is just one of the possible secondary goals. Understanding the intended message is always the first goal." Why? Because a person (audience) first must understand what the intended message *is* before it is possible to decide to agree or not. A focus on gaining agreement as your primary goal increases the risk that the audience might misunderstand your intended message, thus might agree with something you never said. That is bad. (Think Smith and Chen in Chapter 2.) No matter what your secondary goal is—audience agrees with your point, does what you want, follows your instructions or answers your question—the audience must first understand your message 100% clearly. It makes sense to me.

Difference Between Selling And Marketing Messages

Audience is more important than the speaker is maybe the most crucial principle to remember in all forms of communication. No matter the level, content or situation, the person (audience) you are communicating with is more important than you are. What does that mean in real life? It means a lot, but it is going to take me a roundabout way to explain. Impolite again, I start with a question: What is the difference between sales and marketing? I know this does not sound relevant to communication but if you can be patient, I will make it so.

Is there an actual difference between sales and marketing? European audiences are usually quiet when I ask, a little unsure, and tend to say that sales and marketing are just different aspects of the same job. American audiences are the opposite, and hands go up as soon as I ask the question. Americans tend to say there is a difference, a clear difference. This is not a business school text-book though, so I dodge the debate by saying I believe both sides have a point. What is important is that you think of the differences between the two jobs, slight though you think these may be.

For teaching purposes, I have my own way of describing the differences between sales and marketing. Sales is active on the part of the speaker. When you sell you focus on your needs; you do whatever you must to convince the audience to do what *you want* to satisfy *your* needs. Sales is a selfish act. When you sell, you want the customer (audience) to adapt to your needs. Yes, yes, I know all about customer satisfaction and selling just what your customer needs, and it's all true, most of the time anyway. Maybe not so much at the end of the month though.

Let me use a pen example. I sell pens. It is the last day of the month and I am visiting the last customer of the day. I need to sell ten pens to this customer in order to reach quota and get my sales bonus. I am very motivated to make this sale. There is a problem though: I sell felt pens but the customer really is looking for ball-point pens, not felt pens. With my quota looming large in my mind I set out to convince the customer that they actually need (or can use) felt pens. True or not, I focus on *my* needs (meeting quota) rather than *customer* needs (getting the pens they really want).

Sales can only sell products they have, not products they might like to have. In that sense, sales *is* selfish.

(This is perhaps too much of a black-hat view of sales and I apologize for the unfriendly generalizations, but you get the point. Sales means you ultimately worry about your needs, not audience needs. Sales' goal is to convince the customer to do what the sales-person needs: buy my products!)

Marketing is the exact opposite. As a marketer I analyze my customer's needs and see that felt pens are not what the customer really wants or needs. Instead of focusing on my needs (sell the pens we have) I communicate with production and design, asking if they could produce ballpoint pens as well. In other words, I try to change or adapt in order to meet the needs of my customer. While doing this is perhaps uncomfortable, perhaps meaning lost sales and increased capital investment, it pays off. Good marketing means easy sales.

To summarize, I define sales as focusing on your needs and convincing the audience to adapt to your products or pitch, and marketing as focusing on audience needs and adapting your products or pitch to meet their needs. If you don't agree with my definitions … I understand, but please try to live with them. Now, turning back to communication and using my definitions, should you *sell* or *market* your messages? Not just in cross-culture situations, but in all situations.

The right answer is marketing. You do it every day. Let's say I am talking to two people, an eight-year-old child and a university professor. Like me, both are Canadians, fluent in English. Can I speak to them in the same way?

No. To communicate with the eight year old I must simplify my language, use small words, easy examples and very basic logic (if at all). If I don't do this the eight year old will not understand (or even listen to) my message: communication failure. Now, what would happen if I spoke to the university professor as if he/she was an eight year old? Oops, no fun. Thinking I was talking down to him or her, the professor would not be happy and would not listen properly: communication failure again. To speak success-fully to the professor I must use the big words professors tend to like so much, phrases like the corollary of the concomitant dichotomous relationship, or jargon of some sort. Back to the eight-year-old, if I used 'professor words' to him or her I would fail yet again.

I change my way of talking to match the communication needs of the audience. I market my message, not sell it. In order to satisfy *my* needs, that the audience clearly understands my message, I adapt my communication style to meet the *audience's* needs. We do this all the time without thinking; it's just the natural thing to do. If you are married, remember the first time you met your wife's father (or husband's mother). You were probably very polite and respectful. Now compare that to the way you speak to him/her now: after 10 years of successful marriage, you are able to speak on a far friendlier, almost-equal basis. If, however, you would have spoken to him or her *then* as you do *now* ... you would probably have married someone else.

We market our messages without thinking about it, changing the way we speak to match the communication needs and expectations of each different audience. Do you speak to your boss the same way you speak to your secretary? Not likely: you 'tell' your secretary what to do; you 'suggest' to your boss what he should do. Be it to your wife, best friend, boss, coworker or gas station attendant you change your communication style depending upon whether you are asking a favor or making a complaint. You market your message.

If you know *Situational Leadership*[32] you know this principle, that there is no one 'right' way to lead, that your leadership style should change to suit the needs and expectations of the person you are leading. It is exactly the same principle when you communicate: there is no one 'right' way to communicate. You must change your communication style to match the needs and expectations of the person with whom you are communicating. To me it is a no-brainer, but then I have an eight-year-old daughter and have university professor friends.

When we are in our own culture we tend to market our messages (adjust to the audience) very naturally, almost without thinking. When we are with Chinese Asia though, we tend to sell our messages (focus on our needs), not market. Why? What is the difference? We market messages within our own culture because we understand the audience's needs and expectations: we sell messages outside our culture because we don't know what audiences need or expect. It is that simple.

A key first step in marketing is to understand your target customer. To understand your target customer you must do market research. If you don't understand the target customers' needs, all you can do is to sell, that is, focus on the only needs you know, your own. If you don't know Chinese needs or expectations, you will sell your messages to them.

I supply the missing market research. I explain what Chinese communication needs and expectations are. All good, but I can't do the most important step: I can't make you market your message. That is up to you, and your success depends on it. If you don't understand the need to market, to adapt to the Chinese audience, you will never get a pair of Chinese glasses.

To me this is obvious, yet some refuse, saying it is too tough to adjust to the Chinese, or that the Chinese should adapt to them.[33] Well, I agree that marketing your message in Chinese Asia is not always easy and not always comfortable, but so what? If you want to succeed, you have no choice but to adjust. If you agree so far I have one more piece of advice. Try to adjust willingly, with a smile on your face. Mistakes are inevitable, and smiling reduces (but does not eliminate) frustration.

What follows is a look at the difference between selling and marketing messages in the Chinese context. Later chapters explain how to use these principles to achieve communication success.

Selling Your Message

All else being equal, which is better, a one-step or a two-step process? Murphy's Law (whatever can go wrong will go wrong) suggests that a one-step process is better, less chance for something to go wrong. When you sell your message, it is two steps for the audience, one for the speaker.

Two steps for the audience, one for the speaker, the opposite of what should happen. Why? Well, if it is true that the goal of communication is the clear and complete transfer of message, and if it is true that communication success is measured between the ears of the audience, then the speaker should make it as easy as possible for the audience to 'get' the message. It should be two steps for the speaker, one for the audience.

Selling your message looks like this:

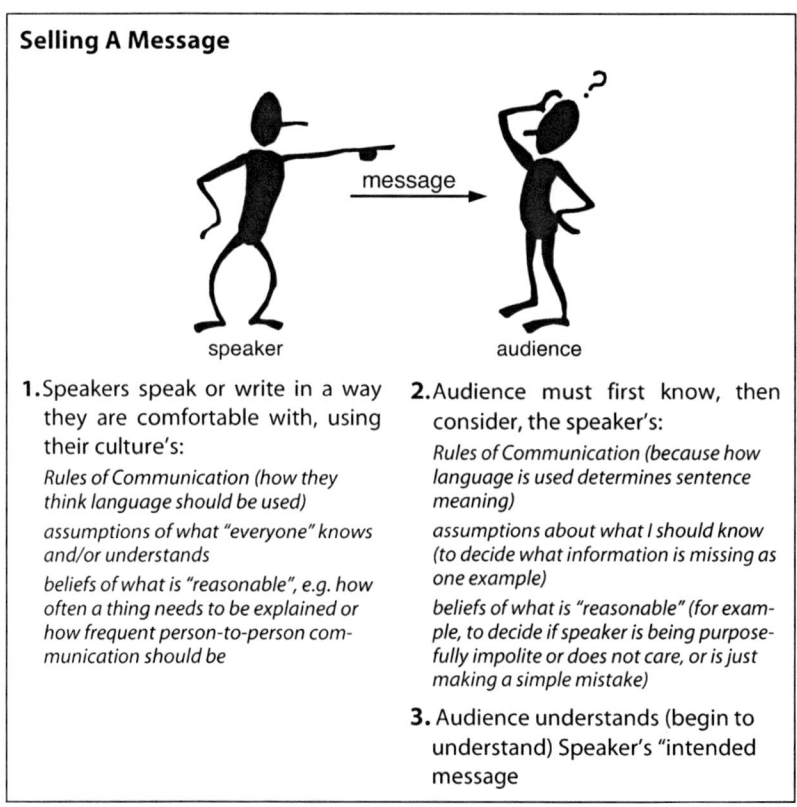

Selling A Message

speaker   audience

1. Speakers speak or write in a way they are comfortable with, using their culture's:

   Rules of Communication (how they think language should be used)

   assumptions of what "everyone" knows and/or understands

   beliefs of what is "reasonable", e.g. how often a thing needs to be explained or how frequent person-to-person communication should be

2. Audience must first know, then consider, the speaker's:

   Rules of Communication (because how language is used determines sentence meaning)

   assumptions about what I should know (to decide what information is missing as one example)

   beliefs of what is "reasonable" (for example, to decide if speaker is being purposefully impolite or does not care, or is just making a simple mistake)

3. Audience understands (begin to understand) Speaker's "intended message

Table 4. Selling A Message

How about an example? Let's go back to my buying a briefcase, a good example of how a culture's Rules of Communication determines sentence meaning. Being a good Westerner I expect disagreement to be clear and direct. I listened to my wife raise two objections (possible problems) with my purchase, one about price, the other about size. I answered each objection in turn. After answering her objections I asked for her thoughts; she was silent, which to me meant agreement (or that I'd satisfied her objections). Even though I was (or thought I was) sensitive to Chinese *ways* in

general and her feelings in particular, I never once heard, or sus-
pected, disagreement. Expecting disagreement to be clear, straight,
some variation of 'I don't think you should buy it; Don't buy it; I
disagree; No,' when I didn't hear anything resembling disagreement I assumed my wife agreed.

She was trying to disagree though, and in her mind had
clearly communicated disagreement to me. The language she used
is irrelevant (see below); while her words were in English, her
communication style was pure Chinese, based on Chinese Rules of
Communication. Oops: my ears were tuned to Western Rules so I
never heard her *Don't buy it* message, thus went ahead and bought
it. As I tried to explain to her during our argument, if she had told
me 'don't buy it' I never would have; she argued back that she
had told me 'don't buy it' and I had defied her. Our marriage now
moved in the dreaded 'go broke' direction due to the start of mutual questions about mutual trust.

The problem was my wife *sold* me her message instead of
marketing it. Being Chinese, she was uncomfortable with open disagreement so she used one of her culture's ways of communicating disagreement without being open about it (raising objections
to show disagreement). I failed to get her message because I had
to do two steps, first I had to *understand* Chinese Rules of
Communication *and consider them*, and only after that could begin
step two, getting her message.

I must stress this problem has **nothing** to do with language.
Recently some of my wife's Chinese friends stayed with us for a
few days. Their English wasn't very good so we used mostly Chinese. Recent immigrants to Canada, they were preparing for their
oldest child to enter university. One evening the subject of university came up. I realized that her friends had some mistaken ideas
about Canadian universities. Like many Chinese, our friends were
more familiar with American things and had based their plans on
the American university system. I could see that their plan would
cause them trouble, time and money. I felt it was my duty as a
friend to prevent them from making a mistake, so I tried to explain where their errors were, and what would happen if they
didn't change their plan. I thought I had done well.

My wife didn't think so. When our guests had gone to bed my wife jumped all over me about what I had said to them. I asked her, "Well, what was wrong, my grammar, my pronunciation?" She said it was not my Chinese skills (for a change), it was that "you should never have asked your questions that way. You were extremely impolite." Her point was that I had used Chinese words but spoken like a Westerner, direct and to the point. She worried that I had offended our guests by telling the husband *in front of his wife and children* that his information on Canadian universities was incorrect. You know, she was right. I should have used the Chinese way, should have used an indirect, roundabout way to 'suggest' that maybe the husband could look at the university plans again. As my wife told me, stopping him from making a mistake was not my job; not hurting his feelings was. (I continue this point later in the book.)

Different University Systems and Buying A Briefcase are two examples of how different Rules of Communication can cause problems. Three Invitations To Dinner is another example: the problem happened because my friends used a Chinese way of inviting. I expected any invitation to be in the classic Western, yes/no question format, so did not realize I was being invited Chinese style, thus misunderstood, three times! I return to this example in Chapter 7. For now, I hope you see that my friends sold me the invitation, used English words but not a Western way of using language.

More than just different Rules of Communication cause problems though. An equal, maybe even larger, problem is caused by assumptions about what 'everybody knows.' Time for yet another embarrassing story. I have lots of them.

Assumptions Are Dangerous

In the late 80s I was tired of Taipei (the Big Smoke as I called it) but not of Taiwan. Wanting to see Taiwan countryside, I moved south 90 km to Bao San (Treasure Mountain), a very small village on the outskirts of the Hsin Chu Science Park, Taiwan's Silicon Valley. The Science Park that now dominates Hsin Chu was just starting up and the city was still a sleepy, conservative place. On a trip home to Canada I purchased a bolt of suit fabric, a nice light wool blend, dark gray with light pinstripes. On my return to Hsin Chu a Chinese friend recommended a tailor to me. "Oh, very nice fabric," the tailor said as he fingered the material. He measured me and told me to come back in few days for a fitting. When I returned I was in a true rush so paid little attention to what he did. A week later I returned for the suit. He had done an excellent job; well tailored, it fit perfectly. Too bad I couldn't wear it. Can you guess why?

In a pinstripe suit, how do the stripes go, north-south (vertical) or east-west (horizontal)? North-south of course, unless you are in prison. Though not a convict, the pinstripes on my beautiful new suit ran east-west, not north-south. I had not told the tailor to make the stripes run north-south, assuming that "of course everyone knows that."

Who was wrong, the tailor or me? Me. Using Western glasses I assumed *everyone* knows that pin stripes always run north-south, so never thought to tell him to make the stripes go that way. It never crossed my mind that stripe direction was an issue! Why didn't he already know to make the stripes vertical? Why should he? What type of suits did Chinese businessmen (especially outside the big cities) wear? Solid color suits, most-often dark blue. Pin stripe suits were (are) rare outside of financial centers like Shanghai and Hong Kong. What other clothes did Taiwan tailors make? School uniforms, all solid color or some type of tartan, never stripes, pin or otherwise. Of course he didn't know to make the stripes vertical. It was my responsibility to tell him but, as I was looking at the suit through Western eyes and basing my assumptions on what happens in the West, I never even considered the stripes issue … until too late.

(The only time I now wear the suit is when I teach Westerners, but only if I can take it off during the lunch break. I enjoy watching students see my suit and, too polite to say anything to me but too amazed to be quiet, watch them poke other students and whisper, "Look at his suit." It really helps me drive home the point that assumptions about what *everyone knows* can kill you.)

The same troubles arise over what is 'reasonable.' We all have an idea about what is reasonable, yet just like how we think words should be used and the hundreds of other assumptions we carry with us, our ideas about what is and is not reasonable are determined by our culture (in large part: personality can play a big role too). This is best explained by an example, but for a change not one of my mistakes. Finally.

Who Decides What Is Reasonable?

In the early 90s I led a team that reengineered a famous British-Dutch multinational's 'order, delivery, billing, payment' business process. A huge, complicated job, we had to restructure entire departments, change job descriptions and work flows, and introduce new ways to measure performance, changes that affected promotions and compensation, always a sensitive and tricky task. Company employees were understandably quite nervous by what we were doing, nervous and worried.

My boss was British, smart (Oxford graduate) and demanding, a great guy. At project kickoff, the boss wrote a memo to calm staff fears: he explained what we were doing and that no one would be fired because of the project (something I insist on before taking such jobs). About two months into the project we started to make our first changes. I asked him to send another memo to all staff; like the first, its goal was to tell them not to be nervous about the changes. The British boss refused.

He told me that he had already sent such a memo, and that sending another one was "not reasonable." Huh? I explained that yes, from an Oxford-educated, Western-culture point of view sending a second, nearly-identical memo *may* be 'unreasonable,' i.e., not needed so a waste of time. But the audience here was not made up of Oxford-educated Westerners. I explained that his Chinese staff may not have understood everything he wrote in his first memo (written as it was in very bureaucratic, educated English … but I never said that) and needed things explained again, needed reassurance about their job security.

He would not move. "It's just not reasonable Greg. I have already explained everything once. Once is enough. They work for XXX company." I tried and tried to change his mind. I told him that not only was a second memo needed, we might need a third or a fourth as well, that his staff still were unsure about what was happening and that project success depended on staff cooperation. My pleas fell on deaf ears. I had to write the memo myself, and a consultant's memo is not nearly as powerful or as reassuring as one from the boss. Sigh. I wrote two more memos after that.

Frequency, or how often things should happen, is another difference between Westerners and Chinese. More than a few Chinese have told me that Westerners are very selfish, that they only care about themselves. Why? Because, "The only time I hear from my Western partner is when he wants something." Discussed in more detail in a later chapter, for now just think about what the Chinese said. The only time we write/call/email/fax our Chinese partner is when we want something, information about a shipment, a change in an order, a problem we want solved. We think of this as correct, efficient; Chinese see it as being selfish, that you are interested in your gain only.

The above examples have two points in common: the speaker's communication and actions stemmed from his/her ideas of what was the right thing to do, and all failed. Selling messages and actions does not work! To improve your chances of success in Chinese Asia you must think marketing. So, what does the Chinese audience want? Expect? Require?

Marketing Your Message

Marketing your message puts the pressure (and the extra steps) on the person who already knows the message, the speaker. This is where it belongs.

Marketing is two steps for the speaker, one for the audience. As the speaker marketed the message the audience it is likely (nothing is sure) to understand it because the message is offered in the way the audience understands, contains all the information the audience needs and is offered when or how often the audience expects. Marketing means making it easy and comfortable for your audience to understand your message. Just common sense.

If my friends and Chinese family would have marketed their dinner invitations to me—used the yes/no question format to invite me—I would have accepted the first invitation and declined the next two, less embarrassment for all concerned. If my wife would have marketed her disagreement to me—directly telling me her thoughts—I would not have bought the briefcase, less argument for both of us. If my client would have thought marketing

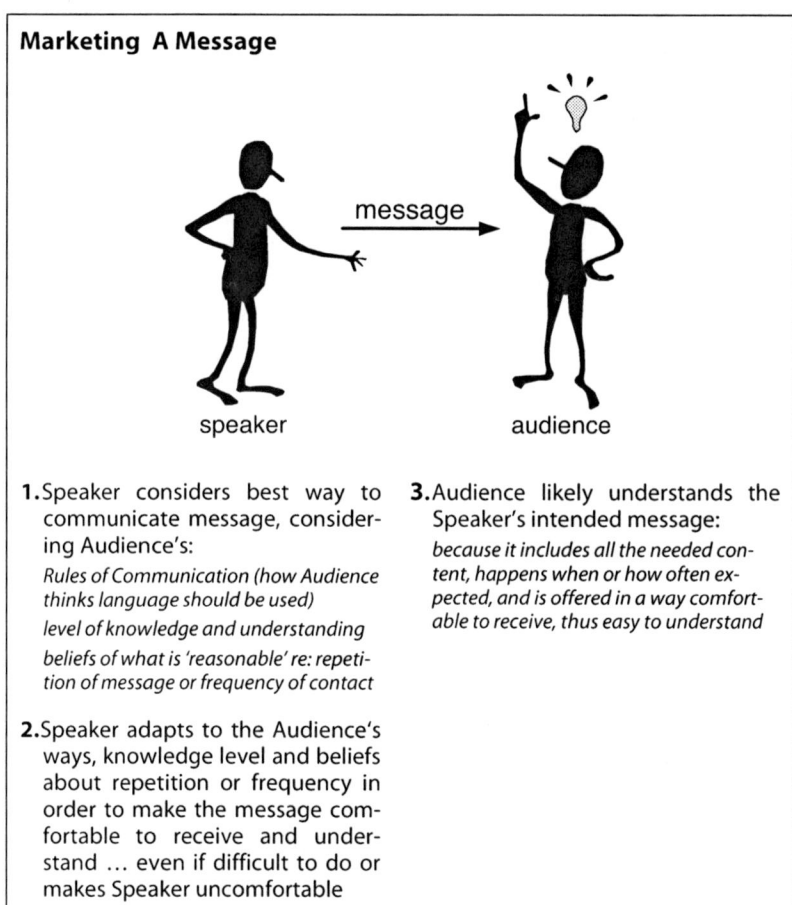

Marketing A Message

message

speaker   audience

1. Speaker considers best way to communicate message, considering Audience's:

    Rules of Communication (how Audience thinks language should be used)

    level of knowledge and understanding

    beliefs of what is 'reasonable' re: repetition of message or frequency of contact

2. Speaker adapts to the Audience's ways, knowledge level and beliefs about repetition or frequency in order to make the message comfortable to receive and understand … even if difficult to do or makes Speaker uncomfortable

3. Audience likely understands the Speaker's intended message:

    because it includes all the needed content, happens when or how often expected, and is offered in a way comfortable to receive, thus easy to understand

Table 4: Marketing A Message

he would have sent the second memo, making his staff feel better thus leading to better results for his company and less work for me. And finally, if I would have marketed my fashion request to my tailor—stripes go up/down, not left/right—I would have bought a suit I could regularly wear instead of using it as an expensive stage prop.

Faxing Frustrations

Another example. An American friend in Hong Kong got involved in a situation. A Chinese company was renovating a big hotel on Hong Kong side and was getting the new carpet from a US carpet company. The Chinese had sent a fax asking for a carpet sample. No answer, no sample. They sent a second fax; no reply, no sample. A third fax again produced no results. Deadlines were slipping and the Chinese company was worried. My friend got involved in the situation.

He looked at the faxes and quickly knew what the problem was. He asked the boss if there was an English-language contract with the US company. There was. He wasn't a lawyer but could read a contract, and it looked like the American company should have already sent the missing sample. He wrote a new fax. This all took him at most 15 minutes. It took him the rest of an hour to convince the boss to send the fax. What was the problem? All sales, no marketing.

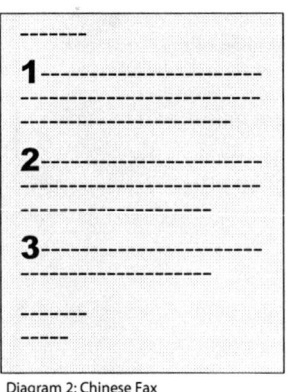

Diagram 2: Chinese Fax

To the left is a normal three-paragraph Chinese fax. In a Chinese fax, letter, email, what is the first paragraph for? Polite language, compliments to build the relationship from the past until now, words like 'How wonderful it is to do business with your well-respected, famous company.' The third (or last) paragraph has more polite language, building the relationship from now into the future, how much they look forward to working with such a fantastic company etc. The actual message is in the second or middle paragraph, and put into polite language as well.

The message was in the last sentence of the second paragraph, words like, 'We look forward to receiving a sample of your carpet as soon as you find it convenient to ship it.' Is that an urgent message? No? Are you sure? Maybe it depends on what glasses you wear. Looking through Western glasses it is not urgent, I agree, but if I wore Chinese glasses I'd consider it an urgent message.

Certainly the Chinese boss meant it to be urgent. A key principle in Chinese communication is *the more important the situation is the more important it is to be polite.* When the first fax did not work the second fax was more polite, the third even more so.

The Americans looked for the Chinese company's message in the first sentence of the first paragraph, and found instead polite garbage, overly-polite garbage to boot. Not finding the message at the start, only meaningless, too-polite words, put the Westerners in the wrong frame of mind. By the time the Americans saw the actual message (bottom of second paragraph), their eyes were probably a little glazed over. The message was in the wrong place and written in an unclear, polite way, so they missed it, their eyes likely moving swiftly to the too-polite last paragraph.

The Americans had probably never seen a fax quite like it. There's a good chance it was shown to co-workers, asking, 'Can you believe what this says about our #*!!& company?' Being such a novelty the Chinese fax might have ended up pinned to the lunchroom wall, complete with arrows, circles and comments. Not quite the outcome the Chinese wanted.

When no one responded and no sample arrived, the Chinese sent a second fax, but as it was now more urgent, it was even more polite. I can only imagine the American reaction to it, and to the third, more urgent thus even more polite, fax. Being busy (shipping departments always are) I suspect the American manager's reaction was something like, 'Hell, when the Chinese figure out what they want they'll

Diagram 3: Western Fax

tell me. For now though I'll just put these in the 'round file' (garbage can).'

Before going on I need to repeat a point: like all previous examples, this was not a language skills problem. The fax was written in Chinglish (Chinese English), but good Chinglish. There was nothing wrong with grammar or vocabulary, just how Chinese used language. The Chinese followed their Rules of Communication, not Western Rules.

Back to Hong Kong. My friend knew what the problem was and reading the contract showed how to solve it; he wrote the short fax shown above. Quite simple, he wrote, "Dear M., please send carpet sample ABC123 as soon as possible or we will consult with our lawyers. Thank you for your kind attention." Simple, polite (it did say please) and with the message both clear and in the proper place for Westerners. My friend was happy with it. The Chinese boss was not.

The Chinese boss did not want to send it because, "It is not polite." My friend explained the situation for almost 50 minutes! He finally convinced the Chinese boss to send it by explaining that yes, while it was not polite for the oh-so-polite Chinese, it was being sent to rude Americans, not polite Chinese, and that this format was polite to barbarians. *"You dao li, you dao li"* he answered (that makes sense). He sent it.

What happened when the Americans received the short fax? The manager probably went something like, 'What? Lawyers!?!' Checking the contract and discovering the sample should have already been shipped, the manager made getting the sample out the door the first priority. Exactly what the Chinese wanted in the first place, and what the Western manager wanted from the start.

Okay, who is at fault here? The Chinese: instead of *marketing* the message, writing it in a way that met American (audience's) expectations, they *sold* the message, writing in a way they thought correct and appropriate, in a way they were comfortable with. Only after my friend got involved did the Chinese market the message, making it comfortable for the Americans to understand.

What Way Is Right?

If there are two (at least) different ways to write a fax (to communicate) what is the right way, the rambling, overly-polite way or the direct, threaten-a-lawyer way? I can't answer: it all depends on who the audience is. About now I ask Western students how they communicate with Chinese staff, friends, partners and/ or officials. Looking guilty, most say they use some variation of the direct way. Very understandable, considering that like all Westerners, the students have been taught, again and again, to be direct, that direct=efficient=polite. This raises another question though, which is the *polite* way, overly-polite or brutally-direct?

Again the answer depends upon who the audience is. I communicate differently to Chinese and to Westerners, sending the same messages in different ways. A good example is how I promote workshops. I have both Chinese and Western clients. Contacting the Westerners is easy: I write a fax or email with all the information, merge it to my database and wham, it's that easy. Each client gets the same letter, short and sweet, saying that I will be in Taipei, Hong Kong or Shanghai on X dates offering X workshops at X prices, and if you are interested contact me this way. No wasted words.

Emails and faxes to Chinese contain all this information of course, but each is different. I keep good records of every contact I have with my Chinese business relations,[34] and start each email with some personal, build-a-friendship-type of message. It could be that I hope their son was doing well in university, their new car was running well or that my wife had recently tried that noodle shop they recommended and she said they were the best noodles she'd ever tasted. Something that shows I think of the reader as a person, not just a possible source of profit. One or two sentences are enough, then I move to business in the second paragraph, exactly the same stuff I send to Westerners. If I don't have any personal information then I check the news and weather. You can always make some personal comment, like 'I hope your family is fine after Typhoon X' say.

It is not surprising that I enjoy sending letters to Westerners more than to Chinese. Hit a few keys and it's done. The Chinese letters are a lot more work and take a lot more time. Big deal. What is my goal, attracting reader interest or sending easy-to-write letters? In order for Chinese managers to send staff (students) my way, they first must read my email and feel comfortable about it. I care about making them feel comfortable.

Is this callous and calculating, making people think I have some personal feeling for them when I don't? It may be, but I don't think of it that way. I accept that the Chinese feel business is about personal relationships, so I do what I can to create that personal touch.

Look, Chinese are not stupid; they know what I am doing. Why I do it isn't as important to them as the fact that I am trying to follow Chinese ways. Am I manipulating their feelings? Yes, I suppose, but how is that different than taking your wife to a restaurant she likes but you don't, and acting happy all through dinner? Both your wife and my Chinese clients know what is going on, and both appreciate attempts to do what makes them happy. Only the most cynical would consider it in a negative way, or at least that is what I tell myself. Besides, it is what Chinese do. The Chinese boss waiting for carpet did not honestly mean all those nice words written about the American company; he wrote them because that is how Chinese communicate in that situation.

Marketing And Communication

The goal of communication is to transfer messages 100% clearly. To do this you must market your messages, must adapt your communication style and content to match the audience's needs and expectations. Chinese and Westerners have different communication methods. Below is a table that relates cross-culture communication principles to a familiar subject, marketing.

Marketing		Communication
your product or service	=	your message
your customer	=	your audience
successful sale	=	audience understands message
market research	=	communication needs & expectations
packaging	=	doing what audience needs/wants

Table 6. Marketing and Communication

These are the normal marketing steps. First, understand what the product or service is: it is hard to sell something you don't understand. Next, know who the target customers are: who buys our products or services? A successful sale seems simple, but sometimes isn't. Were Japanese car companies in the 80s and 90s interested in maximizing profits or building market share in North America? How they answered that question defined 'successful sale' for them.

Now comes the hard parts. The next step is to do research to understand the target customers: what features and options do they like; how do they normally receive messages, TV, magazines or some other media; and how they expect messages to be delivered, say the difference between comparative and lifestyle advertising. Only after we know customer needs and expectations can we move to the next step, packaging our product or service in a way calculated to match what our customers want and expect.

There are many competitors, and if you make it hard or uncomfortable for customers to buy your product, for example having stores in the wrong location or open during the wrong hours, they will buy from someone else. The same is true if you make your product confusing to use or if your service is rude: customers will buy from someone else. You need more than just a better mousetrap, you must also make it easy for customers to see that it is just the trap they need: that it works, is easy to use and easy to buy. This is the all-important 'buying experience,' the sum total of marketing efforts: pleasing customers by giving them what they want, how they want it. Making it comfortable for them to buy.

This is exactly like cross-culture communication (all communication actually). If we don't make it easy or comfortable for the audience to listen to our messages they won't listen; if we don't tell them what they need to know they won't understand our message and/or won't do what we want them to do. To succeed we must market our messages.

Marketing messages seems just common sense, something you naturally do inside your own culture. You speak in one way to your boss and in another way to your best friend. The message may be identical, 'you are wrong' say, but you would (probably) communicate such a message very differently to the boss than your best friend. In my experience however, as soon as Westerners get off the plane in Singapore or Shanghai, Taipei or Tokyo, they sell instead of market. Why?

My best explanation is they sell instead of market because they lack the necessary market knowledge—they don't know how Chinese tend to want messages communicated. As such, Westerners don't adjust messages to suit a Chinese audience, i.e., don't package their messages properly. Instead, Westerners retreat to known methods and, focusing on what they know, communicate in ways they are comfortable with. They sell their messages.

Communication Principle 4
the audience determines what is polite, not the speaker

Selling instead of marketing happens in more areas than just communication. The concept of marketing—adjusting your ways to match the audience's expectations and giving audiences what they want/need in order to get what you want/need—is crucial in all areas of cross-culture interaction. Later chapters explain how the marketing concept applies to areas like as motivation, meetings and other management tasks.[35] Marketing also applies to politeness and manners. Politeness and manners are very culturally-specific (as are actions, policies and whole range of other things); what is polite in one culture can be impolite in another.

Themes and Lessons

We communicate to others, not ourselves, and the only way we can succeed is if the audience receives our message clearly and completely. To do this we should market our message (focus on audience needs and expectations) rather than sell it (focus on our needs and expectations).

1. The Audience is more important than the Speaker.
2. Communication success is measured by how much of the speaker's message is transferred clearly and completely to the audience.
3. Speakers sell a message when they focus on their needs, speak in a way they are comfortable with, think appropriate or reasonable, and use their assumptions about what 'everybody knows.'
4. Speakers market a message when they: focus on the audience's needs; speak in a way the audience is comfortable with (even if they are uncomfortable doing so); think what is appropriate or reasonable to the audience; and use assumptions about what the audience is likely to know.
5. Marketing a message to Chinese is more likely to succeed than selling it.
6. Chinese believe the more important the message is the more important it is to be polite.
7. As Chinese believe business is more about personal relationships than objective reality, Westerners should take the time to personalize their communication.
8. Westerners can use common marketing techniques to make messages more comfortable for Chinese to receive.

CHAPTER 5

What Is Chinese Culture Anyway?

Culture is a big word. It can mean many things and, in my experience, the more you try to understand all the various meanings of "culture" the more involved (and confused) it gets. So, to reduce some confusion and make what follows clearer (I hope), here is my quick definition.

Culture describes how we live together. At the most basic level culture shapes our values, what we believe are *right* and *wrong*. One way this is applied is in rules, formal (laws made by governments) and informal (social, say when a gift should be given). Culture determines what is polite and what is not, how to make and maintain a relationship and how to treat family members, friends and strangers. Many (most?) assumptions about 'should' are based on culture. Think of culture as the foundation for how we make sense of the world and our place in it. Culture is as common as the air we breathe, and just as invisible.

We see the effects of culture, not the culture itself, in what subjects are taught in school as well as the way they are taught, in the music we listen to, the art we like and food we eat (and how we eat it). Culture shapes our ideas of what we as an individual can do in life, from the American idea that 'anything is possible' contrasted say with (historical) British social or class limitations. We are what our culture makes us.

No one is born with culture; we all must learn it. As children we learn the values, beliefs and rules of our culture from parents, teachers, churches and, yes, TV. Culture places limits on certain behaviors and rewards others so that, in the end, people within a certain culture have more-or-less the same values and ideas, behaviors and beliefs, respond in similar ways to similar inputs, and have the same basic opinions about what is right/wrong and should/should not.

Each culture begins with a central idea, call it a philosophic purpose or goal. All else, values, attitudes and beliefs, stem from that goal, and are adopted or used because they help the people within the culture achieve that goal. This is explained in much more detail below. Yet while different cultures have different philosophic goals, thus different values, beliefs and attitudes, people are basically the same no matter what culture they belong to.

Are We Are All The Same?

No matter from what culture, Chinese, Western or whatever, all peoples have families and friends, emotions, desires and ambitions, all strive to be polite, to succeed and to build a better life for children. Many take that similarity to mean that we are all the same. As one student asked, "We all eat; isn't that more important than whether we use chopsticks or cutlery?"

No, it isn't. It is true that people from all cultures experience emotions, desires and such, all have values and beliefs, all educate their children and, yes, all eat dinner. But if we look only at **what** people do it looks like Chinese are the same as Swiss, Japanese the same as Americans and English the same as (gasp) French. That can't be right, and isn't. Culture is not about what people do as much as about **how** they do it, and **why**. Let's look at raising children for a moment, a key job in any culture.

Parents seek to modify children's behavior so children are polite, well-mannered, able to succeed in school and, finally, in society. Chinese parents tend to focus on the negative, trying to get children to act in the right way by criticizing/punishing them for acting incorrectly.[36] Western parents also punish bad behavior, true, but (normally) not as much as they praise good behavior, complimenting children for correct actions as a way to teach how to act in the 'right' way. The pattern is the same in schools: Chinese teachers tend to emphasize and punish mistakes children make while Western teachers spend most time complimenting children for achievements made.

Tends To

"Tends to" is a key feature of studying culture. China Chinese are different than Hong Kong or Taiwan Chinese for example, just as French and Americans are different types of Westerners. Yet for all their differences, Chinese from Taiwan and Chinese from China tend to believe the same things, have the same values, use the same Rules of Communication and are motivated in the same ways. French and American Westerners also enjoy the same basic similarities (even if neither wants to admit it). There are exceptions and you must be aware of them, but the unique differences are not as important as the broad similarities when you look within a specific cultural group.

You must be cautious not to use "tends to" incorrectly. A common mistake is to say, for example, that as both Chinese and Westerners respect authority then the two cultures tend to be the same. When analyzing different cultural groups the differences are more important than the similarities. Yes, Chinese and Americans both respect authority, but saying that hides a vast difference in the level of respect shown, how respect is gained and maintained, and how respect for authority should affect your actions.

Take two cans of paint, one white, one black. Put one drop of white into the black and one drop of black into the white. While it is true that there are now two cans of gray paint (focus on the similarities), this hides the fact that they are vastly different shades of gray (focus on the differences). Both views are true, yes, but are they equally useful? No. If I were painting my house, I'd care more about the difference than the similarity, just as I care more about how Chinese respect for authority is different than Western respect when arguing my case with a customs official in a Chinese airport.

Table 7: Tends To

Chinese and Western parents and teachers try to teach children to 'fit in' and to 'act properly,' but both the methods used and the outcomes on a child's psychological development are opposites. While it is crucial to remember that the Chinese (or people from another culture) are just people, just like you and I, it is more important to focus on the different methods we each use, our different hoped-for outcomes and goals. The best place to start is the overall philosophic goal for each culture. What are our cultural needs, and why?

What Makes Us Western?

I enjoy this part of my workshop, asking Western students, "Why are you a Westerner? What makes you Western?" I am usually greeted with blank and somewhat embarrassed stares, as if my question is not fair somehow, that I should not be putting them on the spot. But, if you want to understand Chinese you first must understand yourself. What makes you a Westerner?

No, not white skin. No, not because your parents were Westerners. No, not because you were born in a Western country. Not history either: Chinese also have history and they are definitely not Westerners. Christianity? Good answer. Not right, but good.

Christianity or the Judeo-Christian ethic is a key part of Western culture and necessary to know if you want a full understanding of the West, especially our moral center. Nevertheless, it is not what forms us as a culture, and is not where the goal of Western culture comes from.[37] I know some devout Chinese Christians, but their devotion and faith does not somehow make them Westerners. Before you give up how about a clue: who is the father of Western culture? Does that help?

Western culture actually has three fathers: I call them the big three, Plato, Aristotle and Socrates. Of these, the most important is Plato, the author and father of Western culture. Put simply (I hope not badly), Plato said,

> We don't know anything. We don't know what is right, what is wrong, what is good or bad, what is evil, what is truth. The proper role for man [people] is to discover knowledge so we can answer these questions.

While Plato's idea or goal—discover knowledge to answer questions—was mostly lost after Rome fell, from mid 1200s (when Aquinas translated ancient Greek into a modern language) the goal of Western culture has been to discover knowledge and to answer Plato's questions.[38]

A philosophy professor jokingly once told me, "You know Greg, even 2500 years after Plato asked his questions we still can't answer them. Maybe he asked the wrong questions." Be that as it may, the professor's point is a good one: we still don't have clear and/or absolute answers to right/wrong, good/evil and other key issues. A simple yet emotionally-charged example would be *is abortion good or bad?* I have a personal answer, sure, but if I am intellectually honest, I must admit my answer is just my 'opinion' or 'belief,' not 'fact' or 'truth.'

Welcome to Western culture. Unlike other cultures, Westerners don't really *know* anything. Western culture is all about learning and discovery in our (futile?) quest to answer Plato's damn questions. At the center of Western hearts is a question mark. This desire to learn, to discover and to answer questions affects and shapes everything important that we do, the way we teach our children, the way we communicate and interact with others. It is no surprise that science—just an organized search for answers to the physical world—is dominated by Westerners[39], that democracy—just a peaceful way to settle competing answers to society's questions—is the dominant form of Western government. (I can even make the same point about capitalism and Western culture, but I'll let that argument sleep for now.)

Plato set the overall goal or cultural need: where do Aristotle and Socrates come in? From Socrates we get learning by questioning, the dialectic; from Aristotle we get trying to understand the true nature of what we see, logic, and get trying to communicate clearly what we see and know to each other (rules of communication). Aristotle was the world's first scientist and, even if some of his conclusions are strange today, he nevertheless was the first to seek truth from facts and to use the scientific method, the backbone of discovery in the physical world and of decision making in the business world.

It is useful to stop for a moment for a quick look at the course of Western history. Go back 100 years from today and ask, has the West changed during this time? Hmm, that means 1906 to 2006. Yes, I would say the West has changed dramatically in these hundred years. Go back another 100 years, to 1806. More changes. Back to 1706 and still more changes. From the time of Aquinas or the end of the Middle Ages until today, the West has been in a constant state of flux, change, change and more change. Look into the future, to 2106. Do you think there will continue to be changes? I sure do; while I don't know exactly what those changes will be, the one thing I am certain about is that 2106 will look a lot different than 2006.

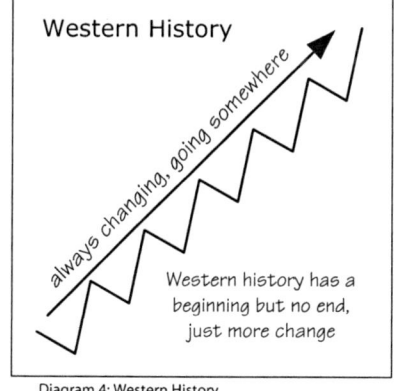

Diagram 4: Western History

A diagram of Western history is very simple. No matter where one argues our history zigs and where it zags, two things are clear: the West has been constantly changing and we are headed in some direction. Different philosophers call the ultimate goal different things, Marx said communism, Hegel said *Geist*, Fukuyama said we've already reached the end,[40] but wherever we are going we know one thing for sure: it will look different than it does today. Who knows, maybe we finally answer all of Plato's questions.

What Makes A Western Hero?

One of the best ways to show and explain cultural differences is to look at what makes a hero in different cultures. What makes someone a hero in Western culture? I don't mean a sports hero, the person who scored the overtime goal or winning basket, or an entertainment hero (if I can use that term), someone who is a celebrity thus treated as a hero. I want a cultural hero, someone remembered fondly for what he/she did long after the sporting event or TV show is forgotten. What makes someone remembered?

Let's start with a list of who I consider Western heroes. Can you spot the common characteristics of these famous people: Copernicus, Galileo, George Washington, Susan B. Anthony, Joan of Arc, Jean Monet, Amelia Earhart, General Douglas MacArthur, and Steven Jobs? Quite a group. What each have in common is they all went against the conventional wisdom of the time and, often at great personal risk, achieved something that changed us and our world, added to our knowledge and moved us further along towards our goal. Personal courage, change and achievement, the stuff of Western heroes.

Heroes don't have to be from politics or the military; business has its share of heroes. I suspect you use a personal computer. Can you imagine work without one? I remember when there were no *personal* computers though, when computers were large machines with big spinning reels, kept in sterile, air-conditioned rooms and tended by white-robed tech druids. Then two men named Steve, Jobs and Wozniak, had a dream, to make computers small enough to fit on a desk, small enough that everyone could have one. Their search for capital was fruitless: large banks and financial institutions laughed at them, telling them that 'no one wants a small computer, computers are big, everyone knows that.' Undeterred, believing in their vision, the Steves set up a company in a garage and changed the world. The little company? Apple Computers.

I could go on. Who in 1950 thought German-French cooperation (let alone today's EU) was possible when Jean Monet proposed the European Steel and Coal Community? Very few, yet he (and others, true) persevered; Monet had a dream of a cooperative Europe, and, in the face of much opposition and Europe's depressing recent history of conflict, changed the world. Who today could imagine a war between France and Germany? George Washington led a rag-tag army against the world's strongest power and helped form the United States. Copernicus, sure that the dogma believed by the most powerful institution of the time, the Catholic Church, was wrong, changed our view of ourselves by arguing the earth revolved around the sun. Galileo braved threats of the Inquisition to defend Copernicus. Susan Anthony braved lawsuits to fight for women's equality and the right to vote.

In each case the heroes believed in something that contradicted the conventional wisdom, current practice or a superior's orders, acted on what they believed was right (instead of being quiet and safe) and succeeded in achieving what they believed in. They produced results. Good committee members are not heroes in Western culture, people who disturb things, affect change and produce results are. Why? I believe it is because only through change and results do we have any chance of answering Plato's questions. If we don't have the answers now then doing just more of the same won't lead us to answers, therefore we need to change what we are doing. Makes sense to me anyway.

Initiative And Mistakes

I became an apprentice electrician right out of high school. Not knowing much, I used to wait to be told what to do. One day my boss told me, "Greg, just do something. Even if it is wrong, just do something." His point was that you don't learn anything by waiting to be told; you learn by doing, even if what you do is a mistake. We call that 'showing initiative,' or deciding by yourself what needs to be done then going ahead and doing it without first asking permission.

Initiative is a key aspect of Western culture, something every Western hero has in ample quantity. Western culture prizes initiative because without initiative nothing ever changes, or changes easily. From classroom to boardroom, those with initiative and independent thinking tend to receive better marks and faster promotions. Yes, of course there are bureaucracy-heavy companies and organizations that penalize initiative, the same as there are teachers who penalize independent thought, but neither are common nor models of what Westerners think should be prized.

Initiative is possible in part because of the Western attitude towards mistakes. While no one likes mistakes, the common Western feeling is that mistakes are as much an opportunity as they are a problem. When someone I manage or work with makes a mistake I learn what he doesn't know, thus learn what I should teach him. He learns something new and I don't waste time teaching things he already knows, a true win-win situation.[41] Mistakes are an inevitable part of change.

Mistakes are also an inevitable part of learning. We call it trial and error or learning from experience, the holy grail of training. A better (or more honest anyway) way of describing it would be 'learning from making mistakes.' The truth is we learn as much (if not more) from mistakes as from successes. With discovering knowledge being the goal of Western culture, mistakes are, and must be, treated as opportunities, not problems.

Closely related to our attitude towards mistakes is how Westerners deal with method (how a thing is done) and results (what is achieved). The ends don't justify the means, certainly, but that rule really only applies in drastic situations. As another boss once told me, "I don't care how you do it, just get it done." Her meaning was that she cared more about the results I achieved that the method I used to achieve them. This is very common in the West, especially in business. We all are measured at work (performance appraisals), with rewards like compensation and promotions based on our performance, on what we achieve.[42] Westerners are results oriented people and rewarded for winning, not on how well we play the game (an idea we can take too far).

Western culture is competitive. Everywhere you look there are winners and losers. A scientist makes a new discovery about how something works: she wins and overnight other scientists who fashioned careers thinking the old way lose. To use an overworked term, paradigm shift always creates winners and losers. Every time we vote in an election one candidate wins and the rest lose. Every time we buy a product we help the company that made it and hurt the ones that didn't. The nature of capitalism, no matter what flavor or how modified, is based on competition: companies survive by offering better products or services at better prices than competitors do. We have and enforce laws to prevent monopolies, this based on our belief that companies will only innovate, change and improve what they sell when they worry that the competition may do it first.

No competition means no change, which in turn means no new knowledge, which in turn means no answers to Plato's questions. It all fits. In the following chapters I look at how the goal of discovering knowledge affects the way Westerners tend to educate children, communicate, build relationships (personal and business), manage staff and solve problems. But before that we need something to compare the Western way to. We need to look at Chinese culture.

What Makes Chinese 'Chinese?'

Again a favorite part of my workshop, though now I get Chinese blank stares, not Western. After some prodding and leading questions, the Chinese get into it and we go through the same lists. No, it's not your parents. Not geography, not the Yellow Emperor. The discussion runs more or less the same as it does with Westerners explaining the West, except when I give in and ask them for the father of Chinese culture. Many hands rise, all eager to say the same answer: Confucius.

Correct. Confucius is, without a doubt, the most important influence in Chinese culture. Although a rough contemporary of Plato (he lived 551-479 BC, Plato lived 427-347 BC), Confucius is still alive and walking the streets of Chinese Asia today. As mentioned earlier, the Chinese believe the direct lineal descendant of Confucius still walks among them. I somehow missed the Greeks introducing the world to Plato's direct descendant during Athens' Olympic Games, which one thinks they would have if they could have. Both cultures have fathers, but Plato is more a ghost figure to Westerners while Chinese think of Confucius as someone who might drop in for dinner.

To understand the effect of Confucius you must look at when Confucius lived and what his goal was. Confucius lived near the end of the Zhou (Chou) Dynasty, a rather long dynasty: it lasted almost 1000 years![43] Confucius lived near the end of the dynasty, a time of growing war and hardship, due in large part to the breakdown in central authority and rule of law that always marks the end of a dynasty. Called losing the 'Mandate of Heaven,' disasters both natural and man-made signal that the Gods have withdrawn support for the ruling family/group.

The Dynastic Cycle

Before continuing with effect of Confucius on Chinese culture, we need to stop for a moment and look at a key aspect of China's history, the dynastic cycle. Every dynasty follows the same basic cycle, some taking a few decades to go from start to end, some lasting many hundreds of years. Every dynasty starts with a strong and vigorous ruler, the winner of the war. There is good government, low taxes and a growing economy. Population increases but food production increases even more, due to people farming empty land.

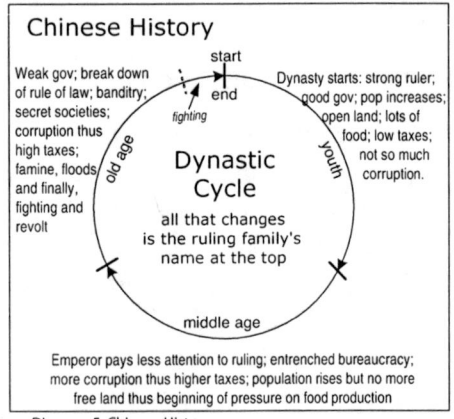

Diagram 5: Chinese History

Over time, decades or centuries depending on the ruling family's strength and stability, the dynasty moves into middle age, a time where emperors begin to enjoy the company of their harem's 1000 wives and concubines more than they do governing. Power drifts to the Court and corruption increases, with officials great and minor pocketing more and more of the tax revenue before it can reach the central government. Skimming causes the government to raise taxes, which places an every larger burden on the population, already disturbed by increasingly venal local officials. All the arable land is now tilled but the population still grows, meaning an ever-lower threshold from famine.

The dynasty then moves into old age, a troubled time. Taxes continue to go up as the court tries to collect enough money to govern, but corruption is now so entrenched that most of the taxes collected never reach Beijing. Population pressure causes local famines to happen, slowly becoming larger and more frequent. Secret societies spring up, often started to help the poor but usually evolving into anti-government activities. In the final stage riots become revolt, fighting replaces farming and millions die during the war to replace the ruling family. Finally, one side wins the war and its leader becomes the new emperor. The circle is complete—a new dynasty starts and the cycle begins anew.

Goals And Rules

Confucius lived during the end of the Eastern Chou, a classic 'end of dynasty' time. The Great Sage, who at that time was basically an itinerant teacher/philosopher going from noble to noble seeking a job, looked around himself and didn't like what he saw. Confucius wanted to create a system that would end this time of trouble and war. He looked backwards in time, to the beginning of the Zhou Dynasty a millennia before, and to the Shang Dynasty (1600 to 1406 BC) before that, and saw, he saw perfection, he saw that the Chinese people had already achieved the perfect society ... but had lost it!

Confucius described this lost perfect society, then said reachieving this known perfection was the overall philosophic goal. According to Confucius, the Chinese people had to create a stable society with harmonious relationships between people. Ah, but how could this be done? Confucius' answer to this 'how' question is his most amazing and lasting achievement, the idea that elevated his ideas to the heights they enjoyed (and still enjoy).

How can the Chinese achieve the perfect society, stable with harmonious relations between people? To Confucius the answer was easy: follow these [his] rules. What type of rules? Not traffic rules, or rules about contracts or commerce. Confucius' rules were all about how people should treat other people in known relationships. Call them rules of behavior: Confucius wrote[44] detailed descriptions of how people should act. Confucius left very little to chance in these rules, describing the four classes of society (from high to low they are mandarins, farmers, artisans and traders/businesspeople) and the five possible types of relationships. Called *Wu Lun* (五倫), the five relationships are ruler-subject, husband-wife, parent-child, older brother-younger brother and friend-friend. (Note there are no relationships including *strangers*.)

A crucial aspect of all relationships is there is no concept of equality. Take twin boys for example: identical in every way and born within minutes of each other, how could they not be equal? Well, as one is born five minutes (say) earlier than the other, the one born first is 'older brother' (哥哥) and one born last is 'younger brother' (弟弟). Younger brother must obey older brother; in return older brother must take care of younger brother. Even twins are not equal. All relationships in Chinese Asia were hierarchical: lower required to obey the higher and higher obligated to take care of the lower. Just another set of cultural rules for the Chinese to learn and follow.

China became a 'rules-obeying' culture, where 'goodness' was (is) measured by how well one followed known rules. Think about that for a moment. When you measure right and wrong by how one follows rules, then the process (following rules) becomes the result (that rules are followed). This is why process, doing things in the right way, is more important in Chinese Asia than results, getting the right outcome. And, as Confucian rules were static and unchanging and all effort placed on following rules rather than questioning them, there was never any pressure on China to change. Confucius had already answered every one of Plato's questions, so there was no need to learn! Each generation learned the same rules so lived the same lives as their predecessors, so ended up with the same society as their predecessors. Again and again, over and over, for thousands of years!

Confucius' ideas were not accepted immediately. Not until the start of the Han Dynasty in 204 BC were Confucian ideals and ideas elevated to the heights of official policy and belief. Yet once entrenched by the Han, Confucius was not challenged until the end of the Qing Dynasty in 1912. The largest philosophical debate[45] in two millennia was between two followers of Confucius, about whether Chinese were basically good or basically bad: both agreed though that if people studied Confucius they could become better.

Think about that for a moment: no debate for more than 2,000 years! Once Confucian rules were established and became official policy, the system was perfectly designed to perpetuate itself: the goal was following rules, and if the rules were followed there was never any desire or opportunity to challenge or change the rules.

Lessons From A Chinese Hero

Unequal relationships and the desire to follow rules above all else is the best way to understand China's greatest cultural hero, *Guan Yu* or, as he is commonly called, *Guan Gong* (關公), literally Lord Guan. Though a real person, Guan Gong owes his fame to his fictional role in a 14th century historical novel, *The Romance of the Three Kingdoms* (三國演義). The novel is set during the Three Kingdom period, 220-263 AD, a time where central government disappeared and rival states fought for control of China. To simplify a very complicated plot, Guan Gong was a leader of one side and *Cao Cao* (曹操) the leader of another side (the third side isn't important here). Both Guang Gong and Cao Cao are Generals, with Cao Cao being of slightly higher rank than Guang Gong.

Three way civil wars are complicated, with shifting alliances and sides changing. Soon into the book everyone (including Guang Gong) knows Cao Cao is bad: totally untrustworthy, Cao Cao will do and say anything to win; he is a man with no honor. In the middle of the book Cao Cao and Guan Gong are on the same side. Cao Cao comes to Guan Gong and says, "Guan Gong, I am worried about my safety. Would you stand outside my bedroom door and guard it tonight so I can sleep in peace?" Being of lower rank of course Guan Gong says yes.

The stage is now set. For many pages the action is now inside Guan Gong's head, standing outside Cao Cao's door, thinking. 'What should I do? I can't trust Cao Cao and if I stay here he will probably go out the window and do something terrible, so I must stop him ... but wait, I can't do that. I gave Cao Cao my word that I would stand here and protect him, and my word is most important ... but if I stand here I won't be able to protect my friends, so I should ... but I can't go, as I said I would stay here ... but my friends are in danger ... but I gave my word ... .' Guan Gong is in mental torture (as are the readers during this section), trying to decide what to do: stay and remain true to his word (do the right thing) or leave and protect his friends (get the right result). He decides to stay.

The next morning Guang Gong discovers his worst fears came true; while he stayed on guard outside Cao Cao's door, Cao Cao had gone out the window and killed someone important to Guan Gong.[46] By the end of the book Guan Gong and his friends lose everything. Cao Cao wins and becomes China's new ruler. My question: what about this makes Guan Gong a hero? Westerners I talk to about this book tend to think Guan Gong is a putz, a loser, a boob, someone who had every chance and opportunity to win but never took advantage of them so he lost, miserably. Why is he a hero to the Chinese?

Simple. Guan Gong is a hero because he decided doing the right thing was more important than achieving the right result. At great personal sacrifice (and sacrifice to all he loved) Guan Gong did the honorable thing and stayed outside the door all night, even while knowing that doing so risked almost certain tragedy. Put in Confucian terms, Guan Gong obeyed his superior by following the rules of correct conduct, even when: a) he knew his superior's words could not be trusted; b) he knew that if he stayed outside the door his superior would probably go out the window and hurt his friends; and c) by obeying he could not protect his friends. In fact, he is such a hero that he became a God, and his willingness to risk poor results in order to do the honorable thing made him one of the few Chinese Gods Westerners recognize. Look for his visage at temples, a red-faced General dressed in splendid clothes with a massive, curved sword. Yet while Westerners may recognize him, do they think Guan Gong is a hero?

Most Westerners say no. Westerners tend to like Cao Cao: he cared about results, did anything necessary to win, and won. I recommend you read this novel as it shows many key parts of the Chinese character, but don't try the full book. Very few Westerners have patience to finish it (think of *War and Peace*, only longer). Read the comic book version instead[47] (often sold in hotels). The comic has the basic principles, which is all you need. (I recommend you read comic book versions of all Chinese classics: Confucius, *The Tao* by Lao Zi, Sun Zi's *Art of War*. They explain all you need to know of the principles, are interesting and easy to read.)

Two Meanings For Relationships

Every book I have looked at on Chinese culture says that relationships are important. 'Yeah, okay,' Westerners might think, 'relationships are important in the West too. I know how to make friends. I know how to network.' The problem is that making friends and networking are not what "relationships are important" means. In fact there are two types of 'relationships' in Chinese Asia, regular and Chinese style.

Networking and making friends is important in Chinese Asia: get to know as many people as you can. But these are the regular kind of relationships, the type of relationships that Westerners understand. These types of relationships are important in the West, at work and at home, but they are not *vital*, not the most important thing. The same is true for these normal types of relationships in Chinese Asia, important but not vital. It is the second type of relationship, the Chinese style, that is vital.

Chinese society revolves around and depends on the Chinese style of relationship, *guanxi* (關係). Normally translated as relationships, guanxi does not mean relationships as Westerners understand the word![48] Guanxi is how business is done, as important to Chinese as contracts are to Westerners. Guanxi is not restricted to business: it is equally important to personal life as well. Guanxi is a big word.

What does guanxi mean? The closest translation I can offer is *mutually shared obligations*, not very helpful I know. Guanxi is complex and hard to describe, and can only truly be understood after living within Chinese Asia for an extended period, years not months. (It took me that long.) I was confused the first time I read about guanxi at school, a 20-page academic explanation that made no sense whatsoever. The best way to explain is to start by looking at the other, the 'normal' meaning of relationships in Chinese Asia.

You can define a Chinese life by a person's relationships, that is, by the groups the person belongs to. Chinese don't think of themselves as individuals but as members of a group, nor are they viewed as individuals but by the groups they belong to and their place in these groups. The group is everything in Chinese Asia. The examples are everywhere. Here is a very common case, finding someone to marry.

When I poll my Western students about how they met their spouse it breaks roughly 50:50, half met their spouse in some type of known situation, belonged to the same club, in the same class, worked in the same office, etc. The other half met in an unorganized setting, in a disco or a bus, buying groceries or doing laundry, a meeting of strangers. No surprise here. But when I poll Chinese students, about 98% met their spouse in some type of known situation.[49] Why? Blame Confucius. The Great Sage forgot to explain the sixth type of relationship, stranger to stranger, so Chinese never learned how to talk to or deal with strangers.

(In Confucius' defense there were almost no strangers in Chinese history. Because of the need to tend to the massive, intricate and labour-intensive irrigation system there was little travel, plus Chinese geography doesn't suit itself to travel. Men died where they were born; women died where their husbands were born: most Chinese never traveled farther than the closest market town. Confucius added to this by making leaving your parents 'unfilial,' that is, disrespectful: how could you take care of them if you were gone? Even when Chinese did travel they never really met strangers, for wherever they went there were family or clan associations to meet up with. And while armies traveled, they did so as a group, not as strangers. But I digress.)

One reason why there is high turnover among single people in Chinese offices is that if a person does not find a mate at the first company it is time to move on to the next. Learning English is another good example. There are three reasons why Chinese love to study English. One is to learn English, maybe 50%. The next reason is just to get out of the house, maybe 25%. The last 25% attend English classes to meet friends or possible mates: when Chinese are in the same class they can now talk to each other. If all else fails there are still professional matchmakers to turn to for introductions to potential mates. Then there is marriage, yet another good example. If you get a chance to attend a Chinese wedding look around at the assembled guests. Normally there will be far more coworkers than friends, often everyone in the company or department. Why? Because coworkers are the key groups that the bride and groom belong to.

What I have always found interesting is that physical foundations for relationships, working for the same company or belonging to the same club, often determines who Chinese spend time with far more than emotionally-established relationships like friends. If a Chinese leaves Company A to join Company B they also tend to abandon their Company A 'friends' for their new 'friends' in Company B. While this group-identity, life-is-only-inside-the-group, can't-talk-to-strangers belief is breaking down somewhat in Chinese Asia (especially in places like Shenzhen), it is still far stronger than any Western-style individualism.

Contrast the Chinese wedding to the West. The only coworkers at a Western wedding are people who have an emotional bond with bride or groom, there because they are friends, not just coworkers. A company in the West is just where we work, nothing more. We may have pride in our company and in our job but we still draw a line between 'work life' and 'real life,' with the people we spend time with outside of work hours normally part of our 'real life,' i.e., friends. If our friends happen also to be our coworkers that is just coincidence, nothing more. Not so in Chinese Asia though, where work is life, the company is a 24/7 part of your life, and much of your free time is spent with coworkers, just because they are coworkers. Changing jobs means new coworkers to spend time with.

I am not saying that Chinese don't have friends. Of course they do. Nevertheless, if I use 'time spent' as my measure, Chinese spend far more time with coworkers/group members than they do with friends. Most relationships are formed through physical bonds (at least initially) like being part of the same class or club, and often last only as long as the physical connection does. Further, all relationships still fit into Confucian rules, even friends or family. There is always rank: no one is equal.

Where Westerners would introduce one friend to another as "George, meet my friend Bill," Chinese rarely use the word "friend." Instead Chinese normally add something about the relationship rather than the use the word friend: "George, meet my elementary school classmate Bill," say. Why? To let George know the depth of your relationship with Bill. Why is this important? Well, if you are all in your 40s and you discover that Bill is your friend's elementary school classmate you can safely assume that Bill is an important person in your friend's life, therefore if you want to remain on good terms with your friend you had better be nice to Bill. It is that simple.

Simple but important, even for family. Where English uses only generic terms for family relationships, brother, sister, aunt, uncle and cousin, Chinese have separate and unique terms for every possible gradation, my 'second oldest brother's third oldest daughter' instead of 'niece;' my 'mother's oldest brother' is one term for uncle, 'father's oldest brother' another, and 'father's second younger brother' yet one more. The reason is so everyone is clear who belongs to who, who is at what rank, who is important, and ... who is not.

Guanxi, The Un-Relationship

Guanxi means you have a duty towards the other person, obliged to help if asked. I began to understand this late one evening. My door rang, I opened it and a stranger thrust a wrapped present in my hands and, as he let himself in, thanked me for helping his son. Huh? Once in he introduced himself as a friend of one of my clients, a client who had just done a big favour for me. Turns out friend-of-a-friend wanted help for his son, a filled-in application to Stanford University … that had to be mailed the next day.

What to do? It was almost 11:00 at night, I was tired from a long day and had to be up early for a big day to follow. All I wanted to do was go to bed. Luckily my roommate was still up. A 20-year veteran of the cross-culture divide, John advised me to help the man. Not only had I already accepted the gift —the bribe coming before helping instead of after, creating an obligation—but, according to my friend, "If you want to remain on good terms with your client you have to help his friend. That's how guanxi works." Damn. I was up until nearly 2am writing the application, including the letter saying what "I" wanted to do with "my" degree. I was tired the next day but (I realized later) I had cemented my relationship with my client, a relationship that continues to this day.

Thanks John. That *is* how guanxi works. Because I had accepted help from my client I now had an obligation to help in return, not to the client himself necessarily but to anyone nominated by the client, someone he had guanxi with of course. Think of guanxi as a circle; once you get inside you now are open to obligations from anyone else in the circle, but also have the right to ask for help from anyone else as well. Mutual shared obligations, the fuel that powers Chinese business.

Guanxi can be wonderful, but often isn't. The good part is that you have a huge circle of friends, strangers actually, that you can call on for help, assistance for which you pay for by opening yourself up to strangers asking you for help. That is not the bad part though. The bad part is that if you want your original relationship to continue (with the person who invited you to join the guanxi circle) you have no choice but to help, even if it is bad business or, in extreme cases, against the law.

Bad business is easier to explain. Once a good friend recommended a printing company to me, "He's my middle-school classmate Greg." I got a good price, the guanxi price, but upon completion the brochure color was wrong and words were misspelled (English of course, the Chinese characters were right). I wanted to reject it but couldn't: I was trapped by guanxi. If I asked for it to be redone (as I would have done in the West) the printer would have lost money and my dear friend would have lost face, perhaps costing me our friendship. I had to choose between accepting substandard work or keeping my friendship. In the end I chose the friendship, agreeing with the printer that yes, I could still use the (incorrect) brochure, and that yes, the red he had used was a nice color … even if my company colors were blue and grey.

Mutual shared obligation: if you accept help from me then you are obligated to help me or someone I nominate, no matter what your personal situation, feelings or opinions are. I had to accept lousy work from the printer because my dear friend had previously helped me, plus the printer had given me the guanxi (reduced) price. I had to work late doing a favour for a stranger because the stranger was a friend of my friend. Doing things because you 'want to help' is replaced with 'must help,' the 'must' coming from the idea that no matter what else happens, nothing must be done to hurt a relationship.

Law or Relationships

情
理
法

These three identical characters show the difference between Western and Chinese thinking about law and relationships.

Read one way they say human relations are more important than law, read the other way they say law is more important than human relations.

法
理
情

Diagram 6: Law or Relationships

Not just Westerners become trapped by guanxi. Chinese get trapped by guanxi too. In the early 90s a well-known media industry Chinese couple bought a small, up-scale hotel near Beverly Hills, California. Business soon boomed, rooms and restaurants almost-always full, how money is made in the hotel game. Excellent you would think. Not this time: the couple had to sell the hotel because they were going broke! Why? Blame guanxi. More and more Chinese friends came to stay but, as it was impossible for them to charge their friends (and their friends never thought about insisting to pay) the more friend-guests in the hotel the more money the couple lost. Mind you, the couple now had lots of favors to call in from their well-fed, well-rested friends.

Let us look at something more serious than profit, loss and bottom line (yes, there are more important things). Guanxi can pit ethics and law against protecting a relationship, a stern test. What

should a government worker in charge of issuing restaurant li-
censes do when a good friend's license application is incorrect?
How about a fireman who spots a dangerous situation in his uncle's club or a building inspector who sees poor-quality work in an
office tower being built by an old friend? Or an extreme case, a
son who accidentally discovers his father was a serial killer? Each
case a dilemma, a choice between relationship and result.

The Chinese recognize this dilemma with a three-character
saying that poses the question, 'what is most important, protecting
a relationship or following the law?' Guanxi says protecting the
relationship is more important, which can and often does lead to
breaking the law and/or poor results: my extreme examples include a dangerous fire, building collapse and a serial killer free to
keep killing. Too dramatic? Possibly, but consider, what would
the son do? No Chinese lesson prepares a son to consider the good
of the whole, the good to all society of putting a killer behind bars
or of protecting strangers. Chinese lessons say protecting the relationship is the most important goal, that a son must obey and protect his father above all else, and that strangers, well, as Confucius
never spoke of strangers then they can't be very important.

This would be an extremely difficult situation in the West, I
agree. What should a son do? Yet in the West the son would have
been taught about the good of the whole, the basics of the Social
Contract and the Christian story of the Good Samaritan, plus the
importance of following the law above all else. When I add the
son being taught to think for himself and to make independent
judgments of right and wrong, I think it is safe to assume that a
Western son would be more likely than a Chinese son to call the
police. Sure, it would still be a very hard decision in Paris, Pitts-
burg or Perth, but in the West at least the son would be comforted
by church and society with words like "you did the right thing." I
am not sure that is true in Chinese Asia.

I have gotten off the subject, or too deep into it actually. The
importance of relationships and guanxi are crucial to understand
but are damn tough ideas to explain with words. It is much easier
to grasp when you live it rather than read it. Oh well. I end this
part with two points: 1) 'relationship' means a lot more than 'I

know him' and 'networking' as most Westerners define it; and 2) the Chinese believe that maintaining relationships is one of most important goals in life.

No Initiative In Chinese Asia

Chinese show no, or very little, initiative, something that often makes Westerners (like me) crazy. Instead of seeing what needs to be done then going ahead and doing it, Chinese will usually wait to be told to do it, even if it is obvious what should be done next.[50] Asking Chinese why they don't show initiative is frustrating; the normal response is embarrassed silence. Be sympathetic: the Chinese don't even have a word for initiative! The concept of initiative, that is, of *independently deciding what needs to be done then going ahead and doing it without first getting permission* is alien in Chinese Asia. Blame Confucius, again.

Confucius' system is based on following orders or rules, always. Young obey old, women obey men, subjects obey the Emperor (or in modern terms, staff obey managers). Even the Emperor had to obey the wisdom of past Emperors and scholars. In such a top-down, hierarchical system there is no room for initiative, just obedience. This do-what-you-are-told attitude is still the essence of Chinese Asian education, formal and informal.

Chinese graduate from school with almost no experience making decisions about anything more important than what music to listen to, then enter the workforce never having being asked their opinion on anything serious; if they work for a traditional firm or bureaucracy they might never be asked until they reach a senior position. At home, parents tell children what to do and to think, teachers do the same at school: neither parents nor teachers are interested in asking or knowing a student's opinion. Students don't choose what to study: their parents do, or it is chosen by their score in the University Entrance Exam.[51] Neither in the school nor the home are Chinese students taught debate or discussion skills, or asked to explain what they think about a subject. Chinese tests are almost all memorization: tell the teacher what she told you to tell her, and you pass. The people with the best memories go to the best schools. The best of the best become doctors.

To be fair Westerners also can have trouble showing initiative. Yet imagine how hard it would be to act independently if you had no experience making decisions for yourself and had been trained from birth to obey, not act, to memorize, not think. It would be very tough. Other aspects of Chinese culture would make it even harder.

Chinese are rewarded for following rules (how things are done) first, but initiative is all about achieving results (what gets done). It is possible in Chinese Asia to get an excellent result and still be penalized for how you did the thing, say for not asking permission first. Chinese are practical people and many have told me, "Why show initiative? It is too risky. It is easier to be quiet and wait to be told." As much as the Chinese lack of initiative often frustrates me, it is hard to argue with their point: it is easier to show initiative when good results are rewarded and bad results are not penalized too severely, and almost impossible to show initiative when even good results can be penalized.

This leads to the way Chinese treat mistakes, another way initiative is discouraged. Chinese grow up learning to fear making a mistake. Parents and teachers pounce on and penalize mistakes, using this to teach proper behavior or study habits. The focus on mistakes is another side of the 'punishment' teaching methods common in Chinese Asia, that if a child does not make mistakes he/she behaves properly: no mistakes = good behavior.

Well, maybe: it depends on what you define 'proper behavior' to be. I think a Western definition would include the good things children do as much as the bad things they don't do. One thing is sure though, Chinese children (any children) brought up with such methods will not show much initiative. More, children will likely try to hide mistakes and be reluctant to speak up about things they don't know or are unsure of, afraid of anything that might put focus on them. Such children would tend to be quiet, sometimes a good thing with children.

Being quiet is not so good for adults however, especially those who work for or with Westerners. We expect coworkers, team members and partners to have at least *some* initiative, and to do at least *some* of their own thinking. Westerners think it is bad to hide mistakes as they always come back to bite you, plus you can't train people until you know they have a problem, like their making a mistake. As far as speaking up/asking questions is concerned, it must have been a Westerner who first said, "The only stupid question is the one you don't ask." Westerners encourage questions, especially from children; it is how you learn and how you ensure achieving a good result.

Over the years I have heard a beer glass full of complaints about the Chinese, maybe two glasses full. Some of the most common complaints are lack of initiative, waiting to be told, hiding mistakes and not asking questions. These cultural behaviors make working with Chinese frustrating for Westerners. In later chapters I look at these problems and what they mean in daily work. The good news is that there are ways to get around or minimize these problems, either by becoming more sensitive yourself or by helping Chinese to change: a little bit of both works best. The bad news is that both ways take patience and effort, and maybe more than two glasses of beer.

In A Nutshell

It is hard to think of two cultures more different than Western and Chinese. What works for one is the opposite of what works for the other. Yet while the differences are many they all stem from one basic source, the vastly different goals of each culture. Your ability to work with or build any type of relationship with someone from Chinese Asia depends upon you understanding the goals of Chinese culture and how they affect Chinese actions and expectations. To grasp fully the importance of Chinese cultural goals you need to know how Western cultural goals shape your actions and expectations. True understanding requires a clear culture contrast.

Chinese culture has many uncles but only one father, Confucius. For over two thousand years China and the rest of Chinese Asia tried to achieve Confucian goals using Confucian methods, and to a very large part succeeded. Confucius said that the goal was to re-achieve or regain a past perfect society that had been lost. The perfect society was stable, i.e., unchanging, and characterized by harmonious relationships between people. To succeed all the Chinese people had to do was follow Confucius' rules about how people should treat other people. China became a rules-obeying culture, where the means (following rules) became the end (rules were followed). Goodness was found in how things were done rather than what was accomplished: the means were not the way to achieve the end, they were the end.

Key points include the absolute importance of relationships in Chinese life. No matter the situation or the cost, the greatest good was maintaining the relationship. This led to Chinese praising those who endured or sacrificed in order to 'do the right thing,' that is, to put maintaining the relationship in front of other considerations. For China's great cultural hero, Guan Gong, this meant losing a war and watching his friends die so he could 'honor his word' to his enemy (follow the rules).

Western translators use 'relationship' incorrectly to translate two different things: one is the normal know-each-other type of association Westerners think of as 'relationship;' one is something not really found in the West, an association based on mutual-shared-obligation, guanxi. Westerners must understand at least the basics of guanxi; it is the oil that greases the gears of Chinese society, business and life. Perhaps the hardest thing for Westerners to grasp is that guanxi is not win-win as much as it is you-help-me-win ... and you will get help when you need to win.

Adding to the mix and to the complexity is the fact that there is no concept of equality in Chinese social culture, meaning that all relationships are between people of unequal rank. Even twin brothers are not equal; higher rank is first born 'older brother,' lower rank is 'younger brother' born five minutes later. To ensure harmony between non-equals Chinese developed elaborate ways to act and to communicate.

Confucius succeeded. No matter what else you say about Chinese culture, you must salute its longevity: Confucian Chinese culture did not change for over 2,000 years, and would likely still exist if not for the steam engine, the Industrial Revolution and Western culture's drive to expand. China's stability came at the price of not knowing how to change though, a problem that continues to plague every Chinese Asian society.

A society is what it teaches its children to do. Chinese, Japanese and Korean teachers and parents teach children to conform, obey, follow and be quiet. No emphasis was or is put on Western (and business) virtues like initiative, independent thinking, speaking up or asking questions.

Westerners reading the last sentence should recognize the key problem in West-China relations: the very virtues Chinese culture lacks are among the most prized virtues in the West (the opposite is true as well). Can you imagine living or working with people with **no** initiative, people who always waited to be told and never asked questions?

Western culture is a 'knowledge seeking' culture, the overall goal discovering enough knowledge to answer Plato's questions. Assisted by two powerful uncles, Socrates' dialectic and Aristotle's logic, Westerners agree (mostly) on the goal and on how to learn but on little else, arguing continually about whether these are the answers, what the answers should look like or how close we are to them. Because of this struggle to learn, Western culture has been/is locked into a state of constant change, the irony being the more we learn the more pressure we create to change even more (and the farther we get from answers?).

Western heroes are people who went against the group, against the conventional wisdom of the time and often against the political authorities of the day. Western heroes believed in themselves and their idea or plan, often courting great personal risk in order to prove that they were right. Western heroes added to our knowledge, moving us along our line of history a little bit. How they did things is not so important; we marvel at what they achieved, their results. Western heroes are the agents of change.

Not every Westerner is a potential hero-in-waiting. Many Westerners are like good committee members, patiently waiting until they see the consensus before deciding how they think. Does every Chinese wait to be told what to do and think? No. I have met some very confident, do-it-now-and-damn-the-consequences Chinese. Starting your own business is almost pure initiative, and entrepreneurs are maybe the most important 'manufacture' in

Chinese Asia. The joke is that in a five-person Chinese company, one person is the boss and four plan to be.

This chapter has used black and white to describe a very gray environment, and I apologize if I have hurt anyone's feelings doing so. I readily admit exceptions exist, and that not all Chinese are X nor all Westerners Y. But learning culture (at least in my opinion) must start with understanding the sources of culture and the tendencies thus created, the black and the white. Once we understand the why that creates the 'tends to,' students can and must move to the gray. Living in black and white means you pre-judge, (the root word of prejudice) something to be avoided at all costs! Each person and situation is unique, and each deserves to be judged on merits alone, not with some preconceived notion. Nevertheless, it is true that Westerners 'tend to do X' and Chinese 'tend to do Y,' and these tendencies are the best place to start in deciding what a person means, what the possible solutions to a problem are and what actions should be done. Just don't base everything on the black and white picture; add some gray for color before you print the picture in your mind.

Themes and Lessons

Phew. Culture isn't easy to explain. I went into detail (too much?) as understanding why and how Chinese and Western cultures differ is necessary to wear Chinese glasses. I recognize the repetition—blame the teacher in me—but don't apologize for it: this is the most important chapter of the book.

1. Culture is a set of rules, values, beliefs and attitudes learned from parents, teachers and the social environment we grow up in.
2. Each culture seeks to achieve an overall philosophic goal. The Chinese goal (mainly from Confucius) is to create a stable society based on harmonious relations between people. The Western goal (mainly from Plato) is to create a dynamic society where individuals can discover answers to questions about the world around them.
3. Culture is not about what people do so much as how they do it, and why.
4. Understanding cross-culture begins by seeing the similarities between people within a cultural group (China and Taiwan Chinese for example) and the degree of differences between people from different cultural groups (Chinese and Westerners say).
5. What makes a hero is a useful way to look at differences between cultures. Western heroes add to our knowledge or development, frequently by going against the group and/or conventional wisdom. Chinese heroes put doing the right thing (following Confucian rules) in front of achieving the right result, even if doing so means they sacrifice themselves and/or their group.
6. Chinese culture is process driven, where the good is measured by how well a person follows the rules (about human relationships); Western culture is results driven, where the good is measured by what is achieved.

7. Western culture is based on the idea that people are equal (so each is equally able to add to society knowledge); Chinese culture on the idea that all relationships are unequal and hierarchical (so each knows their status and what rules to follow).

8. Western culture prizes individual initiative, as only through showing initiative can a person change or add to society's knowledge or development; Chinese culture prizes following the rules and obeying those above you, as only through following rules and obeying superiors can society be harmonious.

9. Western history is all about undirected change, with the only constant being that tomorrow will be different than today; Chinese history (since 204BC) is all about successful directed stability, and did not change for over 2000 years.

10. Chinese social and business culture is based on two types of human relationships: the networking, 'I know him/her' type of relationship understood in Western culture, and a unique, 'mutually shared obligation' type of relationship called guanxi. Of the two types, guanxi is by far the most important.

11. Guanxi is based on mutual obligation: because I helped you now, in the future you must help me, or someone I nominate. Think of it as a way to trade favors. A key part of guanxi is that once you accept a guanxi favor you are obliged to help in the future, even if helping is not in your immediate interest, i.e., it is not 'win-win' but more an 'I win now, you can win when you need to in the future' strategy. Once you are on the guanxi chain the only way to get off is to hurt relationships.

CHAPTER SIX

Rules of Communication

Communication is just a tool used to transfer messages. Every culture communicates differently, both in what language is used and in the *way* language is used. Every culture creates a 'proper' way of communicating, their unique Rules of Communication. Rules differ between cultures because each set of Rules is designed to help the culture achieve their overall goals. Consider Chinese and Japanese, two very different languages; while grammar and vocabulary are different both use almost identical Rules of Communication, this because both have almost identical cultural goals (stability and harmony). The same is true for English, Swedish and Italian, three very different languages that nonetheless use almost identical Rules of Communication, again because all three have almost identical cultural goals (discovering knowledge). A culture's goals determine all else. Actions and attitudes, beliefs and behaviors are all governed by Rules that help a people achieve its particular cultural goal. Keep the relationship between goals and Rules in mind as we look at Chinese Asian and Western Rules of Communication.

Children learn their culture's Rules of Communication at the same time they learn the language. As soon as your children begin to talk (able to use basic words and grammar), you begin to teach them how to talk politely (Rules). Learning to be polite is a key goal of a culture's Rules of Communication. We learn that just because we know how to say something—like how to disagree with a parent or how to use a loud voice—does not mean saying it whenever we want to is 'right' or 'proper.' Teachers reinforce the politeness Rules and introduce new Rules, these to help people learn the skills needed for achieving the culture's overall goal. For example Western students learn that asking questions is a necessary skill in discovering knowledge while Chinese students learn that expressing negatives in an indirect way is a necessary skill in maintaining harmonious relations. When children graduate and start to work they use these Rules in their jobs, reinforced by supervisors and bosses, paychecks and promotions. Eventually the children become parents themselves and pass these Rules on to the next generation, completing the cycle of learning how to communicate 'properly.'

Western Rules

It is best to start with Rules you know (Chinese classes start with Chinese Rules). If you want to understand the effect Chinese Rules have on how Chinese communicate, it helps first to understand Western Rules, what they are, why they are that way and their effect on communication. Below is a list of the Western Rules, followed by a short look at each of them.

Western Rules of Communication
• offer as much information as you can
• be as truthful as possible
• make sure that what you say is relevant
• don't make people guess your meaning
• be brief, orderly and logical
• get to and keep on the point
• state your honest opinion even if you disagree
• ask questions if you don't understand
• being clear is most important

Table 8: Western Rules of Communication

Most Westerners agree with the list; the only real disagreement I recall was from a European audience, something about the Rules looking "too American," and that "Europeans were more polite." I am not sure what that means (nor were the people who said it). Two points, first is that as a Canadian I am neutral in any American-European, ah, disagreements, and have never found Americans or Europeans any more or less 'polite' than the other. Americans can be a little loud perhaps, or not as strict about formality and titles as Europeans can be, but if 'impolite' is the same as 'blunt' I would say the Dutch are most direct, business-first people I have worked with.[52] The second point is that only Chinese with lots of experience working with different types Westerners would see any real difference between the different flavors of Westerner. Thus for the sake of argument, I hope you can live with my list.

How did the West end up with these Rules of Communication? Because each Rule helps us learn, share information, analyze facts and reach conclusions, helps us achieve our culture's goal, discovering knowledge. In the following section I describe each Rule, what it means and what its effect on 'discover knowledge' is.

Offer As Much Information As You Can

This Rule does not mean 'tell everything you know in a business meeting.' It has nothing to do with secret or sensitive information, or blurting out your bottom line in a negotiation. This Rule has a two-part meaning: don't offer information only one piece at a time and add all relevant details. To return to school (one of the best sources for examples) Western tests frequently ask subjective questions, the dreaded 'why?' question. Around the time we reach adolescence, (if not a little before) tests ask us to explain why, say "Why did WWII start?" or "Why did feudalism end?" To answer 'why' questions we must add as much relevant information (see below) as possible.

We also must supply as much information (proof) as we can to prove our answer to a 'why' question. Not just in tests either; when someone asks a question in an area you know, you don't just answer the specific question, you also consider other related information the questioner should know and, without being asked, supply as much information as you can. This is the *efficient* way to exchange information.

Be As Truthful As Possible

Once again this Rule does not mean tell the questioner everything: if you work for Coca Cola and someone asks you for the 'secret formula' you are under no obligation to tell him or her. What this Rule means is that you must try to tell the truth and to be honest: no lies please! If I am going to work with you, I need to trust that what you tell me is the truth.

There is also a personal or moral component to this Rule. Telling the truth is morally correct, even if the truth hurts you. George Washington is a hero not just because he led the American forces to victory but also because he told the truth about cutting down the cherry tree. Instead of lying and saying he did not cut the tree down (to save himself from punishment), he told the truth and thus risked receiving punishment. My parents stressed the need always to tell the truth, no matter the consequences.

Make Sure What You Say Is Relevant

Relevance is perhaps the most important concept in Western communication, making sure that what you say is relevant to the situation or issue being discussed. If you are listening to a person talk and have to ask yourself, 'why is he saying that, what does *that* have to do with *this*?' you start to feel uncomfortable, a clear signal you question the relevance of what is being said. You will likely either stop paying attention or will ask, "Hey, what has that got to do with this, why are you saying that, how is it relevant?"

We value relevance so much that we have developed sayings or communication formulas to deal with the issue. One example would be a sentence like, "I know this doesn't sound relevant but just bear with me and I will make it relevant." This shows that know your words don't appear to be relevant; your goal is that the audience remains patient (and keeps listening) until you can join what you are saying back to the original point. Relevance is so important that Westerners equate *irrelevant* with *unimportant*, a judgment that leads to huge problems communicating with Chinese (see below).

Don't Make People Guess Your Meaning

If I listen to someone talk for ten minutes and still don't know what their point is, what they are telling me, why or what they want, I find it very uncomfortable. If it is my boss, client or father speaking I often keep quiet and hope I figure it out eventually, but with others I don't wait long before asking, "Why are telling me this? What is your point?"

Many of Western culture's key communication situations or outcomes depend on clarity: contracts (anything that involves lawyers), scientific formulas, engineering specs, job objectives; it is a long list. We combat the effect of Murphy's Law for communication—*anything that can be misunderstood will be misunderstood*—by being aggressively clear and by not making people guess.[53] Except in the rarest cases, misunderstanding adds cost, never a good thing.

The upshot of this emphasis on clarity rather than ambiguity or indirectness is that Westerners tend to be poor at guessing meaning. At least once a month (week?) I say to my Chinese wife, "Look honey, I am a lousy guesser. Just tell me what you think, yes or no, don't tell me a story." I think on average Western women are better guessers than men are, yet Western women are not even in the same class as Chinese women … or even Chinese men. More on this later.

Be Brief, Orderly and Logical

Brief does not mean short, it means accomplish your communication goal in as few words as you can. If you need 50 words then use 50, not 100. Being orderly helps audiences follow your message. One way is speaking in lists, like saying 'there are three reasons: one is, two is, three is.' Another involves time, for example starting with the past, moving to the present and ending with the future. Being logical is, well, about being logical: offering a cause for an effect or premises for a conclusion, making sure all your facts are just that, facts, not opinions or beliefs.

Get To and Keep On the Point

In Western business the number one rule for written communication, fax, email or letter, is the first sentence must tell the reader what your point is, what you want or what the subject is. Time is money so we say, and if you don't get right to the point you are wasting time. Keeping on the point is critical to keeping audiences listening: if you give an audience a chance to lose interest, they will. Related to this is the benefit of step-by-step communication: making one point at a time truly helps most audiences follow your message.

Ask Questions If You Don't Understand

I would like to thank the person who coined the phrase, 'the only stupid question is the one you don't ask.' While in my classes and teams I certainly have heard my share of stupid questions, I honestly appreciate every question. Why? Because I can't look inside the audience's head to know if they understand, thus I depend on their questions to accomplish my goal, that they understand.

Most presentations end with the same sentence, "Are there any questions?" Westerners tend to disapprove of someone who has a question but does not ask it, thinking them foolish (or worse) to live with confusion or uncertainty rather than speaking up and asking a question. From childhood to old age Westerners are trained to ask questions, and are expected to ask questions. To end impolitely, if we don't ask questions, how can we learn?

Being Clear Is Most Important

Unless messages back and forth are clearly understood communication will fail. No matter how much information is offered, how relevant the points are or how many questions are asked, if the messages are not clear they will likely be misunderstood, the graveyard of good communication.

Emphasis on achieving 100% accurate transfer of message stems from the Western goal of discovering knowledge. While the brilliant insights and flashes of inspiration that propel our culture forward come mainly from heroic individuals and not committee groupthink, the only way to turn brilliant insight into gritty reality is by sharing information accurately, that is, sending clear and correct and messages.

Consider a very common business activity, deciding how to solve a problem. Four people meet and talk. None know all the answers or have all the necessary information, but if they can pool what they know they would have all the information needed to arrive at a solution. To pool the facts, thoughts and opinions effectively the 4-way communication must be clear, orderly, relevant, questions asked and disagreements expressed. Communication must follow all the Western Rules in order to create the real goal of group discussion; knowledge synergy, the group knowing more than the sum of what each individual knows.

Western results-driven culture depends upon the accurate, effective and clear transfer of knowledge from person to person, top-down, bottom-up, sideways. Our education system teaches two seemingly contradictory skills, how to learn as individuals and how to communicate clearly with others. The Rules of Communication used in the West are perfectly suited for both of these tasks.

Chinese Rules of Communication

Now the fun begins. Below are the Chinese Rules of Communication (Chinese Asian actually; these Rules work just as well for Japanese and Korean communication as they do for all flavors of Chinese). Take a first look at the Chinese Rules then we will look at each in detail.

Chinese Rules of Communication

- try not to disagree openly
- don't ask the people above you difficult questions
- don't let people know you don't understand a thing
- communicate negatives in an indirect way
- keep the conversation smooth
- don't embarrass someone in front of a group
- if what you say might cause problems, don't say it
- don't disturb the harmony of the situation
- being polite is most important

Table 9: Chinese Rules of Communication

Chinese Rules are very different from Western Rules. Before looking at Chinese Rules in detail though, some Westerners have challenged me on them—"they can't be right"—so let me deal with *bona fides* first. I have taught and talked about these exact Rules to, oh, well-over one thousand Chinese, in workshops, restaurants and beer houses, in China, Singapore, Hong Kong and Taiwan, and I can't remember *anyone* telling me they were wrong. The only close-to-disagreement comments I recall are: 1) these are more bottom-up Rules, and boss Rules are a little different, more direct and less polite; and 2) something like "Chinese society is changing and as it does the Rules need to be changed," usually part of a larger discussion about the problems of change in Chinese Asia. Even in the latter cases though, Chinese argued that they need to change their Rules (often mentioning education system too) to match the changes in the Chinese world, not that my description of current Chinese Rules were incorrect.

Chinese have told me they don't like the Rules, but no one has ever said, "These Rules are not true." Of course all that may mean is the Chinese have followed their first Rule—try not to disagree openly—and I missed their disagreement. But I don't think so. In my *Logical Thinking and Communication* 3-day workshop I train Chinese students to disagree openly, and by the last day of the workshop they get very, ah, happy and comfortable disagreeing with me. If I was wrong about Chinese Rules I am sure I would have heard about it, clearly and with a smile—my students love to find my mistakes! All this is a long-winded way of saying that I believe these Rules to be accurate, a belief I live by in all my dealings with Chinese. So, again for the sake of argument, let us live with my list.

Why do Chinese have these particular Rules of Communication? Simple: these Rules are perfectly suited to achieve the Chinese goal of a stable society based on harmonious relationships between people. Remember, there was no Chinese goal about discovering knowledge—Confucius already answered all of Plato's questions—or promoting change. The Chinese goal was (is) to follow Confucian rules: obey those above you and be polite. Below we look at each Rule in detail.

Try Not To Disagree Openly

Chinese do disagree openly. Publicly even, very obvious in political arenas like Taiwan's young and free-wheeling democracy and Hong Kong's slightly more subdued political struggle. You also see more open disagreement in business settings, especially in Chinese offices of Western multinationals. A traffic accident is followed by a high-volume disagreement about who is at fault (Chinese open disagreements are often loud). Even so, open disagreement is considered to be bad, impolite and incorrect; indirect or hidden disagreement is considered *proper*, and is still what happens in most areas of Chinese society.

Why do Chinese not like to disagree openly? Think about the two key goals of Chinese culture, stability and harmony. Open disagreement helps achieve neither harmony nor stability. People disagree openly because they care, because they think they are right and what they are disagreeing with is wrong and should be changed; they disagree openly because they believe change is more important than other goals, like maintaining stability and harmony; they disagree openly in order to win, to beat another, a goal that helps neither stability or harmony. None of the reasons for disagreeing openly fit into Chinese culture.

Why bother disagreeing at all? In traditional Chinese society there were precious few opportunities to disagree, openly or otherwise. When wisdom comes from age, children have no reason to disagree with either teacher or parent. When power comes from seniority, workers have no reason to disagree with supervisors or managers. Moreover, disagreements that did occur were between relative equals. As such, and as the relationship had to endure, disagreements normally were kept discrete and polite. Moreover, if a person did not care about an issue or about winning, why would he bother disagreeing at all, especially openly?

Two points about the open disagreements starting to occur in Chinese Asia. First, open disagreement is not done particularly well. Disagreement (productive disagreement anyway) is a learned skill complete with rules; call them the rules of debate or of meetings. One example is *Robert's Rules of Order*,[54] the manual for parliamentary debate and meetings in general. Westerners learn discussion, debate and disagreement skills as children, formally in classroom debates and informally arguing with parents at the dinner table. We learn to respect the rules—don't interrupt, don't yell, wait your turn—and to respect the other side's arguments; we learn that the actual goal is not necessarily to 'win' (that everyone agrees with you) but to explore an issue to find the best answer or solution. Chinese children don't have these advantages or opportunities to practice discussion and constructive disagreement, so have limited skills in these areas. Maybe most crucial,

Chinese have a different concept of what 'to win' means. To Chinese, 'win' means to 'defeat the other side,' any way possible.

You can see this 'win in any way possible" attitude to debate when Chinese do disagree openly, which brings me to my second point. Open disagreement happens primarily in areas where Chinese have been forced to change, not in areas where traditional forms still apply. There is still no debate or open disagreement in Chinese classrooms or around Chinese dinner tables, yet you can hear frequent (often loud) open disagreement in performance-related businesses and in democratic politics (open or nascent). Education is still traditional but business (especially Western-influenced) is not: in a growing number of companies promotion and compensation depend more on individual performance than seniority, a *huge* change. Domestic life is still traditional but politics is not. Even in China (though so far still at village level) individuals are tasked with becoming informed voters with the responsibility to decide whom to select as ruler, as far away from traditional Chinese politics as possible to be.

I am in danger here of writing a different book, so back to disagreement and Chinese glasses. Chinese do disagree, just not openly. Over the millennia Chinese have developed a way of communicating disagreement that protects a person's feelings, a way of disagreeing without disagreeing. Way back in Chapter 1 my wife disagreed with my buying the briefcase, was passionate about stopping me from buying it, but not once did she say "I don't think you should buy it" or any other type of open (clear) disagreement. Instead she used two objections as a way of communicating total disagreement. Later in the book I describe this technique in more detail and add a couple more common techniques Chinese use to disagree without disagreeing. For now what is important is you become aware that disagreements may be happening all around you, but unless you use Chinese ears you will miss them. You must pay attention. Don't just look for clear, Western disagreement code words.

Don't Ask People Above You Difficult Questions

People 'above you' are those senior to you, not simply taller than you: bosses, teachers, parents are all 'above' you. A difficult question is any question that may embarrass the person being questioned. Some typical examples are questions that ask for a judgment, that put a person 'on the spot' or that asks a person to prove or explain a decision. Most questions that start with 'why' are difficult questions. Indeed, one of the few ways Chinese fail to graduate from university is embarrassing a professor in class (a story I have heard numerous times).

Don't Let People Know You Don't Understand A Thing

If there was only one thing I could change about Chinese communication this would be it. Not only me: every Westerner who has asked "Do you have any questions?" only to be answered with blank, smiling faces agrees with me. Please, a rule you *must* live by: just because a Chinese does not ask a question does not mean he or she understands!

The examples are so numerous I could probably fill a book with just this one topic. Sitting in on a meeting where the boss explains what he wants the team to do, thinking it was my poor Chinese that made me unsure about what he was asking them (us) to do. Then, meeting over, asking my teammates what we were supposed to do only to be told they were not sure. Instead of asking the boss a question about what he meant the Chinese huddled together after the meeting, trying to guess what the boss wanted them to do. Not the best way to conduct things you say. Perhaps, but a good strategy for the boss: if the team accomplishes great things the boss can say it is exactly what he wanted, if the team fails the boss can say that they didn't do what he asked them to do. Empowerment through confusion, a technique not taught at Western MBA schools.

Why won't Chinese ask questions? I am not really sure. It must have something to do with face though, as Chinese will eagerly ask questions … as long as someone else asks a question first. The key to efficient feedback (people asking questions) is getting someone to go first; once he or she does everyone else will follow. One way I have done this is to plant a person in the audience, someone who trusts me: I give them a written question and assure them it is a 'smart' question, and ask them to ask it (read it aloud) when I finish my presentation. It works. The whole room knows what the person is doing, simply reading my question back to me, but the ice is broken and the dam is burst, someone went first and that is all that is important. Now everyone will ask questions.

Never forget that the Chinese are just as intelligent as you are, just as curious and just as eager to advance. The problem is how Chinese are educated: to sit back, listen and memorize, all passive learning. Not once in K-12 are Chinese trained to, or even expected to, ask questions. Now grown up, Chinese co-workers, partners and friends understand the cost of misunderstandings and of uncertainty, yet remain burdened with the lessons of youth: listen and memorize, don't be active or ask questions. In a later section I look at what else you can do to ensure feedback (a necessity in business), but for now please remember the rule: no questions does not equal understanding!

I once met a group of Western financial advisors happy their presentation had been a success. I asked how they knew. "Because no one asked questions," they answered, a metric I suppose works on Wall Street. They were so happy I did not have the heart to tell them that no questions probably meant the Chinese audience had not understood anything they said.

Communicate Negatives In An Indirect Way

By now you get the idea that Chinese are, ah, reluctant to communicate negatives in an open, direct way. What else is open disagreement but clearly communicating a negative? We in the West are often reluctant to do this too, say in marriages or when talking to superiors. No matter how ugly I think my wife's new haircut/shoes/dress is, I will do everything I can to let her know without actually saying my opinion clearly. Basic survival skills: as in Chinese Asia, my number one priority is maintaining our relationship ... and not sleeping on the sofa.

More interesting is that Chinese also have trouble with positives. The Chinese HR Director of IBM told me years ago, "You know Greg, Chinese have just as much trouble giving compliments as they have expressing negatives." Over the years I've realized just how true that is. Perhaps it comes from childhood experience, that neither parents nor teachers did much positive reinforcement, like giving compliments for good behavior or praising a child in front of the class. As my wife tells me (when I complain that she doesn't compliment me enough), "good behavior and accomplishments are expected: why should I have to compliment you for them?"

Tell a Chinese woman "You look good today," and she could easily answer something like, "Does that mean I don't look nice every day?" Now I worry she thinks I insulted her! To get around this I usually say something like, "Mary, you always look good but today you look especially nice." That compliment is always happily accepted. In a later section I deal with the whole issue of using positive reinforcement to encourage good behavior. You have to learn to use a 'public secret.'

Keep The Conversation Smooth

You don't want highs, you don't want lows, you just want everything to keep moving along smoothly. The Confucian goal for Chinese culture was stability, just another way of saying smooth. Once you get off the plane in Singapore, Seoul or Shanghai you have no reason ever to raise your voice; no matter what the provocation, you will be in the wrong. Loud voices don't make the conversation smooth.

A key skill to learn is to keep your temper. If the Chinese see that you have every reason to go crazy, to yell and scream and stomp your feet … but you don't, and instead keep your anger inside and keep the conversation smooth, well, your stock will rise tremendously in their eyes. If you can keep 'smooth' without eyes bulging, face turning red or smoke coming out from your ears all the better. Try to learn Chinese body language, which in difficult situations is no body language at all, just the Chinese mask.

Don't Embarrass Someone In Front Of A Group

How big is a group? More than two: five, fifteen, fifty, it makes no difference; once you go past one-on-one it is a group, and the entire dynamic changes. If you want to find out something at all sensitive don't do it in a group, do it in a series of one-on-ones. It takes more time, true, but you are results-oriented Westerner, so measure what you achieve (results), not what you have to do to achieve it (process).

What types of things might embarrass someone in front of a group? Result items, all the good stuff that we want to find out. Taboo subjects would include asking a Sales Manager in front of his staff why sales were down, asking a Production Manager in a staff meeting why the quality targets were not being met, or asking a Marketing Manager in a department meeting to give reasons for his marketing plan. In each case the potential for embarrassment is high: the Sales Manager might have to admit his staff is poorly trained; the Production Manager forced to say the factory's machines were old and poorly-maintained; the Marketing Manager reluctant to answer as he didn't create the plan, a low-level assistant did. In all cases answering the question in a group setting would cause big loss of face for some or all the Chinese, especially in front of the Western guest.

This tendency to keep silent about all the important bits in group situations is frustrating; time is short, good hotels are not cheap and you traveled to Tianjin or Taipei to deal with the important bits, not for polite conversation. You just want to get on with it. Get all the relevant people together and deal with the issues one by one. Western managers in Chinese Asia have the same desire, and the same frustration. Raised with the idea that time is money, Westerners believe efficiency is more important than embarrassment, and besides, we all make mistakes so what is the big deal.

It is a big deal to the Chinese. If you push and force the issue, well, you may find out what you are looking for, but maybe not. More likely you will hear what people think you want to hear, or what is likely to stop your questions. Even if you do get exactly what you want it will come at a cost to the relationship: you'll be put into the 'ugly Westerner' category, a classification that will affect how the Chinese deal with you.

Is there any way not to worry about this? There may be, but I don't know it. I suffer through Chinese meetings rather than participate in them, even when I am the chair. I use the meeting to let people know what is on my mind or what I want us/them to do, to gain clues and to set up the one-on-one meetings after the meeting is over. Takes time sure, and a **lot** of patience, but I focus on the results I achieve, not the methods I (have to) use.

One-on-one meetings are where you find results. While you still can not be as blunt, direct or candid as you would with another Westerner, you can be to-the-point in a one-on-one setting. Stripped of Confucian Rules and out of the hearing of the group, Chinese can be very forthcoming. You will be surprised. Just show some respect and don't come back to the group and say, "Now Mr. Lin just told me the real situation, and … ." To paraphrase a key principle from another type of relationship, 'don't learn and tell.' Everyone may know that you found out X from Mr. Lin, but as long as you don't mention his name he will not have too big a problem with the group. Remember, the Chinese also want good results, just not at the expense of good relations.

A following chapter looks at meetings in Chinese Asia in more detail. For now let's leave it with the fact that Chinese meetings are frequently dull and frustrating, even (or especially) if there is an urgent problem to resolve or policy to be decided. Success comes from playing the Chinese meeting game in their way, using the group meeting to set up one-on-one meetings that follow.

If What You Say Might Cause Problems, Don't Say It

This Rule is hard to explain. Basically it means that given the choice of their words causing a relationship problem or of speaking up to stop a result error, Chinese often choose silence, so to preserve harmony and the relationship. Still confused? An example is the best (only?) way to explain.

When I started my first company I had Chinese investors and lots of help from Chinese friends but still led the effort myself. A friend and investor was boss of a good-size law firm so I went to him to do the legal startup stuff. Of course you go to a lawyer for the legal stuff, right? Well it took a long time—almost three months!—to finish the paperwork and get all the chops needed to incorporate. I was very frustrated by this, frustration I often vented with another good Chinese friend/investor. He would pour me a good scotch (he owned the company) and I would bitch about the process, about how long it was taking and how it was costing me/us money and opportunities.

Finally the last paper was chopped. I had an actual company! I went directly to my friend's office to celebrate. Over a generous scotch I told him I could not believe how long and complicated it was to start a new company.[55] His reply? "Well Greg, that is because you used a lawyer to set it up. We use accountants, not lawyers, and it normally takes only 3-4 weeks, not three months."

I could not believe my ears. My friend had watched me make a mistake (use a lawyer not an accountant) that cost me (and him) time and money, and had not said anything about it, had not tried to stop me from making the mistake! It took all my effort not to stand up and punch him. Through clenched teeth I asked him why he didn't tell me I was making a mistake. His answer? "I tried to warn you Greg, but when you insisted on using a lawyer ..."

Huh? I did not 'insist' on a lawyer, I just thought using a lawyer was common sense, and as I had a Chinese friend/investor who happened to own a law firm, well, it seemed the right thing to do. Later, after I was home and cooled down I thought back to our first conversations, trying to find where I had 'insisted' and where he had 'tried to warn me.' I recalled my friend mentioning way back at the beginning that he knew an accountant we could use to set up the company, and something about lawyers having different roles in Taiwan than in the West. I paid no attention to this though, thinking the accountant would be useful only after my lawyer friend finished the incorporation. The 'different roles for lawyers' sentence never even registered in my head, competing as it did with something a professor back in college had said, that the smartest thing you can do when starting a company was to get legal assistance. I wanted to be smart, wanted to do the *right* thing—use a lawyer.

My 'insistence' on using a lawyer put my Chinese friend on the spot: either clearly say I was making a mistake and risk hurting my feelings and maybe our relationship, or watch me make a mistake and say nothing in order to protect the relationship. Once again the choice between pride and profit. My making a mistake was just a result error that would only hurt profit, while telling me I was making a mistake was a process error that might easily hurt my pride. A much different calculation than in the West.

A Western friend has a responsibility to protect me from making a mistake. If a good friend or a family member sees me about to make a serious mistake he/she has responsibility to do whatever necessary, shout, slap my face, whatever, to make sure I clearly know about the mistake I might be making. Anything less is just not right in the West: friends protect friends from making result errors (mistakes). Our friendship depends on it. Not so in Chinese Asia.

No, that is not quite right. Chinese have friends and do try to protect them from making result errors. But where Westerners pay little or no attention in these cases to how their words might hurt a friend's feelings, Chinese must and do pay attention. Other communication Rules come into play, communicating negatives in indirect way, not disagreeing openly and keeping everything smooth for example. Within the confines of these Rules the Chinese do warn friends about result errors, they just do it, ah, politely. Indirectly.

In retrospect and with my Chinese glasses on I realize my friend did warn me I was making a mistake, twice, just as he said he had. My friend told me he knew an accountant that could help, and that lawyers had different roles in Taiwan. Add them together and voilà, a Chinese-style warning. When I continued to say we would use the lawyer my friend interpreted that as me 'insisting' on doing it my way, so he dropped the subject. Exactly the same as in the West: a friend's responsibility is to warn me, then to shut up about it if I don't listen (true friends don't say "I told you so" after I make the mistake). My friend did warn me, just in an indirect, polite way.

Did my friend do enough to warn me? No, I don't think so. Or I didn't think so at the time: I do now. True, he never shouted nor slapped me in the face, forcing me to recognize his warning, but I can't expect that in Chinese Asia. My friend did try, twice, to warn me, which would have been enough for another Chinese, or for me if I had been wearing Chinese glasses and paying attention. Every word has meaning, a crucial point I discuss later in the book.

This *don't say it if it might cause problems* Rule is difficult for Westerners to accept, brought up as we were in a 'speak up, good results matter most' culture. Yet to succeed in Chinese Asia Westerners must accept that Chinese are trapped in a 'don't hurt someone's feelings' culture, meaning that ideas, opinions and advice contrary to yours may be hinted at, not shouted. Listen as if every word has meaning: they frequently do.

Don't Disturb The Harmony Of The Situation

This Rule explains itself, especially with all the words above about the other Rules. You can think of it as an applied form of "keep conversation smooth," referring to all situations, not just conversation. A good example is raising your voice. Once you get of the plane in Shanghai, Seoul or Shenzhen you should never, repeat never, raise your voice. This includes cries of joy and happiness as well as the more-obvious screams of anger. If you get a hole-in-one don't shout out with joy; doing so will disturb the harmony of the situation and, by making everyone look at your group, embarrass your playing partners. (It's okay to be happy though; you can do a little song and dance, as long as it's quiet. Don't cause a scene.)

Being Polite Is Most Important

Can this be true, that being polite is more important than being clear? Westerners have some trouble accepting this. Remember, communication is just a tool used by people to achieve the overall goals of the culture they live in. The Western goal is discovering knowledge, making clarity of message the key consideration. The Chinese culture goal is not to discover knowledge but to maintain stable, harmonious relationships, making politeness much more important than clarity. When faced with a choice between being clear or hurting someone's feelings, politeness wins in Chinese Asia, even if it leads to bad business results.

"But how can this work?" Westerners often ask in class, "How can Chinese run a business like that?" It's hard to grasp, I agree. A huge but well-hidden drag on Chinese Asian business is poor Chinese-Chinese communication, caused not by the Chinese language (though that has an effect) but by Chinese Rules of Communication. The goals of modern business (good results) are in daily conflict with the goals of Chinese culture (harmonious relationships). How Chinese companies succeed when their business communication has to serve two opposing masters is a subject for a later day. For now you just need to realize the difference between Chinese and Western (or modern business) Rules of Communication. To do that let's look at the respective communication Rules in a different way.

Garbage In, Garbage Out

Do you know the 'garbage in, garbage out' principle? From computers, it means that no matter how good a program is (a budget spreadsheet full of related formulas say), if you key in incorrect information (garbage in) you will always get incorrect results (garbage out). We can use this principle to look at communication, shown below:

Two Parts To Every Message	
every message has two parts: message content and method of delivery	
Content	Delivery
• information quality	• how-to communication skills
• are the facts relevant?	• grammar and pronunciation
• are the facts accurate?	• effective sales techniques
• are they facts or just opinions or beliefs?	• making a persuasive and clear business presentation
• are all the needed facts included (sufficient)?	• writing polite business letters, faxes and emails
Method Used	Method Used
using the rules of **logic** to analyze the nature of the information and the sufficiency of proof in a message	using the techniques of **rhetoric** to be both effective and efficient in any type of communication situation

Table 10: Two Parts To Every Message

Every message has two parts. First is 'what' you are going to say, the content of the message, next is 'how' you communicate it, both the method (fax, email, shouting) and the quality or skill level (writing ability, voice volume) used. Both are needed: you must have something to say (content) and then you must actually pass it on (delivery) in order to communicate. Content without delivery is just thinking, delivery without content is, well, much of what we see on TV, that and political messages.

If every message has two parts and both are necessary, are both equally important? No. The 'in' part of a message is the content, what you try to communicate; the 'out' part is the delivery, how you try to communicate it: in comes before out. Communication goes *what* then *how* (speaking without thinking the possible exception). No matter the message, request, thought, opinion, question or order, we have to know what it is before we can choose how to communicate it. It's common sense to me, if not always immediately to my students. One countered with, "what if I decide to give my wife a romantic Valentine's card (how I'll say my feelings) before I buy the card (which is what my feelings are)? Isn't that the *how* before the *what*?" Clever, but no. The desire to communicate an "I love you" message (what you wanted to say) came first, followed by the decision to give a romantic card (how to say it).

Consistent communication success depends upon doing a decent job in both the what and the how, so in that sense they are equally important. Nevertheless, if there is enough time to focus only on one part, facts beat delivery. In almost all cases lousy facts equal a lousy message, no matter how well delivered. Look at a key business and life activity, decision making.

Which is most important to a decision, the facts in front of you (content) or how you received them (delivery)? Of course delivery is important, you must understand the facts before you can use them, but you make a decision based on what the facts are, or you should. The reality is many of us are too easily swayed by fancy presentations and famous speakers into basing decisions on the delivery. Used car salespeople excel at this verbal sleight-of-hand, as do politicians. Other pressures make you focus on delivery too much, like office politics forcing you to use your boss's pet facts even when they are wrong, but that's life, not communication.

I teach Chinese (in my *Logical Thinking and Communication* workshop) there are seven major types of business communication: persuading, requesting, instructing, describing, explaining, questioning and ordering. Communication success in each depends upon good content, on facts being accurate, relevant and sufficient. Let's say you receive an unclear request, partial description or confusing instructions. You first try to clarify the content: if you can you have communication success. But the reverse is not true: even beautiful delivery can't save poor content. Even if your coworker sings you the description in a voice kissed by angels, even if the request is written in gorgeous script on parchment, even if the PowerPoint presentation is actually interesting, incomplete information or unclear writing still equals a lousy message, open to mistake and misunderstanding.

Content, Delivery And Culture

I hope you see that messages have two parts, and that both are important. Without looking at the book think about Western and Chinese culture and its effect on each group's Rules of Communication, and answer these questions:

1. Do Westerners and Chinese both have content and delivery Rules?
2. Do Chinese focus most on one part of communication? If so, what is their primary focus?

The quick answers are: Westerners have both content and delivery Rules; Chinese focus only on delivery, not content. Look at Western Rules of Communication: which are content Rules and which delivery? The first are about content, then come delivery Rules: Westerners include both content and delivery. Look at the Chinese Rules: how many are content and how many are delivery?

Western Rules of Communication	**Chinese** Rules of Communication
• offer as much information as you can	• try not to disagree openly
• be as truthful as possible	• don't ask people above you difficult questions
• make sure that what you say is relevant	• don't let on you don't understand a thing
• don't make people guess your meaning	• communicate negatives in an indirect way
• be brief, orderly and logical	• keep the conversation smooth
• get to and keep on the point	• don't embarrass someone in front of a group
• state honest opinion even if you disagree	• if words may cause trouble, don't say them
• ask questions if you don't understand	• don't disturb the harmony of the situation
• being clear is most important	• being polite is most important

Table 11: Western and Chinese Rules of Communication

Chinese have **no** content Rules—**all** are delivery Rules! Hard to believe, I know. Why are all Chinese Rules about delivery? To understand we need to look at why we need content at all.

The key reason to focus on content is to achieve results or change things. If your focus is on stability and harmonious relationships (like in Chinese culture … and large bureaucracies) there is no real need for content. If goals (what to do) and processes (how to do) are not questioned, just repeated, there will be no disagreements about change, and deciding about change is when facts are most needed. If you don't have anything to prove (like "we should make this change") you have no need for facts. Strange for Westerners, yes, but it worked for the Chinese.

How well did it work? Chinese culture didn't change for millennia, that's how well! Yet it was success at quite a price, the inability to adapt to a world shaped by the industrial revolution and new currents of political, economic and social thought. The Chinese almost lost control over China, and did suffer for decades or more because of their difficulty to adapt. It continues to hurt Chinese businesses today.

Chinese Rules of Communication add a huge, hidden cost to business, from waste and extra work caused by misunderstandings, from not asking questions, being polite instead of clear and such. Moreover, not just business with outsiders is hurt; efficiency and effectiveness inside and between Chinese companies is hurt as well. Yet Chinese businesses are still successful, even with such a communication, ah, weakness.

Add in the limiting effect of Chinese education—lack of initiative, no experience with debate or discussion, no training in logical analysis or in independent thinking—and Chinese business success is even harder to understand. I always think, 'what could Chinese do if they were actually prepared for business?' Add proper training to the Chinese cultural desire to 'get ahead and make a better life for my children' and willingness to work hard and, well, if you think the Chinese are fierce competitors now, you haven't seen anything yet! Let the Chinese throw off the shackles of dead Confucian goals and redesign education to prepare students for an uncertain future and, well, I am glad my daughter speaks Chinese.

Themes and Lessons

There are two (at least) things needed for successful cross-culture communication: a common language and a way of using language in common. All cultures have unique Rules of Communication, rules about how language should be used. To communicate with Chinese you must understand Chinese Rules of Communication, both to understand what their written or spoken words actually mean, and to adjust your words to match the way Chinese expect messages to be sent.

1. Communication is just a tool to transfer messages. Every culture creates ways of using language—their Rules of Communication—that assist the people to achieve the overall culture goal.

2. Chinese Rules help people have stable and harmonious relationships (key Chinese culture goals).

3. Western Rules help people change, learn and discover (key Western culture goals).

4. **Be as polite as possible** is the key Chinese Rule

5. **Be as clear as possible** the key Western Rule.

6. One example is disagreement: each culture expresses it in different ways. Western disagreement is expressed clearly, Chinese disagreement expressed indirectly. Both ways work, as long as the respective audiences know which method is used.

7. Messages have two parts, what the message is (content) and how it's communicated (delivery). Western communication has both content and delivery Rules, Chinese only have delivery Rules.

CHAPTER SEVEN

Communicating in Chinese Asia

No matter why you are in Chinese Asia, for work, travel or whatever, nothing hurts you as much as communication problems. It does not matter how nice you are, how hard you work or how polite you are, if you often misunderstand what you hear and/or Chinese often misunderstand what you say, you will be in one 'going broke' relationship after another. Almost every cross-culture problem, personal or business, includes at least some bad communication and misunderstandings. Misunderstandings add huge hidden costs to business, especially international business.[56]

This chapter looks at some common communication problem areas, why they happen and what you can do to (try to) prevent them. Overcoming communication problems is a necessary building step to culture-to-culture success. Poor communication affects everything.

Not all communication problems are West-East: Chinese recognize communication problems within their own culture. Two of these problems are *Play Piano to the Cow* (對牛彈琴) and *Duck Hears Thunder* (鴨子聽雷). What do they mean? Nothing to do with cows, ducks, weather or a piano of course, instead each expresses a common communication problem.[57]

Play Piano to the Cow describes wasting your words on someone who won't or can't understand or appreciate your message. Just like if you played piano to a cow, a waste of time and effort.[58] The Western expression, 'speaking to deaf ears,' has somewhat similar meaning.

If you *Play Piano to the Cow* it can lead to *Duck Hears Thunder*, and here I can't think of any Western approximation. *Duck Hears Thunder* describes a situation where a duck hears thunder then becomes afraid, not knowing that thunder is harmless. In other words, the duck misunderstands what it hears and reacts incorrectly. A common real-life example of this (described below) is a Chinese misunderstanding a Westerner trying to be 'Western polite,' and thus reacting incorrectly. Equally common are Westerners misunderstanding Chinese messages, thus reacting incorrectly in turn.

Duck Hears Thunder is the most common problem Westerners and Chinese have communicating with each other. Innocent misunderstandings often lead to Big Problems. Misunderstandings normally occur when both sides focus on just *their* way of communicating, and use only *their* culture's Rules of Communication. It works both ways: Chinese want to be polite too, but are as guilty of using the wrong Rules as Westerners are.

Western Polite And Mixed Messages

Contrary to what many Chinese think, Westerners *are* polite, or at least try to be. Westerners often forget, though, that 'our' way of being polite is not necessarily the same as 'their' way. You must market manners just like messages. Consider this: if I think I am polite but my Chinese friend does not, then in his eyes (which at that time are the only important eyes) I am not polite. In order for me to be polite in his eyes, I must act or speak in a way *he* recognizes as being polite. The best way to explain this is to look at an actual example (for a change one that didn't happen to me).

Western Polite

Tom Brown is in Taiwan to visit some factories. At the end of the third day he was tired and wanted to take a rest. On the way back to the hotel his guide, Li-chen, told him tomorrow was a holiday. Their conversation went like this:

Li-Chen: Well, tomorrow is a holiday.

Tom Brown: Too bad. I was really looking forward to seeing that other factory. Oh well, it's not important. Another time.

1. What do you think Tom meant by what he said?
2. Are there one or two messages in Tom's words?
3. Any idea what happened next?

Case Study 1: Western Polite

Any idea what happened next? The worst possible outcome (of course): as Tom lay in his big hotel bed looking forward to doing nothing all day, the phone rang. It was Li-chen who, in an unhappy voice, said, "I'm in the lobby. Let's go." Confused and not at all happy, Tom dressed and went downstairs. Tom was in a bad mood all day, but was not sure why Li-chen and the factory manager seemed to be in bad moods as well. As Tom thought to himself, 'It's not as if *I* asked *them* to work today.'

Tom *did* ask them to work on their day off; he just did not realize it. Take a close look at Tom's words. The first part has no real meaning, just Tom being polite: the meat of the message is the last part, the 'not important' phrase. Most Westerners would understand Tom's message to be something like, 'Good: I need a day off.' Not Chinese. Most Chinese would misunderstand. Why?

No Sarcasm In Chinese Asia

Sarcasm is saying one thing to mean another. Chinese tend not to use or understand sarcasm as Westerners use it, even very innocent and obvious sarcasm.

I often mutter, "Oh great," or "That's wonderful," when I hear some bad news or when something bad happens. Most Westerners would understand my message to be the opposite of what the words meant, i.e., that my real meaning was disappointment or anger, not happiness or joy.

Chinese will **not** understand. If I say something like "That's great," Chinese who hear me will, in a serious voice and manner, correct me: "It is not good Greg, it is bad." While there must be exceptions, must be Chinese who do understand such innocent, *say one thing to mean another* messages, I can't think of one I know. After 15 years of marriage and 8 years living and working in Canada, my Chinese wife still misunderstands my innocent sarcasm.

Chinese don't use sarcasm like this. You shouldn't either.

Table 12: No Sarcasm In Chinese Asia

Chinese don't usually offer confused or mixed messages, saying one thing to mean another, but Tom did. To Westerners Tom's first words, "too bad ... really looking forward to," means something like 'you are doing a good job; I am happy with what we are doing,' some type of positive message anyway. Just being polite. Tom's real message came last, the "not important ... another time," meaning something like 'good.' Just making conversation.

Chinese don't just *make conversation* like we do, at least not with strange Westerners. A rule I use with Chinese (even those I know well), especially when speaking English, is 'every word has meaning.' Chinese think Westerners follow the same pattern, that every word we say has meaning. This is especially true at beginnings of potentially important relationships, like Tom and Li-chen's is, or could be. (See later this chapter for more on this.)

Adding to Li-chen's confusion was the sequence, meaningless words first then the actual message. To Chinese, the first words spoken will likely be the message, followed by meaningless, polite words to soften the blow. Go back and reread Tom's words with this in mind. You get a very different message. First Tom seems to say, 'I don't care about the holiday; I want to visit that factory tomorrow,' then adds, 'not important; another time,' which seems to mean ... I'm not sure what Li-chen would think it meant. Moreover, he (and most Chinese) would probably not have paid much attention to the last sentence, and would remain focused on the "don't care about holiday" part (also continued below).

Be Direct: Say What You Mean

Tom should have answered by saying what he meant, directly but politely. Something like, 'Tomorrow is holiday? Good. So, we'll start again the day after tomorrow, right?' Direct, to the point, no confusion possible. Everyone is happy, Tom with his day off and Li-chen with his holiday.

Even better, Tom confirmed when the factory tour would start again, a definite win-win: eliminating uncertainty (always a good thing in Chinese Asia) and any possible misunderstandings. Yet even as good as Tom's direct words would have been, he still missed a number of excellent chances to build the relationship with Li-chen.

First, Tom could have added, 'You've worked me hard and I need a day off' after saying 'Good.' Tom wasted a wonderful chance to make Li-chen feel good about himself and his work. Even more useful, Tom could have asked at the end, 'What holiday Li-chen? Could you explain it to me?' I look for these opportunities, look for chances to ask Chinese to talk about themselves and about Chinese culture. You should too.

Why? Because Chinese love to talk about things Chinese. (Positives, not negatives, not pollution, laws, politics, traffic etc.)

To paraphrase Dale Carnegie's advice,[59] Chinese love to talk about Chinese culture and traditions.[60] A key reason I know as much as I do about things Chinese is that I constantly ask questions (sometimes when I already know the answers). Tom should have ended by asking, 'What holiday Li-chen? Can you explain it to me?' It was Tomb Sweeping Day, a fascinating day when families clean, paint and restore their ancestor's graves, sometimes ending with a barbeque on top of the dear departed.

Whatever the holiday though, you should never pass up a chance to ask Chinese about the Chinese, their ways, culture and traditions. It shows you are interested in learning about Chinese things, and is a wonderful way to build a relationship. More will be needed, of course, but showing the Chinese you respect their ways enough to want to (try to) learn them is a great start.

Remember, Westerners are barbarians, outside Chinese rules, a true advantage in many ways, being direct is just one. Westerners can be direct and, as long as they are polite as well, Chinese have no problems with it. The truth is that even Chinese can have trouble guessing what other Chinese mean, and understand the benefits of direct talk. Certainty is a good thing, in any culture.

But He Didn't Disagree

Chinese make as many communication mistakes as Westerners do, mistakes normally caused by Chinese using English words but Chinese Rules of Communication. Westerners, hearing English thus using Western Rules of Communication to understand the messages, get confused all the time. Below is an example.

Didn't We Decide That?

Dave is in China meeting Yen-ping, manager of the JV between their two companies. Below is part of their discussion about whether to import parts or buy them in China.

Dave: Part #212 should be imported. Taki Co. in Japan has very high quality, and #212 must be of the highest quality. Everything else depends on it.

Yen-ping: I don't know if buying from Taki is a good idea. The duty will be very high.

Dave: But good quality is more important than low price for #212. And besides, we've got enough margin to pay a premium for it if needed. You agree?

Yen-ping: Dave, Taki Co. it is very difficult to deal with.

Dave: Aren't all Japanese companies though Yen-ping. You'll have no trouble. Solving tough problems is what you are good at, right? Don't you agree?

Yen-ping: (looks away and says nothing)

Dave: Good. That's settled. Now, about Part #213 . . .

> Six months later Dave finds that Part #212 is not coming from Taki Co. but instead was being sourced from a local Chinese company. Dave phones Yen-ping to ask why.
>
> Dave: Yen-ping, about Part #212. I'm pleased and puzzled. It's good quality and cheap, but I thought we decided to import it from Japan. Why the change?
>
> Yen-ping: Well, the high duty made buying it from Taki in Japan very expensive.
>
> Dave: But I remember we talked about that, and agreed we could afford to pay more for it. Part #212 is crucial, and had to be top quality. Didn't we decide that meant it should come from Taki? I'll admit you've surprised me by finding it cheaper and good quality locally, but I'm still puzzled why you didn't buy from Taki as agreed.
>
> Yen-ping: Dave, Taki Co. is very hard to deal with.
>
> Dave: I can't believe it was too hard though. That's what you are good at, dealing with tough companies. What's the real reason Yen-ping?
>
> Yen-ping: Taki was just too tough to deal with.
>
> Dave: I can't accept that. Taki is a company just like ours. It wants to make money. What is the real reason? I'm not angry—I just want to know why.
>
> Yen-ping: Dave, Taki Co. owns one of our big competitors; they won't sell to us.
>
> Dave: Since when?
>
> Yen-ping: For at least six years now.
>
> Dave: But if you knew when we talked months ago why didn't you say something? I only suggested we buy the part from Taki. You should've told me.
>
> Yen-ping: I tried but you kept insisting, even after I said we couldn't get it from Taki.
>
> Dave: I can't remember you insisting, or disagreeing. I really can't.

Case Study 2: Didn't We Decide That?

In a strict Western sense, did Yen-ping **tell** Dave, *We cannot buy the part from Taki*? No, he did not: Yen-ping's 'disagreement' was indirect and unclear, breaking a number of the Western Rules of Communication. Yet every Chinese I ask think Yen-ping clearly told Dave, *We can't buy from Taki.*

How did Yen-ping tell Dave, *No, don't buy from Taki;* why did Dave miss this clear (to Yen-ping and to the Chinese) message? Why does Yen-ping think Dave *insisted* on using Taki? Dave does not recall insisting, nor can most Westerners see how he insisted.

To understand we need to look at disagreements in each culture. In Western culture few people like disagreeing exactly, nevertheless it is an accepted part of life. We expect disagreement to happen, and expect it to be clear. In Chinese culture, disagreement is a serious thing: Chinese try to avoid disagreement but, if they must express disagreement, think it should be indirect.

The most common type of indirect disagreement is to use objections to communicate disagreement. In Chapter One I told the story of buying a briefcase. My wife and I argued over it, she angry because she was sure she had told me not to buy it but I didn't listen to her, me angry because I was sure I had done no such thing—I had asked her and she said it was okay to buy it. Now is the time to explain this argument and Dave/Yen-ping, for the cause of the problem is the same: Chinese using the wrong Rules of Communication, and Westerners listening with the wrong ears.

Let's start with the Chinese point of view. Look at Yen-ping's words through Chinese glasses. Twice, first about the high duty and then about how difficult working with Taki would be, Yen-ping expresses clear objections to Dave's idea to buy from Taki. In Yen-ping's mind, these objections communicate clear disagreement. When Dave does not pay any attention to the objections/disagreement, it means that Dave insists they use Taki.

Now, through Western eyes. Dave attempted to satisfy Yen-ping's first objection, then asked Yen-ping what he thought. Yen-ping could have said he was not satisfied, that he disagreed, but instead he changed the subject (offered another objection). Dave took the change of subject to mean Yen-ping was satisfied about his first objection. Dave then tried to satisfy Yen-ping's second objection, and again gave him a chance to disagree after he finished. "Don't you agree?" Dave asked. When Yen-ping was silent, Dave thought it meant he must agree about using Taki.

Dave and Yen-ping heard the same words but each reached different ideas on what they words meant. Meaning depended upon what glasses each wore.

The rule I live by in Chinese Asia is **Two Objections Means Disagreement**. Whenever I communicate with Chinese, by email or phone, fax or face-to-face, if I hear two objections I immediately assume the actual message is *no* or *I disagree* or *we shouldn't*, whatever negative the context requires.

Greg's Tips – No. 1
Two objections usually means disagreement.

If Dave had understood that Yen-ping was not 'objecting' but 'disagreeing' he could have tried to deal with his 'don't buy from Taki' message: he might have asked for more detail about Taki, about why they would be so hard to deal with for example. If so, I expect Yen-ping would have told Dave about Taki being owned by a competitor and unwilling to sell to them. Yen-ping was (probably) not trying to hide anything from Dave; indeed, he attempted to be clear about his disagreement.

The audience now asks how to tell the difference between a Chinese simply trying to raise an objection and one trying to disagree using objections. I answer that I don't know, and that if they ever find out let me know and we'll all make more money. This always brings forth nervous smiles.

No *Yes* Or *No* In Chinese Language

There is no one word for *Yes* and no one word for *No* in the Chinese language. Instead there are numerous ways of saying Yes, and as many ways of saying No. Chinese choose how to say Yes or No depending upon the situation, the context.

My Chinese students disagree, or try. I ask them without talking to their neighbor to write down one word for 'Yes.' We then compare answers. The three most common words for *Yes* are *is* (是), *good* (好) and *right/correct* (對). All <u>can</u> mean Yes, but none necessarily do: the meaning totally depends on context. For example, if I ask, "Is he Chinese? (他是不是中國人?)," the literal question is "He is/not is Chinese person?" If he is Chinese, I answer "is" (是), if he is not I answer "not is" (不是). The audience receives a *Yes* or *No* answer by understanding the context and how Chinese use words, not because of a clear one-word Yes or No answer.

Chinese are often terrible with yes/no questions. Instead of a clear Yes or No the Chinese often tell a story, then from the story you must guess whether they mean Yes or No. I ask my wife if she wants to go see a movie. She answers with something like, 'Well, we haven't seen a movie for a long time and I have heard there are lots of good movies on.' I think that means Yes. Or she answers, 'It is a long drive to town, we don't have a babysitter and movies are so expensive.' That sounds like No. I must guess her meaning.

> **Greg's Tips – No. 2**
> Answers to Yes/No questions come from the story, not as one-word answers.

Always pay attention to the story. Westerners look for a Yes or No answer first and, if they don't hear one or the other, they tend to stop paying attention. Without a Yes or a No, a story is not relevant to the question. As a later section explains, looking to relevance first is bad habit when communicating with Chinese. Instead, learn how to listen the Chinese way: learn how to guess.

High and Low Context Languages

In a high context language you need more than the meaning of words to understand the message. Listen to longtime coworkers talk; you might understand every single word they say but still have no idea about what their actual messages are. We all develop and use high context languages, with old friends and family, longtime coworkers, people we know well.

You can call high context language a type of verbal shorthand, where you can say a lot in a few words. The reason why you need only few words is that you and your audience have experiences in common, and you can use these shared experiences to fill in the gaps. Best friends and longtime married couples don't even need words; they can use a raised eyebrow or a small cough to communicate a message.

Language Systems

High Context Languages

- need to know more than the dictionary definition of words to understand the meaning of what is said/written (the message)
- can be very efficient (much said in few words) but, as the message must be *guessed* it can be ineffective (high risk of misunderstanding)
- *consistently successful guessing* depends on shared experience and using non-verbal clues
- married couples, best friends, long-time coworkers use High Context communication (a verbal shorthand others can't easily understand)
- Confucian-Asian cultures (China, Taiwan, Japan, Korea etc.) use what are considered the most High Context languages in the world
- Confucian-Asians use clues like who says it, when and how it is said, who is present, people's positions, what the situation is and such to add meaning

Low Context Languages

- knowing the meaning of the words and the grammar rules is all that is needed to understand the meaning of what is said or written (understand the message)
- is very effective (misunderstanding is rare) but, as everything must be clearly said, not very efficient (not many shorthand clues)
- communication success depends upon clarity of language used
- examples are engineering, science, computers, legal documents, much of business and most communication between strangers
- European languages (German, Dutch, English for example) are considered very Low Context
- Chinese tend to think Low Context communication rude and unskillful

Table 13: Language Systems

High context is very efficient (when it works!), as much can be said with just few words. The problem is that high context language *always involves guessing*.

Low context language, on the other hand, needs no guessing whatsoever. All you need to understand a low context message are grammar rules and the dictionary definitions of the words.

We all use low context language. A recipe in a cookbook uses low context language; you don't (or shouldn't) have to guess whether "1T" is one teaspoon or tablespoon. Cookbook language is clear, 1Tbl or 1Tsp. The same is true for chemical formulas and engineering drawings; the language used is 100% clear. We don't want bridge builders having to guess what the drawings mean!

Low context is very clear, but at the price of efficiency. As every word and idea must be 100% clear, low context language is slow and cumbersome. Look at a contract. Lawyers add all those little words and strange vocabulary to ensure that the contract has one meaning only! Why? Because a contract with more than one possible meaning is a contract decided in a court by a judge.

Chinese is a very high context language, and regularly involves guessing. Chinese use clues, who said it, when, how, who else was there and such, to add meaning to the few words used. English (Western languages in general) are high context, and normally require little guessing. The premium is on being clear, even if that takes a little longer.

Westerners are lousy guessers. Chinese are expert guessers. If you try to use the Chinese low context way to communicate you will likely fail, or at minimum will create unnecessary problems. Western women are better guessers than men, probably, but even Western women are no match for Chinese men.

Remember, we are barbarians, outside Chinese rules. We can be direct and, as long as we are polite as well, Chinese have no problems with it. The truth is even Chinese can have trouble guessing what other Chinese mean, and understand the benefits of direct talk. Certainty is a good thing, in any culture.

Living With Uncertainty

Westerners think Yen-ping should have offered all the relevant information without being asked, and should have made his disagreement clear. If Chinese did so it would make Western lives in Chinese Asia easier, but being clear and offering information unasked is not how Chinese communicate. Chinese are very careful with information, mindful of the Chinese Rule of Communication, 'if your words might cause problems don't say them.' A common Chinese saying goes:

The more you say the more mistakes you can make (cause more trouble)
The less you say the fewer mistakes you can make (cause less trouble)
If you don't say anything you can't make mistakes (cause no trouble)

Chinese are careful with words and facts. The normal pattern is to say the least amount needed to accomplish a communication goal. Indeed, Chinese see ultimate talent as the ability to communicate without speaking and to understand without hearing. People should just *know*.

Westerners have trouble with high context communication, but there is little you can do about it. I see two broad choices. The first is learn to adapt, learn to infer (guess) Chinese meaning from contextual clues, how it is said, by whom, to whom, when, who else was there, when was it said, etcetera and etcetera. The second is to try to change Chinese you meet, maybe by making their using Western Rules of Communication (going against Chinese Rules) a requirement of communicating with you.

Well, the latter is possible if you are the Biggest Boss or have a monopoly on something Chinese desperately want. Even then it will be an uphill struggle likely to end in pyrrhic victory; you will receive only filtered, sanitized, carefully-considered facts and opinions, whatever the Chinese figure you want to hear.

(There are two other times you can force Chinese to do it your way, but both are bad news. One is when you are leaving so much money on the table that the Chinese will do anything to make you happy, the other when the Chinese are setting you up for a fall, perhaps by having no intention of following through with the deal once they get their benefit first.)

The only realistic choice is to do it their way, for Westerners to adapt to the Chinese. Remember, your goal in China is NOT to change the Chinese, your goal is to achieve the results you want. This leads to another tip:

> **Greg's Tips – No. 3**
> Do it *their* way to get *your* result: accept *how* it is done if you get *what* you want.

This tip is useful in more areas than just communication. Managing, building relationships, finding your way through Chinese bureaucracy, even getting your laundry done, all are easier and go smoother (and usually more successfully) if you do it the Chinese way to get your desired result.[61]

Accepting uncertainty, in communication and other areas, is a price Westerners must pay for success in Chinese Asia. The good news is that the more you wear your Chinese glasses, understand how the Chinese think and why they do things the way they do, the clearer the Chinese picture becomes. The bad news is

Peeling the Chinese Onion
Learning Chinese culture is like peeling an onion. You cry your way through a layer and think, good, I'm done. I get it. I understand. Then something happens and you realize, Wham, I don't get it. There's more to learn. One more layer of Chinese onion to cry your way through. I don't know how many layers there are, I just know to carry tissues.

Table 14: Peeling The Chinese Onion

your that vision never gets 20:20, or at least mine hasn't (yet anyway). I've no idea how many layers the Chinese onion has.

But Their Answer Was Irrelevant

Relevance is crucial to Western communication. We have internal radar that beeps when we spot irrelevant communication, written or spoken. If something is not relevant to the issue at hand it is, well, not important, not now anyway. We stop considering it, at least until we move to a subject or issue where it is relevant.[62] Judging relevance is maybe the most automatic communication response Westerners have. Before we begin to judge true Yes/No, we have already decided relevant Yes/No, and if we judge not relevant well, we don't waste any more time on it. Why would we?

The automatic Western response to irrelevant communication—unimportant so there is no need to consider it—hurts us in

Chinese Asia. The best way to explain is by example, another time I cried through a layer of Chinese onion.

Below is a favorite case study; we spend an hour or more in class discussing it. After reading it, look at the questions at the bottom. In a strict Western sense did Meiling answer my, "Do you like my beard?" question? No. Not once did she say, "No, I don't like it," or "Yes, I do like it." Why did she (at the end) look strangely at me?

What Does She Really Think?

Greg and Meiling are friends. Greg went back home for three months and came back with a large full beard (rare in China). He looked forward to surprising her with his beard. Their first conversation is below.

Greg: Hi Meiling, how are you?

Meiling: Fine, and you?

Greg: Great. Notice anything different about me?

Meiling: Let's see. New Glasses? No. Hmm, you've put on some weight.

Greg: Yeah, mom's cooking. But my beard Meiling? Do you like it?

Meiling: Your beard? Well (she pauses) it'll make it harder to sell your customers.

Greg: Yeah, well, maybe. But do you like it?

Meiling: (looking strangely) Well… are you hungry? What do you want to eat? Did you miss Chinese food?

Did Meiling answer Greg's question?

Why did Meiling look strangely at Greg?

Case Study 3: What Does She Really Think?

She looked strangely at me because in a strict Chinese sense, she had clearly answered my question, numerous times actually, but I kept asking a question she has already answered. No wonder she looked at me strangely. (This exact kind of strange look happens all over Chinese Asia every day, and for exactly the same reason: Chinese puzzled, thinking, 'Huh? But I've already answered that.')

Huh? How did she answer my question if she did not answer my question? Back to uncertainty, guessing, and the Chinese communication rule, communicate negatives in an indirect way. Most Westerners (and all Chinese) can see that she did not like my beard, but explaining just how she communicated that is a little tricky. Meiling used many ways actually, but the technique I want you to learn here involves relevance.

About half way through the example, frustrated with her re-
fusal to tell me anything about my beard, I force the issue, asking
the direct, clear, can't-avoid question, "But my beard Meiling. Do
you like it?" She now has no choice (so I thought); she must tell
me what she thinks.

Her answer? "Well … it will make it harder to sell your customers." I thought, 'Huh? So what? That has nothing to do with
my question!' I try again, this time blunt, clear: "But do you like
it?" I never got a direct answer. I also never get a relevant answer.

In Western argument logic, the two common relevant answers to a 'Do you like my beard?' question are Yes or No, period.[63] You can explain your answer, say for example, 'No, I don't
like it because it will make it harder to sell your customers,' and
that is fine; anything if acceptable as long as Yes or No comes first.
But no Yes or No means the answer is irrelevant to the question.

What happens in Western minds when we get an irrelevant
answer to a question? We dismiss the answer as unimportant: the
answer is, after all, irrelevant. We consider the question not answered, so, a bit frustrated perhaps, we likely ask the question
again. And again. The more times we don't hear Yes or No the
more our frustration increases; we are not satisfied until we get a
damn answer, a Yes or a No.

After Two Objections Means Disagreement, this is probably
the most common way the Chinese say No without saying No.
What is 'this?' The rule is:

Greg's Tips – No. 4
Irrelevant answers are relevant if they are negative; an irrelevant negative answer usually means No.

I call the technique **Irrelevant Negative Answer**. You must
learn to look for negative/positive, not relevant/irrelevant. Why?
Take another look at Chinese Rules of Communication. There is
absolutely nothing about relevance. In my experience, Chinese
don't understand the concept of relevance as Westerners do; it
does not occur in Chinese schooling or their communication
method.[64] (If you will allow me a short advertisement, I spend
roughly one third of my three-day *Logical Thinking and Communication* workshop for Chinese teaching the concept of relevance;

that relevance describes the relationship between information and the key point.) The Chinese lack of a concept of relevance also has huge affects on other areas, some described below. For now though, let's stick to communication.

Look at the Irrelevant Negative Answer technique from a Chinese point of view. It is a win-win strategy: it won't risk hurting a relationship because the words, even though negative, are irrelevant thus have nothing to do with the subject, and the audience will still receive a negative, 'No' message. Win-Win.

Are there still other ways Chinese say No without saying No? Yes. How many are there? I have no idea. Lots though, and I seem to learn a new one or variation on an old one from every client/student/official I meet. Even now I don't know how layers there are in the Chinese onion, but armed with my Chinese glasses I don't cry through the layers any more. Why? Because each time I put a Chinese in a yes/no position I pay close attention to what they say, don't say and how it is said/not said. I don't miss many messages ... any more.

> **Greg's Tips – No. 5**
> If a Chinese says anything other than Yes, he or she likely means No

Earlier I said that I live by the rule, Two Objections Means Disagreement. Well I do, but I also live by a much-stricter version, that **Anything Other Than Yes Means No.**

Some Westerners tell me this Tip is cynical, unfairly critical of Chinese communication even. I don't agree, and no Chinese has ever complained to me about it either. Those who criticize base their critique (I think) on the Western assumption that 'being clear is most important,' and as the 'Anything ...' Tip is the opposite of being clear, it must be bad. Yet viewed through Chinese eyes, where 'being polite is most important,' the ability to communicate negatives simply by adding any words or qualifiers to Yes is good, in fact very skillful! Start with a different assumption and you get a different result.

When Your Taxi Doesn't Come

Another time Chinese desire for harmony over clarity bothers Westerners is requests, when Chinese don't say No to a request ...

but don't do what you request either. Westerners don't know how to deal with this. I didn't either, until … time for another story.

After five years in Taipei I moved to Taiwan's version of Silicon Valley, Hsin Chu (literally 'new bamboo'), about 90km south of the big city. No traffic, pollution or crowds, my new home was very small, about 100 people (mostly one extended family) huddled beside a lake framed by the same craggy, mist-shrouded mountains so loved by Chinese landscape artists. It was beautiful, literally Treasure Mountain (寶山). For a year I worked in the nearby Science Park, traveling to Taipei only when necessary.[65]

Traveling anywhere was a pain. There was only one bus each day, at 4pm. I could either walk 4km to the main road to catch a bus, or call a taxi service. Not a liveried or metered taxi company, just a dispatcher and drivers using their private cars. It was a good service, not cheap but reliable, with nice cars and friendly drivers. I was a frequent customer and over time got to know most of the drivers. We would talk on my way to the Science Park or the bus station where I'd catch a freeway bus up to Taipei.

One time I had a 9am start in Taipei so called dispatch the evening before and requested a taxi for 5:45am the next morning. "Should be no problem." I was ready to go at 5:45. No taxi. 6:00. No taxi. 6:15. No taxi. I called the dispatch number. No answer. Oh no. I started walking, hoping to see the driver pass by. No driver. I reached the main road around 7:10, caught a bus and arrived at the main bus station at 7:25. With no time for the freeway bus, I flagged down a normal taxi and, making the driver's day, took him to Taipei, a 90 minute, US$75 ride. I made the class on time, but what to do about the missed taxi?

Once back home I had a choice of four actions. I could:

1) phone and complain
2) phone, complain and ask for compensation[66]
3) phone and ask what the problem was
4) act like nothing happened

Before answering, keep in mind two things: I depended on the taxi service and I was 100% positive the dispatcher received and clearly understood my 5:45 pickup request. What would you do if this happened in your country? What should you do in Chinese Asia? If there is a difference, why? Take a minute to think about it, then compare your answers to mine below.

Let's start by eliminating some choices. I can see a Chinese maybe inviting me to lunch or dinner because of this—food, the fix-anything Chinese apology—but handing over money? Not a hope. Asking for cash compensation works only in Chinese Asian dreams, not in the real world. That choice is out.

Next, what about phoning and complaining? Besides making you feel better, what else would complaining likely accomplish? Westerners might think that complaining would improve future service, the logic being the Chinese would not want to hear complaints again so would improve their service. This might work, but I doubt it. Why? Put your Chinese glasses on and imagine the scene in the dispatch office. The Chinese answering the phone would likely think he had done nothing wrong, and would think, 'It's not my fault. I'm not the driver. Why get angry at me?' How will that help improve future service?

For the sake of argument let's say the person you complain to knows the driver made a mistake. Do you think that the Chinese will therefore apologize, offer you a free ride or something? Not likely. In cases like this Chinese will almost-always defend each other, group solidarity let's call it. Besides, all they did was forget to pick you up, a result error; it is not as if they were impolite or anything! Your complaints would be impolite though, breaking any number of Chinese Rules of Communication: communicating negatives in a direct way, disturbing harmony, not keeping the conversation smooth and quite likely embarrassing someone in front of another. Phoning and complaining is a bad idea.

(Another reason why 'complain now to improve future' will likely not work is Chinese don't think into the future very well, thus any logic that goes 'doing X now will have an Y effect in the future' is, well, faulty. This point is discussed in greater detail in a later chapter.)

Phoning and asking what happened is an acceptable choice, but still has problems. Asking what happened—why did you make a mistake?—is just a polite way of complaining! Still, by complaining by not actually complaining you would be communicating negatives in an indirect way and preserving harmony, all good things. Chinese would appreciate your sensitivity, tact and manners: you did the *how* in the right way.

The best choice though? Do nothing. Act like nothing happened, which is what I did. The Chinese knew they had made a mistake, and expected me to phone and complain, to get angry, use a loud voice, to be an insensitive Westerner (what the drivers thought about most Westerners). My non-reaction surprised them. I think it even pleased them. All I really know for sure is that their service improved.

Acting-by-not-acting only works when you have some type of existing and ongoing relationship with the Chinese, one they want to continue. Like in all the types of relationships and communication scenarios I describe, Chinese will look at your actions and words through Chinese eyes. By not acting in an emotional way I preserved harmony, showed a willingness to do things in a Chinese way. While I was still a barbarian, I was a polite one.

Requests

What does the taxi episode say about Chinese communication? Why shouldn't I be angry at the no-show taxi? To answer we need to look at the situation from a larger perspective, asking and fulfilling requests.

If someone asks me to do something that I don't want to do, I have four choices, four possible courses of action. They are:

Requests You Don't Want To Do
You are asked to do something you do not want to do. Your choices are:
1. don't argue about doing it; you agree to do it, and do it
2. argue about doing it (no time, ability etc.), but agree anyway, and do it
3. argue about doing it, finally saying you will not do it
4. don't argue about doing it; then don't do it

Table 15: Requests You Don't Want To Do

Most Westerners say that Nos. 1, 2 and 3 are acceptable, depending on the situation. But No. 4 is unacceptable. Why? Because to a Westerner No. 4 looks a lot like lying—you had a chance to say 'I won't do it' but didn't speak up, your silence thus meaning (appearing to mean) that you agree to do it. On the surface, No. 4 looks to be the same as No. 1.

What is a frequent (I hesitate to say typical, but ...) Chinese way? No. 4, though I am not sure it should be called a lie. Let's look at it closer through Chinese glasses.

You ask me to do something I don't want or can not do. If I use either Nos. 2 or 3, argue about it openly, I risk hurting our relationship. Even if I end up agreeing to do it, I have already disagreed openly, communicated negatives in a direct way and disturbed the harmony of the situation. I may have even embarrassed you in front of a group. Nothing about arguing openly is *smooth*. If I can't openly argue about it I have only two other choices, either I do it without arguing about it (No. 1), or say nothing one way or another and don't do it (No. 4). It seems that No. 4 is best for all concerned. I don't have to do it and I don't hurt our relationship. No one gets hurt.

No one gets hurt? Huh? Wearing Western glasses it is obvious someone got hurt: the person asking me the request. Our relationship also is hurt as she now can't trust me. Silence means agreement; my silence in No. 4 meant I agreed to do it, but then I didn't do it. Case closed ... for Westerners. Looking through Chinese glasses makes it not so clear.

(Before going further, of course Chinese do use Nos. 1, 2 and 3, and the more you know them, the deeper your relationship, the clearer they will be about their intentions. Chinese do use No. 4 however, often in the start of a relationship or when a junior asks a senior for something. Or when a Westerner makes a request.)

The issue has two parts, the process (communicating 'I won't do it' without hurting the relationship) and the result (fulfilling the request). Forced to choose between process (how) and result (what), most Chinese will choose process. No matter what else happens, the relationship must endure. Chinese relationship Rules must be followed.

Besides, I never actually agreed to the request. I was silent, and as anything other than Yes means No, and I did not say Yes, then I could have meant No. Remember, silence does not mean agreement in Chinese Asia.

One more example. Say I ask you to help me, and you answer, 'Greg, I will do everything I can to help you.' If your name was Smith or Schmidt, I would think I have found someone to help me. If your name was Chang or Chen however, I would thank you and immediately start looking for someone else to help me. Why? Couldn't the words mean, 'I'll do what I can but as I can't do much I won't do anything.' If Chen or Chang say 'yes' I'd take it to the bank, but if not ... anything other than Yes means No.

Three Invitations For Dinner

At last, the details of my very first example, Three Invitations For Dinner (see pg. 4). To recap briefly, soon after I arrived in Chinese Asia three different Chinese groups invited me to dinner on the most important night of the year, Chinese New Year's Eve (CNY). Each group thought I said yes. I was unaware I had been invited at all, and had no idea I had said yes to all three groups.

My conversations were similar with all three groups. Using English, they told me of Chinese New Years traditions, which I compared to our Christmas. Each group asked if I was doing anything for dinner on CNY Eve; I answered No. Each group told me restaurants closed on CNY Eve. With all three groups there came a time where I was **sure** they were about to invite me to dinner, but they never did. Yet according to each group (and every Chinese I ask) they did invite me, clearly too. Let's look at how. After they told me about CNY traditions, each conversation went like this:

Greg: *Christmas traditions, etc., my family Christmas Dinner, etc.*

Group: *Are you doing anything for dinner on CNY Eve?*

Greg: *No, I'm not.*

Group: *There are no stores open, no restaurants open, nowhere to eat dinner that night.*

Greg: *Oh.*

Group: *(after describing CNY Eve dinner at their house) You would probably enjoy coming to our house for dinner, and I know my parents would enjoy having you.*

Greg: *Yeah, sounds wonderful.*

Have the Chinese invited me yet? I say no, not a Western invitation anyway. Western invitations all use clear a yes/no question. I thought the invitation would be the next sentence, something like, "Well, would you like to come?" That is a clear yes/no question, so it would be the invitation.

In Western communication, the conversation described above would be *preparing to invite*, not *actually inviting*. Westerners would still be looking for the yes/no question. Not so in Chinese Asia. Every Chinese gives the same answer about this example, that the Chinese clearly did invite me and I clearly did say yes. Chinese see no need to add a yes/no question.

Oh? Just how did the Chinese actually invite me? Even better, just how did I say Yes? As I related earlier, it took me two years to understand what happened. Let's put on Chinese glasses and see how it works.

I had just met each of the groups, therefore our relationships were in beginning stages, the riskiest time for a relationship. Chinese are always most polite at the start of a relationship, careful not to do anything that might give offense and hurt the relationship before it even begins. New feelings are fragile.

Inviting someone with a direct yes/no question is risky. What happens if they want to decline? If an invitation is clearly offered, a clear 'no' reply is needed. Yet as a negative response could be embarrassing for one or both sides—dangerous in a new relationship—the Chinese frequently use a no-invite invitation, a way to invite without actually inviting. Then, if the person wants to decline they can decline without actually declining, this because the invitation was never actually offered.

Confused? I was too. Let's go back to actual conversation. The invitation is in the last Chinese sentence, not, as many assume, in the "are you doing anything?" sentence. The last sentence is really a proposition about something positive in the future that I would likely enjoy … and their parents would enjoy … my coming to dinner. I answered this proposition in a positive manner, "sounds wonderful." There you have it, invitation and acceptance.

The rule is that Chinese don't need a clear yes/no question to offer an invitation. Instead of a clear, yes/no question Chinese can use an optimistic, positive statement set in the future to offer an invitation. In such cases, Chinese use a positive, optimistic answer to accept the invitation.

Another Chinese win-win situation: saying No doesn't hurt the relationship because the invitation was never actually raised (so both sides can act like it never happened); saying Yes without saying Yes causes no problems as both parties know the invitation was offered and accepted. No muss, no fuss.

Greg's Tips – No. 6

An invitation can (not will) be offered as an optimistic, positive statement set in the future. Look for this in new relationships.

How do you decline such an invitation? The first step has to be to pay attention! Every time I hear Chinese make a positive, optimistic proposition about the future that includes me, my internal radar starts making noise. You must develop similar radar. If you don't pay attention you will discover too late that you are expected at three dinners in one evening. Once you think you hear an invitation you can turn it down many ways, anything other than a positive, optimistic reply works. Another possibility is to change the subject. In the above situation, I might have told the second and third groups something like, "Yes, it sounds wonderful. Too bad I am busy that night."

Every Word Has Meaning

Are Chinese ever direct with you, will they ever clearly say *No* or *I disagree* to you? Of course they will (and not just after marriage either). But, Chinese will usually only be direct or clear in extreme relationships. One extreme is stranger-stranger interaction. Get into an accident on the street and you will hear the taxi driver being quite clear and direct with his, "You were wrong; I am ruined" loud lament. Enemies also have no trouble being direct with each other; why be polite in a zero sum game?

The other extreme is close relationships, like good friends or family. Brothers and sisters can be direct with each other, at least when parents can't hear. Best friends in China enjoy much the same comfortable directness as best friends do in the West, innocent joking, friendly insults and such. Note that these are almost-equal relationships, with the Rules of Confucian hierarchy just a small shadow in the background.

Which relationships are important to you in Chinese Asia, the ones on the extreme or the ones from the vast middle? The middle ones: time spent with strangers is limited and non-repeating, and most Westerners are not in Chinese Asia long enough to get married, to make enemies or best friends. Nonetheless, your goal is to achieve 'old friend' (*lao pengyou* 老朋友) status.

How do relationships start and grow, how is 'old friend' status achieved with Chinese (Westerners follow a similar but not identical path.) First meeting: neither side knows the other so the sensitivity level is high, each being careful not to hurt the 'feelings' of the other. Both sides will be polite, at their indirect best.

Once past the awkward first-meetings the relationship moves on to a long, slow period of getting to know each other, of getting closer. Even here the emphasis will be on politeness over clarity, especially when anything negative is communicated. Why be direct and possibly hurt a new-acquaintance's/co-worker's/partner's/supplier's/vendor's feelings when it is easy to be indirect and still communicate the negative message? After a foundation of trust and respect grows—in part from showing you can be polite and sensitive to the other person's feelings, that you know how to build a relationship—language can become more direct, more focused on result rather than process.

Most Big Noses[67] never reach 'old friend' status, and remain somewhere in the vast middle. Certainly there are exceptions, and strong, close bonds can form between, say, a longtime vendor and supplier, yet even here I'd pay attention to the rule, every Chinese word has meaning.

Greg's Tips – No. 7
Listen to everything as if every word has meaning.

Chinese genuinely want to make Western friends and to develop long-term ties with business partners. But, they want to develop these relationships on Chinese terms, which means how you do things is as (if not more) important than what you do. Do you pay attention to feelings, take care not to embarrass them in front of a group, communicate negatives in an indirect, non-threatening way? Do you keep your ears open and catch their meanings the first (or second) time, or do you force them to be direct and/or to act dumb? Neither are good for achieving 'old friend' status.

Some Westerners argue this point to me, telling me I overdo it about the importance of relationships to the Chinese. 'Business is business Greg, and all the Chinese really care about are chances to make money.' I strongly disagree (not about Chinese wanting to make money though!) but no longer argue back. There is no point. For more on *Good, Bad and Ugly Westerners* see Chapter Ten.

Make One Point At A Time

Looking inside Chinese minds is hard; knowing how much of the message your Chinese audience understands is neither science nor art, just damn difficult. Westerners frequently make the mistake of thinking Chinese audiences understand everything they say. Why? One reason is the Chinese don't ask any questions, and look (and act) like they understand everything. Another reason is that Westerners hear near-fluent (or at least passable) English so it is natural to assume Chinese can understand near-fluent English as well. Many Chinese have excellent English speaking/listening skills, but remember, understanding a message involves more than understanding the meaning of words.

For reasons of efficiency or just out of habit, Westerners often combine two or more logically related points into one sentence or short presentation; more points in less words means less time used. A partial list of when this happens might include combining steps in a sequence, a cause and effect relationship, reasons for a conclusion or issues that need discussing. If possible, Westerners should resist the impulse to combine.

Why? What often happens is Chinese hear the first point but stop listening to what follows, their mind working to process the first point rather than mentally moving to the next point. This tendency is very common if the first point made is at all surprising, complicated or controversial. Trained in the 'don't let people know you don't understand' Rule of Communication, Chinese are highly skilled at not showing confusion or non-comprehension— they appear to be following along but actually will be stuck sorting out the first point you made. It is frustrating.

Greg's Tips – No. 8

In spoken communication, make your points one at a time.

The best way to overcome this problem is making your points one at a time. Make a point, give the audience a chance to comprehend it fully, then make your next point. While this looks like you waste time, the opposite is true. More time is lost dealing with misunderstandings or unheard points than by taking the time up front to ensure Chinese understand a point before moving to the next. Much less frustrating too … once you are used to doing it.

Themes and Lessons

Nothing hurts in Chinese Asia as much as communication problems. If Chinese often misunderstand you or you often misunderstand Chinese you will be in 'going broke' relationships. Preventing misunderstandings is your first communication goal.

1. Western 'polite' is different from Chinese 'polite' in language as well as in actions.
2. It is fine to be direct as long as you do it in a sensitive, polite way. Being direct can prevent many misunderstandings.
3. Chinese use language differently than Westerners. A common example is how Chinese disagree: instead of disagreeing clearly (as Westerners expect), Chinese often use two objections to show disagreement. You must pay attention to this!
4. There is no (or very little) sarcasm in Chinese Asia. Don't use any type of sarcasm.
5. Irrelevant answers are relevant if they are negative.
6. There is no word for 'yes' or 'no' in Chinese: their answer will be in a story instead.
7. Chinese is a High Context language: you need to pay attention to more than the words to understand the message.
8. Don't ask the Chinese to adapt to you; do it their way to get your desired result.
9. Saying nothing can often be the best way to communication a message.
10. Chinese can extend invitations with an optimistic, positive statement set in the future. Look for this in new relationships.
11. Listen to what is said as if every word had meaning.
12. Anything other than yes means No.
13. Make your points one a time.

Communication success depends far more on paying attention to how Chinese use language (their Rules of Communication) than it does trying to be fluent in Chinese.

Listen With More Than Your Ears

Complex Chinese characters are often formed by combining other characters; looking at the combination can give a large insight into both the meaning of the character and Chinese thinking.

The Chinese character for 'listen,' *ting*, (聽) includes three characters, an ear, a pair of eyes and a heart. This shows that to understand Chinese messages you must do more than hear the words with your ears; you must also listen with your eyes (who said it, to whom, when, where, body language) and with your heart (how did it make you feel, what were the emotions). Only through such a holistic, whole-body approach will you have success communicating with the Chinese.

Table 16: Listen With More Than Your Ears

The more you do the more mistakes you can make.

The less you do the less mistakes you can make.

If you don't do anything you can't make mistakes.

common Chinese saying

CHAPTER EIGHT

Managing and Motivating

Chinese who work with Western managers share a common defense mechanism, the idea that *Westerners come, Westerners go: if I don't like this one I'll just keep quiet and hope the next one is better.* Some Chinese spend most of their careers repeating this under their breath. It does not have to be like that. Western managers can be effective in Chinese Asia, respected and liked.

The most common reason why Chinese don't like a Western manager is because of *how* things are done, not because of *what* the manager wants staff to do. If Western managers adjust how they do the typical manager 'people' tasks—communicate, motivate, reward, punish, delegate, enquire—their actions will become more comfortable for Chinese to receive, thus accept. *How* always comes before *what* or *why!*

In this chapter I offer some insights on Chinese-friendly management practices, why some things work and others don't, followed by some tips on management and motivation. To understand the tips you must wear Chinese glasses; if you wear Western glasses, they will not make sense.

Three Times To A Meeting

Western business lives by meetings. If you define an organization as people working together in a common way for a common goal, the key role of meetings is clear: to create the common ways and to communicate the common goals. Yet valuable as meetings are, one common thread among employees from different types of organizations is most people dislike meetings. A quick Google™ web search for the phrase 'meetings are bad' gets 50,300,000 hits[68]. Nevertheless, Westerners come to Chinese Asia convinced of the crucial importance of meetings. How else can we do business? How else can we find out things?

The Western meeting model is to get all the relevant people together, explain the issue, have a free and open discussion of all aspects and points of view, reach a consensus/make a decision, then end the meeting. (Doughnuts are nice but not necessary.) While this ideal is perhaps more often missed than met, it nonetheless is how we measure meetings, by process (were all points of view considered?) as well as by result (was a decision or consensus reached?).

Western managers quickly discover something is wrong with Chinese meetings. There seem to be no differences of opinion, and meetings often end without any decision or consensus reached. Meetings instead are filled with meaningless words and pointless (or off-the-point) discussions, with rarely any rational disagreements, arguments or hard questions, just ... a lot of nothing. All bread, no meat. Yet things still get done. How?

Have Chinese learned how to do business without spending time in meetings? No. Far from it. Rather than doing away with meetings, Chinese add two more stages or times to meetings. In addition to the 'meeting' as Westerners understand it, Chinese offices have 'before the meeting' and 'after the meeting' meetings as well as the normal 'meeting' meetings. Adding to the confusion, the one time Chinese don't openly discuss options and make clear decisions is during the meeting; everything important is done either before or after it. Meetings are mostly *pro forma*, an elaborate play where little of substance is asked, answered or mentioned.

Consistently confusing and frequently frustrating to Westerners, if you wear your Chinese glasses you can see the logic behind the 'three times to a meeting' system. While Chinese want to do the right thing, want to make the right decision and to achieve the right result, they want it done in the right way, in a harmonious way where no one's feelings get hurt.

Remember, the overarching Chinese goal is to maintain harmonious relationships with coworkers, and harmony is hurt by (for example) open disagreement in a meeting. Chinese instead may meet informally before the meeting to discuss options and disagreements in a quiet, safe way. By the time the actual meeting starts, the key decisions may have already been made, leaving the meeting time for general discussion and to make a formal decision on the already-decided decision. Mission accomplished—a decision made after considering different viewpoints—and no one's feelings got hurt. Just takes time, and that is okay.

After-meeting meetings have the same goal—to preserve harmony—but work somewhat differently. I have sat in meetings listening to the boss tell the staff what to do. When finished the boss rarely asks if everyone agrees or understands; if he does ask, staff keep silent and smile. Once the meeting is over and the boss leaves, the fun begins. "What do you think he meant?" one person asks; another says, "I think he wants us to do X;" another recalls a similar situation and wonders if that is not what the boss wants: they talk and eventually make a consensus guess, and the after-meeting meeting is over.

When I ask why they don't ask the boss a question or ask him to be clear about what he wants, they answer me with blank stares or dismissive, you-are-wasting-our-time looks. To Western eyes this seems a poor system, inefficient (wasted time) and often ineffective (considering the high chance of not doing what the boss really wants). It used to bother me a lot, especially as I was often the consultant hired to achieve whatever it was the boss wanted. One day a good Chinese friend explained it to me.

"Bosses do it on purpose: it is win-win for them. If the staff achieve good results then the boss says, 'Great work; exactly what I wanted.' However, if the results are poor the boss can complain, 'Why did you do X? That is not what I asked you to do!' Win-win for the boss." Oh.

Good And Bad Meetings

Western managers should not try to change the three-times-for-a-meeting habit. First off, I don't think you can, at least not without a LOT of patient and consistent effort. Second, you can still get the results you seek—achieving the overall objectives set by your boss—using the Chinese 'three times' method. You just have to change how you think of and use meetings. You just need a willingness to make adjustments. And patience. Lots of patience.

The best way to use meetings is for top-down information distribution. Examples could be explaining a new policy, describing a new product or service, or outlining some new system or procedure sent down from HQ. When finished speaking of course you should ask, 'Are there any questions?' but don't expect them, or worry if none are asked. Ensuring staff understanding is for the 'after-meeting' meetings, not the 'meeting' meeting. Tell staff you would like them to think about it, and that you look forward to hearing their ideas. That prepares them for the individual meetings to come.

The worst use of meetings is for discovery, debate, discussion or anything bottom-up. The Western ideal of getting everyone together to find out what is going on, or to take a critical look at options, two common bottom-up exercises, does not work very well in Chinese offices. Bottom-up success depends on the participants having both ability and willingness to speak out, to offer candid opinions and to focus on meeting result (finding the best answer) instead of individual result (winning the discussion, not admitting ignorance, evading blame,[69] etc.). Neither Chinese education nor Rules of Communication prepare Chinese for the rough-and-tumble, think-on-your-feet, best-idea-wins style necessary for a proper bottom-up meeting environment.

There is a solution. You can get bottom-up input, just not in a group. Instead of thinking group you must create one-on-one situations, times when Chinese can say what they honestly feel or know without risk of hurting a coworker relationship. Keeping your office door open is a great way to start. You need to create both safe physical situations—open office door, taking a person to lunch, going to their office and such—and correct psychological mindsets—you don't embarrass staff say, and are considered fair and open minded— if you really want to find out what is going on. You can't force truth.

Getting Honest Opinions

Following this section are two strategies useful for getting Chinese to speak up and to let you know what they really think about an issue. Before that though, we need to look at a common Western communication technique that hurts Chinese openness. Here is a short case study.

Why Do They Always Agree?

Known as an energetic, effective manager (good at getting things done *now*), George was on a fast track to a high position. Needing some "international" experience, the company sent him to Shanghai "for one, maybe two years." George tackled the job with his normal high energy, and planned using the same management techniques that had worked for him so far.

A favorite technique was starting a meeting by saying his opinion, then asking for comments. Focusing everyone exactly on the point saved his time (what he cared about most). He soon had a chance to use the technique: he called a quick meeting with his new staff to discuss a situation. Here is what happened:

George: *Situation "A" has come up. For these reasons I think it is a wonderful opportunity, something I think we should do. I've called this meeting to hear your opinions. You know China more than me. What do you think?*

No one spoke. A little bit puzzled, George pointed to a manager and said:

George: *Well Hsu-Wen, what do you think? Is my idea good or not?*
Hsu-Wen: *Good.*
George: *How about you Ming-Tao? Good or not?*
Ming-Tao: *Good.*
George: *And you (pointing to a man who's name he had forgotten)?*
Man: *Good.*

No one disagreed: the meeting lasted 8 minutes. George left thinking, "Another good idea, and my technique works just like at home. China is not going to be hard; just a little language problem is all."

- was anything decided at the meeting? If so, what?
- do you think the Chinese staff really agreed with George?
- what type of cooperation can George probably expect from his staff now?
- can Western managers in Asia use the same techniques they use at home?
- how many Western mistakes can you see in this example?

Case Study No. 4: Why Do They Always Agree?

So many problems: let us concentrate on pure communication issues now, and leave other issues until later. First, George uses a common Western technique, beginning a meeting by expressing an opinion as a way to focus discussion on a specific point, issue or course of action. Yet another example of how Western communication emphasizes time efficiency. Comfortable with disagreement and used to a best-idea-wins discussion method, starting with your opinion does make meetings more efficient.

More efficient in the West where people are unafraid to speak up that is, not in Chinese Asia. Notice how his Chinese direct reports answer George's, "Is my idea good or not?" question. All agree with it, all say it is good. Do you think they all truly believe George's idea is good? Maybe, but maybe not, and we have no way of knowing which; neither does George. Once again, Chinese Rules of Communication, especially (but not only) *don't disagree openly*, takes precedence over honest (or candid) answers.

Greg's Tip – No. 9

If you want to know what a Chinese thinks, you can't say what you think first.

No one wants to get in trouble, true for people of all cultures. Trained to think they will get in trouble for disagreeing openly, embarrassing the boss in public and for not making conversation smooth, Chinese will always look for clues from their superiors, signals as to what the boss already thinks. Once they know what the boss thinks the rest is easy; just agree with the boss. While this might not be the best way to find the best answer, it is the best way to maintain a Chinese relationship.

Westerners have to learn to keep their opinions and ideas to themselves, at least in the beginnings of discussions. It is hard, as the typical conversation goes like this:

>Westerner: *What do you think we should do?*
>Chinese: *I don't know. What do you think we should do?*

Around and around the dance goes, Westerners trying to get Chinese to say what they think and Chinese trying to get Westerners to say what they think first, all so they (the Chinese) know the best thing to say. The Rule is, **if you want to know what a Chinese honestly thinks don't tell them what you think first**. Discipline is the key: you must keep silent about your ideas and thoughts, which includes having neutral body language. Force the Chinese to speak up—you are the boss after all, and a barbarian to boot. Just make sure you show respect for the Chinese answer when it finally comes, no matter what it is. If you don't respect their first suggestion, it will become their last suggestion. Finally, this all works best in a one-on-one setting.

Alternative Ways To Get Input

Being patient is well and good, but there are times when you want to know *now*, when you don't want to wait until the conditions are comfortable for the Chinese. I know of two ways to get bottom-up input from Chinese participants without spending time on numerous one-on-one meetings. A warning though: neither way is time efficient. Both involve secrecy, creating an environment where Chinese can speak up without personal risk.

One way is to use democracy, or at least secret ballot. For example, use group discussion to describe alternatives (think mini-brainstorming). Once you have a list of alternatives ask everyone to vote; using some type of weighted voting works best (ranking choices top to bottom say, or giving each person more than one vote). Voting must be in secret; if not, people will likely color their responses to what they think the boss is thinking. Counting the votes gives you a winner, or at least an idea of group consensus, always a good place to start.

Is the voting method time consuming? You bet! But it seems to work. The China GM of an American beauty product multinational ran senior strategy meetings like this. Maybe just coincidence, but during her time senior management made numerous excellent strategic decisions, perhaps the result of truthful bottom-up input. It certainly didn't hurt.

The second method of getting bottom-up input is more high tech than paper ballots, but almost as time consuming. This method involves using collaboration software like Lotus Notes™ to let meeting participants post real-time comments in secret on the issue of the moment. Used properly, software such as Notes can revolutionize meetings in Chinese Asia. One hurdle to effective use of this method is language proficiency though, the difficulty Chinese might have composing comments on the run.

(Western managers must be sensitive to outcomes decided based purely on which person has the best English skills. Good English does not necessarily mean good managerial talent. Also, beware of basing judgments and promotions on who has the best table manners, personal hygiene or fashion sense: all these can be taught, good common sense can't.)

Whichever method you use, ensuring secrecy is the critical success factor. Chinese truly want to participate and have a chance to offer their ideas, just not at the expense of hurting relationships. Find a way to let people speak out while preserving harmony (as Chinese see it) and you will get the ideas you need to make the right decisions in Chinese Asia. Force Chinese to respond in public and all you will get is what Chinese think you want to hear.

Separate The Person From The Problem

Whether one-on-one or in a group, you have to find a way to tell Chinese they are *doing it wrong, making a mistake*, and *this is the right way to do it*. A big part of a Western manager's job in Chinese offices is knowledge transfer, teaching or training Chinese. (If the Chinese knew and did everything like you and other Western global staff did, why would you be managing in China?) Whether for planned knowledge transfer or just correcting a mistake, Western managers frequently must try to get Chinese to change. The problem is how to do this without hurting your relationship with the Chinese. A useful technique is to separate the person from the problem, i.e., to shift the blame from a person to something about the task. Here is an example.

A European company sold a large, complicated printing press to a Chinese firm. Installation was finished, the press commissioned and all was fine, or should have been. The Chinese complained that the output was of poor quality. The Europeans tried to find and fix it by fax, email and phone. Nothing worked. The company sent a senior engineer to fix the problem.

It turned out to be a simple problem: the Chinese operator was not following the instructions (which by chance the senior Western engineer had written). Happy it was such an easy problem to fix, the Western engineer clearly told the operator that he was making a mistake, and that in the future he should follow the instructions. Even better (thought the engineer) was that many people were listening; it was much more efficient to teach all the Chinese at once. The engineer said something like:

> *You are doing it wrong. The instructions are clear and easy; the problem is you are not following them. All you have to do is read them and then follow them.*

The engineer's words echoed in an awkward silence. The Chinese, operator and audience, were unhappy. The Chinese *did* want to know how to do the job right, but they wanted the lesson given in a polite, not-hurt-feelings way. When the Western engineer broke Chinese Rules of Communication—embarrassed someone in front of a group, communicated negatives in a direct way, disturbed harmony etc.—the Chinese stopped paying attention, stopped giving weight or respect to the engineer or his advice. The rule you **must** learn is, if things are not said in the right way Chinese will stop listening to what you say. As was the case here: soon after the engineer left for home, the quality problems started again. Pride is more important to the Chinese than profit.

Greg's Tip – No. 10

If things are not said in the right way, Chinese will stop listening to what you say.

You must keep your eyes on the real goal! Was the engineer's goal to communicate efficiently (method used) or to help the Chinese run the machine properly (result achieved)? I believe it was to achieve result: Westerners care (should care) about results more than method. The engineer could have achieved the intended result if he had separated the person from the problem and, in a one-on-one conversation, had said something like this:

> *Oh, I see the problem. That is a difficult job, and the instructions are confusing. We should change them, but … I think if we work together, we can figure out how to do it. Here, let me show you how I was able to make it work. Maybe you will have a better idea once you try.*

This is not easy for Westerners to do, especially for engineers used to direct talk. It would be especially difficult if you had written the instructions you now had to appear to criticize! Yet even if you thought the instructions were extremely simple and easy to follow, the goal is get the Chinese to follow the instructions and use the press properly (result), not your ability to explain things in an easy or efficient way (method).

You can separate the person from the problem in many areas. A person does not get the report for you finished on time, but instead of getting angry with him, you blame your poor instructions. An official makes a mistake and does not give you the 'chop' he should, but instead of telling him he is making a mistake you tell him how difficult it must be to deal with confusing foreigners all day, and ask if there is a chance he could take another look at it.

Separate the person from the problem is similar to a commonly used Chinese technique, 'white face black face.' You use the white face black face technique to communicate bad news of some sort; the bad news is someone else's fault (black face), not your fault (white face).[70] You put the blame on someone else.

There are times when clearly exposing a person's mistakes is necessary for training purposes, which is fine. The principal behind the 'separate the person' rule is simply that you should pay attention to a person's feelings whenever you are dealing with personal negative (and positive: see below) news. Focus on your goals: is your job to change the Chinese or is it to achieve business results? If your goal is business results then learn to do things their way to get your way.

A Western manager once complained I wanted him to "hold their hands," or in other words, I wanted him to be too easy on the Chinese. "When they are wrong I want them to know it," he said, followed by some words about how he was boss and the company was a Western multinational, therefore the Chinese should adapt to his way, not the other way around.

Am I suggesting you "hold their hands?" I don't think so. I strongly believe in measuring performance (see Chapter 10) and in rewarding or punishing Chinese staff depending on their performance. I strongly believe in teaching and enforcing corporate culture norms specific to a company. Nevertheless, as I asked the above complaining Westerner, "Are you here to achieve business results or to change the Chinese? What is more important to you, that the Chinese do things your way or that they achieve the business goals you set?"

To end this section all I can say is that if your goal is to get the Chinese to do things your way ... you are reading the wrong book. I believe in business results. If you focus on business results the behavioral changes you seek will happen; if you focus on changing behaviors the business results you seek will likely be elusive.

One more small story. The Chinese boss of a very high-tech business unit of a huge Western multinational hired me to design a way to base year-end profit sharing on staff performance. Before this, profit share depended on seniority and salary, the typical Chinese way. Money-for-performance is a very Western[71] idea, as were many of this Chinese boss' ideas. Addicted to Western management trends and business books, the Chinese boss wanted to remake the unit, to change how everyone worked. I tried to tell him he was going too far too fast—even while I was primary beneficiary of his plans—but he would not listen. Business results went steadily downhill; more and more highly trained key Chinese staff left because of the changes to the system: the Chinese boss lost his job soon after. Chinese also fall trap to the desire to change the Chinese at the cost of achieving business results. Results often lead to change, change does not necessarily lead to results.

Using A Go-Between

Continuing with the 'do it their way' theme, what happens in the West if you are the boss and have something negative to say to a person, say about bad recent performance or inappropriate actions in the office? While you might wait until no one else could hear, you would confront the person directly, to his/her face. Doing anything less would be, well, wrong. Certainly this type of confrontation is often hard (for most of us anyway), yet it is both a necessary thing to do as a boss and is considered the correct moral action as well, almost a test of character.

Such confrontation is often missing in Chinese offices. While of course this type of direct confrontation does happen, much more common is an indirect, *maintain harmony and preserve relationships* method. The method is using a go-between, someone else to communicate negative news for you. Many Western students are surprised, even shocked to hear this, and tend to think it is a bad idea. "You can't dodge your responsibility," said one, "That is a cop out," said another, "You will lose all respect in the office," said one more.

Such attitudes are true in Western offices, but not so true in most Chinese offices. Chinese prize the ability to communicate a negative without having actually to say it, that is, without disturbing harmony or hurting a relationship. The Chinese attitude is, 'Why cause more problems than you have to? Less is best.' This method works for Chinese managers, but they are trained in using Chinese Rules of Communication, of saying something (sending a message) while not actually saying it (saying the actual words). Westerners normally are not very good at this method, but can improve if they try. It again comes down to asking what is important, doing things in the *right way* (in the West) or achieving the *right result*.

I don't mean Western managers should use a go-between to communicate all negative (or possibly) negative messages. If the Marketing Manager has done something wrong, you should not ask your secretary to tell her/him about it, or anything so overt. Using a go-between is subtle. Using the Marketing Manager for example, let's say he has not dealt with a on-going problem, perhaps Marketing not cooperating with Product Design to create new advertisements. You have told him about this many times but nothing seems to happen. Now you can pick someone you know is close to the Marketing Manager (not Marketing staff), and 'just happen' to let slip that you are very frustrated with the situation, and unless something happens you may have to find a new Marketing Manager.

That is all it takes. If you have chosen the correct go-between the Marketing manager will quickly receive the 'shape up or you are out' message. No confrontation needed, no harmony disturbed or relationship hurt. Ironically, the indirect, go-between message will be powerful and believable because of the channel used. This is opposite from the West, where (normally) a rumor has less strength and believability than hearing something 'straight from the horse's mouth.' This principle of indirect communication also applies to positive news.

Make It A Public Secret

Motivating staff is a key managerial function. Can you motivate Chinese staff using the same methods used in the West? Some methods, certainly: everyone, Chinese or Western, likes time off or more money. Some methods used to motivate Westerners, however, just don't work so well in Chinese offices. One of the most common 'don't work' methods is public praise.

Westerners tend to like public praise. From childhood on, the teacher/boss/parent publicly recognizes best performers, sometimes with gifts but always with public praise, compliments followed by a 'let's hear it for John or Mary' request for applause and cheers from the audience. Once the room quiets, the boss makes another request, that the audience can or should learn from the best performer's example. The message is clear: if you want to get the reward, public praise, gift and public recognition, you should work harder, smarter, longer.

A popular way Western business uses 'public praise' motivation is some form of an *employee of month* system. Once a month or quarter an employee is selected as 'best' and receives a public reward, a gathering in the lunchroom perhaps, where she receives public praise and frequently some gift. Another possibility is a photo and write-up in a company newsletter, written public praise for being 'best.'

Trained from childhood to accept and expect public praise—and conditioned by the competitive nature of Western culture: think sports and entertainment[72]—even shy Westerners are happy to get their moment in the sun, their chance to be recognized as 'best.' Westerners don't feel that such a fleeting celebrity separates us from our friends and coworkers, or (beyond petty jealousy) harms our relationships.

The opposite is true in Chinese Asia. Chinese (Japanese and Korean) languages are peppered with sayings about not standing out: some examples are *The tallest nail gets pounded flat, The tree that stands above the others gets blown down*, and a personal favorite, *A flea on top of a bald head*. Only rarely in Chinese education, at school or home, is a person singled out for 'public praise.' Chinese do use models for teaching proper behavior, but usually only after the celebrated hero/model is dead.

The most famous behavior model in the modern era is perhaps the "Learn from Lei Feng" campaign in China. A communist (if he actually lived), Lei's short life is an amalgam of traditional Chinese virtues: modesty, self-sacrifice, self-effacement, obedience. Lei's good deeds did not include anything like standing out, being a leader, bringing attention to himself. Lei was a model/hero because of *how* he did things, selflessly and quietly, not for changes he made or accomplishments he achieved.

This Chinese attitude to public praise, to standing out, has a large effect on managing in a Chinese office. Chinese are human and like rewards, especially but not only money; they like gifts and compliments as well, if appropriate and if given properly. It is possible to motivate Chinese by publicly rewarding good performers, just like in the West. The reward presentation just has to be in a different, Chinese-polite way. One of the best ways to present rewards is to use a public secret.

In a public secret, almost everything is the same as in a Western office: you choose and reward good performers, thus making other staff work 'better' so they can be the good performer next time. The only difference is how the reward is given. Instead of some public display or pronouncement, the reward presentation is secret, done in your office say, or in a restaurant.

But how is a secret *public*? How can a secret ceremony motivate staff? First, you must understand that there are no secrets in a Chinese company! Looking just at practicality, the Western manager did not select and buy the gift, nor put together the cash prize from her wallet: either her secretary or the finance manager (both probably) helped arrange the prize so both know what is going on, thus … all staff know. Count on it.

> **Greg's Tip – No. 11**
> Motivate by using a public secret: public (everyone knows it happens); secret (no one sees it happen).

Staff knows that Mr. or Ms. X is this month's good performer, and know that she received a reward in your office with the door closed. Yet as no one actually saw the reward given, all can act as if it never happened. Recipients are not embarrassed or separated from co-workers (the group): they just get the reward! Co-workers see what to do in order to be invited into your office next month. Successful motivation.

An American high tech company let salespersons who sold over quota put a special mark on their business card, a way to recognize and reward the best performers. Two salesmen in the Taipei office sold over quota year after year, but neither ever asked to have the special mark put on their cards. Why? Because adding the special mark would separate them from the group.

Give One Job At A Time

While earlier I said Chinese was a "rules obeying" culture, Chinese people are not always good at following rules or orders. What kinds of rules or orders do Chinese obey? More important, what kinds do they disobey?

Chinese tend to be very good at following rules of relationships, deference to authority, modesty, politeness. Chinese education teaches people to know their place in the social or organizational hierarchy and to know how to act accordingly—each position has rules about how to treat people in higher, lower and similar positions. These Confucian social rules tend to be consistently followed.

Less important are man- or government-made rules. One obvious example is traffic rules. Go for a drive in a big Chinese city and you quickly realize obeying traffic rules seems to be optional, at least whenever white-gloved, whistle-blowing traffic police are absent. Worse is driving in the countryside, roads clogged with newly-rich farmers trading in tractor for Toyota, then driving the latter like the former. Chinese also have trouble following some types of orders in the office.

Western managers strive for efficiency; time is money after all. One way to help staff be efficient is to give them an overall picture or idea of what will happen and what their jobs will be. In this age of flattened organizations and real-time, 24/7 communication, Western managers think the more information staff have the more work they can achieve.

A common situation is communicating a series of sequential, interconnected tasks, with the later tasks somewhat dependent on the results of the early tasks. Western managers try to help by explaining all the tasks—so staff can plan—then telling their Chinese staff, "When you finish task 1 come and see me before you start tasks 2 and 3." It sounds simple and straightforward. It is not.

What frequently happens is Chinese complete all three tasks before coming back to see the manager. Why? Look at it through

Chinese glasses. Not only have the Chinese reduced the number of times they have to see the boss (always a frightening prospect, especially but not only when the boss is Western), staff can show that they have achieved *more than they were asked for!* How can that not be good? Many Chinese have asked me, "Well, isn't that what 'efficient' means, to do more than asked for?" (More on this below.) I tell them no, it is not, explaining that later tasks might have to be changed (or eliminated even) because of the result from the first task. "How would I know that?" is a common reply.

To be honest I have given up trying to explain the logic of the 'do three jobs but come back and talk after finishing the first one' to Chinese. Perhaps influenced by all my years in Chinese Asia I focus on 'getting around' the problem rather than 'solving' it. How? I only give jobs one at a time, not in sequence. This seems to be more work for me because it takes up (wastes) some of my time, but it actually saves me time in the end.

> **Greg's Tip – No 12**
> Give orders or jobs one a time, not in sequence.

Chinese will usually follow orders perfectly, as long as orders are clear and require no balancing between culture and accomplishment that is. Nonetheless, I don't like to tempt fate or invite problems, and giving orders one at a time is my best advice.

Initiative vs. "More Better"

Another source of Western frustration is the Chinese lack of initiative. As seen earlier, the reasons for the Chinese 'wait-to-be-told' mentality are numerous and powerful. Yet most Western managers are uncomfortable giving orders for every action, and still do what they can to encourage staff to have initiative.

Many Chinese are happy to decide for themselves, pleased to be asked to show initiative. Indeed the empowerment-initiative-freedom environment of most Western multinational offices is one of the biggest reasons Chinese want to work there. Yet just because Chinese are encouraged to have initiative, however, does not mean they suddenly know how to decide for themselves.[73] Indeed the opposite is frequently the case, and instead of showing initiative, Chinese try to make something *more better.* You must try to stop this from happening.

The above lines about Chinese not following instructions—not coming back as asked before starting the second task—are an example of more better. More better happens like this: after the discussion is over a Chinese receives a job, complete with boundaries and milestones. Once on his own the Chinese independently decides to *improve* on the decision, a change that makes for a 'more better' (a poor or unintended) result. This is the difference between more better and initiative.

Initiative is pure independent thought, deciding for yourself what needs to be done then going ahead and doing it without first asking permission. It is hard to think of an act more opposed to Chinese culture and education: Chinese learn to listen and follow, not think and lead. True initiative, deciding what needs to be done and then doing it, is daunting to the Chinese (and admittedly to many Westerners). Doing more better is easier. With the overall decision (what to do) already decided, Chinese just have to make changes to it, to tinker with it. Chinese are very good at tinkering.

How do you guard against more better? One way is to give instructions or orders one at a time (as above), but doing so defeats much of the staff development effort Western companies should be exercising. Training works better, that and patience. The rule I teach Chinese is that you can't change a decision or agreement without discussing the change with the people affected by it.

Never assume 'your' Chinese staff (as opposed to other company's staff) either understand and accept initiative, or know the difference between it and more better. Instead, explain the difference to them, clearly. Use examples of more better and how it led to poor results. Find examples of when you used initiative in your career or life, and show how initiative benefited you. Finally, reward instances of initiative, and punish[74] for more better.

Measuring Performance

Many companies have introduced a Western-style management concept into their Chinese operations: increase productivity by measuring, then rewarding good/punishing bad performance.

Called many things, MBO (management by objective), balanced scorecard or performance management, the idea has two basic parts, setting a performance target then comparing actual performance against the target. While I strongly believe in this approach,[75] it is very easy for Western managers to make mistakes trying to introduce and/or implement such a system.

We can use the sales vs. marketing concept introduced earlier to explain. Many Western companies *sell* instead of *market* the new performance management system. By selling, I mean the Westerners pay insufficient attention to the actual realities of Chinese offices, and base their actions, plans and goals on what *Western* offices look like. The result is a performance management system in name and outward appearance only, and decreased instead of increased productivity.

Let me explain using the story of my last major project.[76] My job was to design and introduce a performance management system for an American Fortune 500 company's entire Chinese Asian operation. After some preliminary investigation, I met with the China Region General Manager. The meeting was not much fun; surprising the boss rarely is.

The actual company situation was that no one knew what the actual job processes looked like, and department objectives existed on paper only, and just for show: no one paid any real attention to them. Numbers were, ah, more invented than actual. This was the good news. Worse was that no one had a job description, no one was clear about who was responsible for what, each department manager and supervisor more-or-less made it up as they went along. Minor issues like salary increases, bonuses and promotions were based on ... no one was sure.[77]

This company had operated in Chinese Asia for well over a decade, had factories in three countries and sales offices in all major cities throughout the region. From the start, Western managers had been in senior positions. More investigation showed, however, that Western manager influence (and knowledge) stopped immediately below the level of their direct reports. To make a long story short my job changed from introducing performance management as it was in the US to preparing the company to be able in the future to introduce it. We had to go back to the beginning. Working together with Chinese managers, I sketched rough business processes and wrote initial job descriptions for over a thousand people (over fifty different positions). This was still too advanced. We needed to go further back.

Only a few senior Chinese managers knew of quality management, or understood basic QM tools and concepts like checklists, control charts, process and cycle time, Pareto, fishbone or block diagrams. I designed train-the-trainer programs to introduce the fundamentals to managers and staff, beginning with why quality and measuring performance was a good thing.

I tell this story not to criticize my client but to help Western managers know how to market performance measurement of all types into Chinese Asia offices. In the West all a GM needs to do is explain that from now on the company will do MBO, balanced scorecard or whatever, and department managers can take it from there. That approach is *selling* in Chinese Asia. Marketing means understanding the actual situation and going back to first principles, to preparing the organization to introduce some PM system.

A Western manager recently asked if Chinese sales and marketing staff would accept targets. I said of course, with a few caveats, the most important being that the targets were fair and accurate. "Fair and accurate," he asked, "what does that mean?" In this case fair means that an individual's targets are totally within his or her control, i.e., that Person A's poor performance can't be blamed on Person B's poor work. Accurate means that targets come from the actual business processes.

"But I don't know all of the actual business processes, no one does." I told him he should therefore start by establishing SOPs and business processes, that doing so would increase productivity far more than setting targets. He said he couldn't: his boss at HQ insisted on setting targets, and his performance, promotions, salary increase and bonus amount, were based (in large part) on setting the targets right away. All I could tell him was Good Luck.

Themes and Lessons

Success managing the Chinese depends much more on *how* things are done than on *what* things are done. Managers must stay focused on the goal of producing business results, and must learn to use how Chinese do things in order to achieve these results.

1. Chinese meetings have three stages: before the meeting, during the meeting and after the meeting. Key decisions, consensus building, information gathering and frank discussions happen before or after the meeting, not during it.

2. The best uses for meetings is distributing information and introducing subjects.

3. Chinese are interested in achieving good business results, but not at the expense of hurting relationships.

4. If you want to get an honest opinion, don't give your opinion first.

5. Find a way to allow Chinese to contribute in secret and they will contribute.

6. Separate the person from the problem; blame something external, not the person.

7. If you don't say things in the right way Chinese will stop listening.

8. Using a go-between to communicate bad messages is good management.

9. Motivate Chinese with good performance rewards, just do it using a public secret.

10. Give jobs one at a time, not in sequence. Taking longer up front saves times.

11. Change Chinese by focusing on business results instead of trying to achieve business results by changing the Chinese.

12. Make sure staff understands the difference between initiative and *more better*.

13. Measuring performance only improves productivity when the measurements used are fair: check to make sure before setting them.

CHAPTER NINE

Contracts and Negotiation

Not every company needs to open an office in Chinese Asia, and can succeed with technology and travel instead of people on the ground. Managing and/or working every day in Chinese Asia is a challenge, but so is building a long-distance relationship. Using email, phone, fax and occasional face-to-face visits to create trust as well as to make money presents special difficulties. In this chapter, we look at issues relevant to such 'contract relationships.'

There are many types of contract relationships, covering a bewildering diversity of business types. The most common is the standard company-company, import/export model, a pure buy from and/or sell to business. Some Western companies work with agents or some type of local representatives, while others enter into partnerships with Chinese entities in some type of Joint Venture (JV). Whatever business type or scope, such relationships present unique problems. Even when both sides speak the same language and have the same business customs, it is hard to build a lasting, long distance relationship: it is an order of magnitude harder when they don't.

Translators And Translations

Chinese Asia uses three languages: official Mandarin Chinese, the local dialect of Chinese, and English. No matter where you go in Chinese Asia, Chinese of all ages study English. In schools and companies, on TV and in taxis, English classes are everywhere. It is a true growth industry. One result is that as more Chinese speak English fewer Westerners need to use a translator. Nevertheless, the need for translators still exists, especially in areas and industries just now opening to business with the West.

Travel to Chinese Asia is expensive and business discussions are frequently complicated. Hiring a professional translator is expensive and, if the subject is complicated or confidential, perhaps problematic. Companies with some type of local office arrangement (agent or distributor say) often try to minimize costs and improve effectiveness by using a Chinese from the local office as the translator. While this looks logical, saving money and the local Chinese knows the business situation, it is often a bad idea. The translator can easily be put into a lose-lose situation: translating your impolite words exactly and risking his relationship with other Chinese, or 'modifying' your words to ensure harmony during the meeting (and after you are gone), but at the expense of clearly communicating your intended message.

I recommend using a professional translator instead, usually available through your hotel or country trade offices. Before the meeting, explain your business and goals to him/her. A professional translator is like a lawyer, bound by confidentially (don't take this comparison too far though.)

You may need a professional translator for important written communication as well. A European client encountered ongoing problems with a Chinese customer; the equipment sold (a large printing press) never worked properly, causing complaints and slow final payment. The Europeans tried to use fax, phone and email to discover the cause of the problem, but no luck: each time the Chinese said that yes, the operators were following the instructions perfectly.

The Europeans finally sent two engineers to fix the problem. The engineers learned nothing in meetings so they moved the meeting to the factory floor. While watching Chinese operators work the press, the engineers saw the operators all made the same small mistake in procedure, a mistake that accounted for the problem. When asked why the operators did the wrong step the Chinese were surprised, saying that the operators were following the instructions exactly. The Europeans said that was not possible, the Chinese said it was, and, as the instructions came from the European company, the Europeans had to be at fault. Feelings ran high, and compensation was mentioned.

The root cause of the problem was a bad translation. The instructions went from German to English to Chinese, i.e., to a second language, then from a second language. The instructions survived the first translation with only some loss in clarity, but did not survive the second. Chinese operators were following the instructions *exactly*, very good ... except that the instructions themselves were wrong! Someone had made a bad translation into Chinese, the result being that following the instructions was causing the problem. Once discovered it was easily fixed.

How could this happen? Perhaps a better question would be why doesn't this happen more often. Companies send instructions, product descriptions, training manuals, a virtual and literal forest of paper to Chinese partners. All of it is important, just like the instructions above. What do you think happens when the Chinese receive written English communication?

To be useful the messages must be in Chinese, yet very few Chinese companies have professional translators on staff. Normally the company farms out the instructions, manuals or descriptions to low-level staff. These employees don't have 'translating' in their job descriptions, thus translating is an add-on to normal work, a low priority task. Think of it as selecting the short straw.

Let's say there are four pages of material to translate. A Chinese manager divides the job between four people, each responsible for translating one page (shared pain). One person has excellent English and does a superb job; one struggles all night with an English-Chinese dictionary and does a so-so job; one gives the page to her high school son to translate, who does his best but is confused by terms and context; and one person does nothing until forced, then does a very quick, very sloppy job. The resulting translation is highly suspect at best, confusing and dangerous at worst. Besides no conformity in accuracy and style, paragraphs that straddled two pages would be translated by different people, never a good thing.

If the accuracy of English (or whatever language) materials you supply to Chinese partners is important, hiring a professional translator is a good idea; hiring two is even better. I frequently use two translators. The first translator translates from English into

Chinese, the next independently translates the Chinese back into English: I then compare the English translation to my original text. While never identical, as long as my key meanings are similar it is a good translation. It is an expensive process, but worth it.

Westerners Are Selfish

If I define translation as finding local equivalents for foreign messages, then actions can and must be translated as well. Indeed, we translate actions all the time in our normal lives. A simple example would be translating silence at the end of a presentation to mean the audience understands everything and has no questions. While this is correct in the West, translating silence as agreement or understanding would probably be incorrect in a Chinese context.

Chinese also must translate Western actions. One common area that Chinese translate poorly is what how often Westerners communicate with them actually means. Chinese look at how often Western partners communicate and think it shows Westerners are selfish. Why? How? Put on your Chinese glasses and think of Western communication through Chinese eyes.

As far as Chinese see it, the only time their Western partner talks to them is when *the Westerner wants something*. If you think about it, it is true: we send email to ask if the shipment has been made, phone to ask if the problem has been fixed, fax to ask for missing product information. Every message is concerned with things the Westerner wants, asks for something that benefits the Westerner. We rarely just call to say hello.

Westerners think communication should be clear and direct, and believe that as business is about efficient completion of task, communicating anything other than what is needed to get the job done is, well, a waste of time and effort. Most Westerners see no trouble with this, and believe that clarity, relevance and brevity are the key communication metrics. "Why would I send anything other than a business message to the Chinese Greg?" is a question I hear often, "I am not making friends; I'm doing business."

My answer is that the definition of a business message depends upon how you 'do business.' Chinese 'do business' differently than Westerners do; we depend on contracts, Chinese don't. To explain we have to start by looking at contracts.

What Is A Contract?

What is a contract? *Dictionary.com* defines it as: 1. an agreement between two or more parties for the doing or not doing of something specified; 2. an agreement enforceable by law. Merriam-Webster online dictionary defines contract as: 1a. a binding agreement between two or more persons or parties; 1b. a business arrangement for the supply of goods or services at a fixed price. The key words are "specified, enforceable, binding and fixed." A contract is about certainty, a description of what will happen for sure, or else. A contract is comforting. No uncertainty.

Are contracts about the past, present or future? The future: a contract describes a future reality, that from a specified time (usually contract signing) until a specified time in the future (contract term) 'this' is what will happen. Westerners are so confident they can predict the future with accuracy that they bind themselves or their organizations to future actions, and to penalties if the actions are not carried out properly (as specified in the contract).

How long does a Western business relationship last? The easy answer is as long as it says in the contract. It is also the correct answer. Yes, the quality revolution of the 80s and 90s led Western business (especially large corporations) to do things like choose a smaller number of suppliers and then to develop close, long term relationships with them. Nevertheless, even close relationships are defined and determined by contract terms, and if performance slips to below an acceptable standard (as specified in the contract), the relationship is terminated. This 'you can't deliver so goodbye' attitude takes precedence even if there are strong personal relationships between employees of both companies, this situation leading to that great Western sentence, "Sorry, it is just business." *Chinese don't understand that sentence.*

Contracts And Western Business

Westerners and Chinese have very different ideas of how to do business and how to build a business relationship. Let's start with a review of the Western business model. Are contracts important in Western business? Certainly: Western business is built on contract. Following the contract is how business is done, and a good business relationship is built by efficiently producing the results or carrying out the services as specified in the contract. Contract terms define reality: what must be done, by whom, by when, for how long, and what the final product or service looks like. If it is not in the contract it is not important, or important to business.

Do Westerners need a contract to do business? In almost any situation, the answer is yes. Western business, not to mention society, depends on legally binding agreements, contracts. Earlier in the book[78] I used a three-character saying to describe the different ways Westerners and Chinese use law and relationships to judge which actions are/are not correct. Read one way the three characters mean that relationships are more important than law, that is, a person should act to protect a relationship even if doing so is against the law. Read the opposite way the characters mean that following the law is more important than relationships, that is, a person should follow the law even if that hurts a relationship. The Chinese tend to believe in the former, that relationships are most important. Westerners tend to think following the law is most important. Westerners can't conceive of life without law. In many ways creating of a system of fair and impartial laws that apply equally to everyone is Western culture's greatest accomplishment.

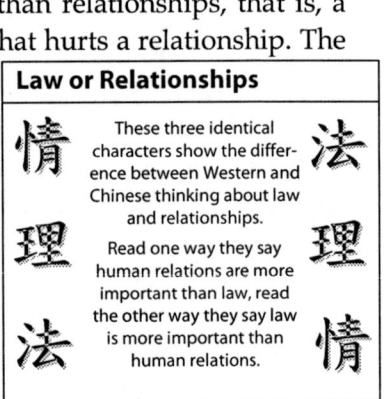

Law or Relationships

These three identical characters show the difference between Western and Chinese thinking about law and relationships.

Read one way they say human relations are more important than law, read the other way they say law is more important than human relations.

Diagram 6: Law or Relationships

European students sometimes speak up about now, saying that I seem to be describing American, lawyer-on-every-corner society, saying that Europe depends much less on lawyers than America does.

Point taken, but what does that mean I ask, does it mean that contracts are not important in Europe? No, it does not: there are more lawyers per capita in America than in Europe, true, but business in Europe depends on contract just as much as it does in the US. When I move the discussion to China and ask, does that mean that Europeans don't use contracts in dealings with Chinese Asian companies, of course they answer no.

No matter the situation, be it personal, say the times you can mow your lawn or take out the garbage, or business, say basing sales compensation on an employment agreement, Western life revolves around legally binding agreements. It starts young: my daughter can't play softball without my signing a contract.

Lastly, following contracts is more than just a legal obligation in Western culture; it is also a moral commitment. When we sign a contract we make an implicit moral commitment, that we *will do what we have agreed to do*. There is an emotional obligation to deliver as promised, feelings that go beyond concern over possible punishment. Indeed, a modern Western hero carries out the terms of a contract even when doing so hurts. It is a point of honor.

Marriage And Chinese Business

Chinese see business much differently. Chinese see mutual, long-term benefit as the goal of business, with business relationships built through developing good, person-to-person feelings. When you think business in Chinese Asia, you should think marriage or friendship, not contract.

Chinese vs. Western Concepts of Business Relations	
Chinese (marriage)	Western (contract)
• give and take as situation changes	• only the give and take written in the contract
• constant compromise	• no real compromise after contract is signed
• meant to be forever	• has beginning and end
• meant for mutual benefit	• can be one-sided (depends on skill drafting contract)
• problems decided by sympathy and forgiveness (Rules of Morality)	• problems decided by impartial third party • (Rules of Law)

Table 17: Chinese vs. Western Ideas of Business Relations

Until very recently Chinese society did not have anything like the Western system of an impartial law applied equally to all. The Chinese legal system (such as it was) depended on virtuous men, mandarins, examining all sides of a case and determining the proper result according to Confucian ideals of inequality and harmony. Chinese had little concept of 'no fault,' that is, person A is 100% right and person B 100% wrong. For a case to be brought in front of a magistrate meant that both sides could not reach a harmonious decision, therefore both sides bore at least some guilt. The last thing Chinese wanted was to go to court. Both sides lost.

The possibility for corruption was very high in such a legal system. With 'right' determined not by impartial law but by personal opinion, the door was open for rich people to sway the decision through, ah, contributions to the presiding official. The 'red envelope' (*hong bao*) tradition of affecting decisions through bribes in Chinese Asia has a very long history, millennia long, one that most observers think continues today.

How was it possible to do business in such a lawless[79] environment? Business depends on at least some certainty about partners' actions, some level of dependability. Without the legal system Westerners use to achieve certainty, how could Chinese business survive? By developing good relationships with partners, relationships with people you could trust to deliver.

Think of your relationship with your best friend or spouse. There is no contract specifying certain levels of performance between the two of you, yet you can trust him or her, trust that goes both ways. Moreover, the relationship is for mutual benefit. You would not become best friends with someone who was always thinking and acting selfishly, would not marry someone who was busy every time you asked him or her for help.

How long does a friendship or marriage last? Forever: at least that is the hope. We put no specified time limit on a friendship, we don't marry for three years then renegotiate. Life and people are constantly changing though; how can a relationship survive the changes? It survives through constant compromise, sometimes I'll change for you (accept something I don't like in order to make you happy), and sometimes you'll adjust your actions to match what I'd like to happen. No one ever *wins* in a friendship or marriage, it is never a zero sum game: it is either win-win or lose-lose.

Relationship problems are inevitable. How do friends solve problems? Let's say you are out of work and I lend you $1,000, and you promise to pay me back in six months. Six months later I ask for my money. You tell me a sad story, about how you had a car accident, have been out of work and can't pay as agreed. Do I now say, "A deal is a deal, you said six months so pay up. If you don't pay up today I'll take you to court?" If I did it would mark the end of the friendship. Instead of using the Rules of Law to decide what to do, a best friend would use the Laws of Morality, would show sympathy and forgiveness. The same is true in a successful marriage: you solve the inevitable relationship problems and disagreements using sympathy and forgiveness, constant compromise, give and take as the situation changes. If just one side shows sympathy or is willing to compromise, or if the other takes but never gives, the friendship or marriage is soon over.

Chinese business, past and present, uses this friendship or marriage model. Business relationships once entered into should last forever. Business relationships are (or should be) for mutual benefit. Neither side should try to take unilateral advantage: it is either win-win or lose-lose, not I win-you lose. Compromise and give and take is how to resolve problems, and each side should take the long-term view that it is better to lose a little now in order to protect the health of the relationship (and gain in the future). Placed within the context of China's overall culture goals, harmony and stability, the friendship/marriage model fit China's needs perfectly.

Does the friendship/marriage business model work today? No, not perfectly, especially between Chinese and Western companies. Even Chinese companies have some difficulty adapting yesterday's win-win model to the competition inherent in modern capitalism. Nevertheless, the ideal is still the win-win friendship/marriage method, and it still characterizes the vast majority of Chinese business deals and relations. Chinese would certainly prefer to do business that way, with trust, not lawyers.

Chinese And Contracts

Chinese do sign contracts, often eagerly. Why? One reason is obvious: Chinese sign contracts because Western firms insist upon it. If Chinese want to play in the international economy, want to belong to the WTO and all that, they need to follow the rules of the game, and that means signing contracts. (It should also mean that Chinese honor contracts and treat both sides in a legal dispute equally and fairly, but ... it often doesn't: see below.)

Yet Western pressure does not explain why Chinese are often eager to sign a contract. Why eager? Because there is often a big banquet after signing the contract, and Chinese love a big banquet! Lots of good food and even more good liquor, toast after toast of *bai ju* (literally white alcohol) and beer, all free. What's not to like?

What does signing a contract mean to the Chinese (beyond the free meal that is)? Do the Chinese feel the same way as Westerners about signing a contract, that there is now both a legal and a moral obligation to carry out the exact terms of the contract? No, not hardly. The Chinese look at a contract as a statement of hope, a description of what they hope happens. Of course, though, if the conditions or business environment changes, Chinese think the contract terms should change also, with compromise and however as much give and take is needed to ensure mutual benefit.

This give-and-take, contracts-terms-are-fluid attitude stems from Chinese ideas about time as well as from traditional ways of doing business. A common Chinese saying, loosely translated, says 'Men may propose what will happen, but it is the Gods who actually decide what happens.' To the Chinese there are two important times, the past and the present. The future, well, to the Chinese the future is unknowable, up to the Gods to decide, thus not something to think about. Chinese are in this sense extremely fatalistic, believing that as people can't control the future therefore whatever happens is whatever the Gods want to happen.

When you add this attitude towards an unknowable future to analytical skills not taught in Chinese schools, the reasons for their poor ability to predict the future becomes more understandable. Analyzing the future requires strong logic skills, specifically (but not only) an open mind to what might be relevant towards affecting the future, and cause and effect analysis of 'if *this* happens it will likely cause *that*, which will likely affect *the other*.' In my experience from over fifteen years teaching logic to Chinese managers and executives throughout Chinese Asia, I believe most Chinese lack these key logic skills.[80] My belief is supported by the numerous comments I have heard from Western managers about their Chinese staff having weak planning skills.

Contract terms are more than guesses to Chinese, but to nowhere near the level of certainty Westerners have about what will happen in the future. When a Westerner signs a contract, he or she believes that the future will be *exactly* as described in the contract. They consider all factors and examine all scenarios, an analytic process that continues until the Westerners are comfortable they understand the future well enough to enter into a binding agreement. As contracts can't change in the middle and must be carried out exactly as written, Westerners are under significant pressure to get the future right.

Not so the Chinese: besides the 'future is unknowable' attitude and lack of logic skills, Chinese feel little pressure to 'get the future right.' *How can we get it right?* Chinese think, *Besides, if the future changes [from what we think it will be when we sign the contract] we will just make changes to the contract.*

When Problems Happen

Chinese wanting to change contract terms in mid-contract is a common problem. Sooner or later Westerners will hear the famous question, 'How can you ask me to lose money?' It goes like this: Chinese want to change the contract, Westerners say No, and then Chinese ask the above question about losing money. The Chinese usually want changes because something else has changed, for example costs are higher than projected, perhaps because of a surprise increase in raw material cost. Chinese explain this to their Western partners; explain that it is *not their fault* that their costs went up, and that they will lose money if they follow the contract as originally written. The conversation might look like this:

Chinese: *Our costs have gone up. We need to raise our prices immediately.*

Westerner: *Sorry, but that is not possible. That is not in the contract.*

Chinese: *But if we don't raise our prices to you we will lose money on the deal.*

Westerner   *Sorry, but that is not my problem. A deal is a deal. Maybe after you complete this deal we can increase payment amount in the next deal. But you must complete this contract first.*

Chinese: *How can you ask me to lose money?*

Westerner: *I am sorry you are losing money. But a deal is a deal. We can't change the contract.*

What do you do now? What can you do? The more you insist on following the contract the more the Chinese will think you only care about yourself, are greedy, selfish and someone who can't be trusted to see both sides of the problem: a person who does not care about mutual benefit and developing a long term relationship. The more the Chinese talks about why he can't follow the contract the more you won't trust him to keep his word, hurting your desire to work with him in the future. You will start to wonder if your Chinese partner is cheating you with this 'surprise' price increase after everything is underway and you are trapped (because changing partners would be very difficult and expensive).

Do Chinese try to cheat Westerners? Certainly, it can happen, but less often than many people think. Do Chinese often ask to make changes to ongoing contracts? Yes, they often do. Most of the times it is not cheating, it is the future turning out differently than what the Chinese planned on; call it an honest mistake. Go back to the chart comparing Chinese and Western ideas about a business relationship. The Chinese are only asking for what they think is proper, some give and take because of the changed situation, some compromise. Did your spouse's character or abilities turn out to be exactly the way you thought, or did you have to make adjustments along the way? Viewed through Chinese eyes it is clear: they will lose money if the deal is not changed, so the deal should be changed—*how can you ask your partner to lose money?*

What can you do? First, you normally **can't** use the lure of a possible, lucrative future deal to make the Chinese follow through on the existing bad (for them) deal.[81] Why? Two complimentary reasons: the Chinese think the future is uncertain, unknowable, therefore your offer is uncertain as well; next, the existing contract (hence the relationship) has a time limit, an end date. How does your Chinese partner know there will be a future 'good' deal like you talk about? He does not, so he will not believe it. Using the future will not work. Only one thing will work, something that has almost disappeared from Western business (though still alive in many other cultures): barter.

During negotiations for the existing deal there were probably things you wanted but the Chinese refused to give, for example let's say you wanted three containers every month but he would only agree to two. Okay, if the Chinese wants something, fine, you can ask for something in return. You offer to raise the price say 60% of what your partner is asking for (he wants an extra $10 per unit so you offer an extra $6), and in return you ask for three containers per month. You and he talk, and in the end settle on increasing the price 70% and shipping five containers every two months. A win-win conclusion, each gets something they want ... in return for giving up something they have.

You **must** take at the same time you give! If you don't, thinking that, 'hey, when we negotiate the next deal my partner will remember how generous I was,' you will likely be disappointed. For people trained to memorize, the Chinese often develop a very convenient bad memory for items like past generosity. The time to take, to get your benefit, is at the same time you give, when your partner gets his benefit.

Building 'wiggle room' into contract terms is crucial. Remember, a contract does not define a certain future reality to Chinese, it simply marks the start of a relationship, one that may go in different directions as things change over time. Pad this, build up that, ask for extra so you can give it away when needed: drafting a contract means looking into the future and anticipating what might go wrong *for the Chinese*, how potential changes in China might affect the terms *for them*. Your legal department might not like it back home, but that is the Chinese reality.

Legal Remedies

Why not take the Chinese to court, why not force them to carry out the contract? That is what you would do in a Western country. After all, it is obvious that you are in the right. And it may be true, you may be in the right, but I strongly advise against taking legal action, even if you are right. Two reasons stand out.

First, you will lose. You can count the number of Western companies that have won in Chinese court on one hand (maybe two). Huge multinationals, Fortune 500 companies with a gaggle of star lawyers and open-and-shut cases regularly lose in Chinese courts. Second, you would lose twice, once in court and once in the marketplace. Chinese companies would now know you as a company that settled disputes in court rather than through give and take. Few companies would want to work with you.

How about suing the Chinese partner in your country's court instead? Fine, let's say you win. Now what? If the Chinese company has direct involvement in your country's market you have a chance of receiving remedy, but few Chinese companies have overseas assets. They buy from and sell to many countries, but rarely *sell in* other countries. Moreover, your reputation as a selfish company with no heart would still spread.

There are other options, arbitration rather than courts is one. Another is writing into the contract a neutral jurisdiction for dispute settlement. I am not a lawyer so I don't want to offer advice beyond my field. Talk to your country's trade office in China, Taiwan or Hong Kong. A much-underused service, in-country trade offices in Chinese Asia are a gold mine of help and advice. The officers there know the market, the players and the laws, and your taxes pay their salaries. Don't be shy. Use them.

Slow To Be Sure

The best way to avoid contract problems and ugly decisions about courts is to get to know your Chinese counterparts before you sign the Big Deal. To use the marriage metaphor again, you should think to develop a business relationship using the same steps you used to woo your husband or wife. Here are such steps.

Marry Your Business Partner		
STEPS	MARRIAGE	BUSINESS
Step 1	meet and talk	meet and talk
Step 2	lunch date	do $0.5M deal
Step 3	dinner date	do $1M deal
Step 4	go traveling	do $5M deal
Penultimate	get married	do $10M deal
Ultimate	have ever happier marriage have wonderful children	do $10M deal every year do new deals with partners

Table 18: Marry Your Business Partner?

Would you marry a man after your first date, propose to a woman after your first coffee together? No, almost certainly not. You would get to know them first, would find out whether their personality fit yours, whether you both had similar values and beliefs, whether you both wanted children perhaps. Marriage is a big step, a legal commitment intended to last forever that is very difficult to get out of if things don't work out. Marriage is not something you want to jump into without looking. Just like a contract.

By going on steadily more complicated dates you discover if you and your prospective spouse are compatible over time, a natural progression actually. The lunch date should come before traveling together, a dinner date is more likely if the initial meet and talk went well. Only once you are sure you can trust the other person and the strength of the relationship would you propose, or say yes to a proposal. Just common sense.

You should try to follow the same deliberate, step-by-step process in building a Chinese business relationship. Instead of trying to sign the biggest possible contract the first time you do business together, try to get to know the person and the company before you make a huge commitment. Do they deliver as promised? Are they easy to work with?

The best way to discover these things about the other side is to work with them, but with smaller contracts first. Why? Because it is easier to compromise on a small deal than a huge one, and a **lot** easier to walk away from a deal if your company won't go bankrupt if you do walk away. We learn trust by how we react to the inevitable mistakes we make. Do we blame the other person? Take responsibility for our own mistakes? Work together to find solutions? All are easier to answer when financial ruin is not looming above you. If possible, go from small to big. Marry your Chinese partner—do the huge deal—only after you have successfully done a number of smaller deals first. Date before marriage.

Negotiation Stages

Negotiation is a crucial step in any business deal. When do you negotiate though? A deal has many stages, from meet and talk to cash the cheque: which (next page) are negotiation stages?

When Do *You* Negotiate?

A typical business deal might go through the some or all of the following stages. Which stages are *negotiation* stages?

1.   **Meet informally in a business setting**
   * *casual business conversation, but mostly of a very general nature*

2.   **Lunches/Dinners/Drinks**
   * *casual conversation, mostly personal (families, hobbies etc.); business talk may be sharing anecdotes, impressions or experiences*

3.   **Phone, fax or email about possible contract**
   * *passing business information, asking and answering business and/or legal questions; discussion of possible contract terms*

4.   **Face-to-face contract meeting in Conference Room**
   * *only serious business topics discussed; legal advisors likely present (or close by); contract either drafted or signed*

5.   **Phone, fax or email during the term of the contract**
   * *passing business information, asking and answering business questions; discussing contract (maybe resolving problems)*

6.   **Phone, fax or email after contract completed**
   * *sending and receiving words of thanks and congratulations*

7.   **Meet informally in non-business setting**
   * *celebration dinner; personal and non-serious business subjects*

Table 19: When Do You Negotiate?

Most Westerners say Step Four is the negotiation stage, and maybe the last part of Step Three as well. Dinner and drinks are just for fun, personal not business, and casual conversation is not negotiation. To Westerners, negotiation is actual discussing of business details, the who, what, when and how of it all, and negotiation ends when the contact is signed. Step Five is order fulfillment, not negotiation for example, just the back and forth needed to finish the deal. Negotiation does not start again until you discuss who, what, when and how of a new deal.

Most Chinese students say that every step is a negotiation stage! Huh? Look at it through Chinese glasses. Chinese don't rely on legally-binding contracts to guarantee performance, instead they depend on relationships they can trust. Going back to the friendship/marriage metaphor, when do you make a friend, while playing football but not while watching a movie, when do you develop the intimacy needed for marriage, during dinner but not while shopping together? Making a friend is a 24/7/365 job, developing a strong relationship prior to marriage—and to maintain a strong relationship after marriage—is a full time job. The same is true working with the Chinese.

Chinese evaluate you from the moment you meet until, well, until your relationship ends. What Westerners call negotiation, discussing specific who, what, why and how details, is just part of the negotiation process. Indeed, what you do to solve order fulfillment problems (for example) will affect whether Chinese feel they can trust you, a factor crucial to their wanting to keep doing business with you. Think of it like a job interview that continues over dinner and during golf; the interviewer already discovered your job qualifications in the office meetings, and now is evaluating your character (do you cheat at golf) and personality (are you rude or respectful to servers). Chinese already know your product is good, they just want to find out if you are.

Hidden Back Office Problems

Chinese might like and trust you, but still have problems working with you. Why? Because of hidden back office problems. In my experience, Westerners working in order acquisition, the ones who come to Chinese Asia and actually meet and work with Chinese people, do a pretty good job adjusting to the Chinese reality. They negotiate a great deal, sign the contract and all is good, or is until the actual work starts.

Problems start to happen, and the Chinese are unhappy. By now the Westerner who negotiated the contract has disappeared, replaced by order fulfillment employees, those who work in the back office and who never see a Chinese. Making this even worse, the Chinese who negotiated the deal has disappeared as well, replaced by Chinese who never (or rarely) see a Westerner.

A common source of problems is Chinese making special requests, which Western back office staff deny. For example, let's say that Chinese are selling the Western company's products in China. The Chinese sales staff goes out into the market, meeting and selling to other Chinese. The Western product they sell is excellent, but even excellent products can be customized, even generous shipping or payment terms can be improved. Being flexible and using the contract terms, price lists, shipping schedules and standard operating procedures (SOP) as a *flexible guide*, not as *laws cut from stone*, the deals offered to the Chinese customers can be somewhat different than what the 'rules' said was possible.

Sales call over, the Chinese salesperson writes up the order and faxes it to the Western office, and waits. And waits, receiving no reply and no shipment. The Chinese salesperson emails to ask why, and receives no reply. By now their customer is unhappy, making the Chinese salesperson unhappy as well. The problem is sent upstairs, and finally a high level Chinese discusses it with a high level Westerner. The high level Westerner then goes downstairs to the person who took the Chinese order. Asking what is wrong, they hear, "Well, what the Chinese asked for is not in the contract so I didn't bother to answer."

A huge amount of friction in relationships stems from this and other similar, quite simple, causes. Neither back office staff, Chinese or Western, is doing anything wrong exactly; each is just following their culture's way of doing business. How can that be faulted? The problem is caused because each are unaware of the other side's way of doing business, so have no reason to alter what they know to be the 'right' way to do things.

Fixing this problem is not easy. Westerners involved in order acquisition (those who know the Chinese) can try to push their knowledge about Chinese ways into their back office organization, say by offering training sessions about the Chinese or by talking to the back office manager. If back office staff know what to expect, and are clear about what to do if X happens, your company can prevent many problems from happening. Yet that only fixes one side of the problem; what can you do on the Chinese side?

The short answer is, not so much. Solutions start with knowledge and awareness, so you can explain the situation to your Chinese counterpart and suggest some remedies. Chinese salespeople are frequently quite divorced from other department staff—more so than in the West—and may not consider educating other staff as part of their job. Of course such an attitude eventually hurts customer satisfaction, thus hurts sales, but that takes time to occur and is in the (unknowable) future, not in the (most important) present. Why worry about something that may not happen? Finally, senior managers may not be aware of the problem either: analyzing and measuring problems and preparing management information reports are undeveloped in most Chinese offices.

Corruption Chinese Style

I would be remiss if I didn't include something about corruption in Chinese Asia. Instead of a detailed look at the many types, methods and levels of corruption and what to do about it—there is not enough room here: that would take a new book—I want to show a key difference between how Westerners and Chinese look at corruption. I call it the lunchbox example.

Anyone who has worked in Chinese Asia for any length of time knows what a Chinese lunchbox is. A disposable plastic or waxed cardboard box about the size of thick paperback book, you pry off rubber bands to open the folding lid to get to the food inside. There will be some meat, a chicken leg, piece of fried fish or a pork chop, a couple of types of vegetables, all on a bed of white rice. Sold on street corners and delivered to offices, Chinese lunchboxes are a preferred lunchtime meal, especially when time and money matter. They are often quite tasty as well.

Let's say we work together in an office of twenty people. I tell everyone I know a vendor who will deliver tasty lunchboxes for US$5 each (a dollar less than normal) if we buy everyday in bulk. Sensing a good deal, you all agree. The lunchboxes start arriving the next day, and every day after for the next three months. One day you discover I am only paying the vendor $4 per lunchbox, and am putting the other $1 in my pocket.

If this was in the West, what would your reaction be? You would be angry, thinking I was cheating everyone. Westerner morality says I should share any savings. Now, if this was in China what do you think my Chinese coworkers would feel? Would they be angry, would they feel I was cheating them? No, probably not.

The Chinese would ask, 'who was getting hurt?' Not my coworkers: they were paying $5 for a $6 lunchbox. No harm there. Not the vendor: he was receiving exactly what he asked for, $4 per box when bought in bulk. No harm there either. Indeed, the only person being hurt is me. Huh? *Me?*

Every day I must take the orders and pass them to the vendor. I must handle any complaints, like the fish is always overcooked or the pork chops are tough (tougher than normal that is). Coworkers sometimes go out for lunch, meaning I order eighteen or less, not twenty, something the vendor complains to me about. Don't I deserve some benefit for all my troubles?

Who is being hurt is a common Chinese way of looking at special deals and altered prices. It affects many ways the Chinese react to prices, schedules and jobs. Remember, the Chinese don't have a system based on a set of laws applied equally to all. Chinese look to see who gets hurt, and who does the hurt. With no concept of equality and all relationships hierarchical, the *who is being hurt* attitude makes sense. Keep this it in mind before you judge Chinese actions as corrupt. Are you truly being hurt, or is it just your Western sense of right and wrong being broken?

Themes and Lessons

Western business depends on contracts; Chinese business does not: if you depend on contracts to succeed in Chinese Asia, you will fail, period.

Westerners already know how to business in Chinese Asia, they just do not know they know. If you know how to make a marriage succeed, know how to make a best friend in your hometown, you know how to do business with the Chinese.

1. Many problems occur because of poor translating, caused by in some way using the wrong person or people to translate. Use professional translators for written as well as spoken communication.
2. Westerners only contact Chinese partners when they want something; this makes Chinese think Westerners are selfish, interested only in their welfare.
3. Westerners believe following the law (like following a contract) is more important than personal relationships. Following a contract is a legal as well as a moral act.
4. Chinese believe personal relationships are more important then following the law.
5. Chinese think contracts are just a statement of what they hope happens; if the situation changes then Chinese believe the contract terms should change as well.
6. When problems happen use barter, not law, to solve them. Use give and take, but make sure to take at the same time you give.
7. A relationship built slowly is more likely to last than one built overnight.
8. Chinese view a business relationship the same way they view a husband-wife relationship: meant to last forever and for mutual benefit
9. Every action you take with Chinese is part of the overall negotiations.
10. Back office problems hurt business relationships and success.
11. Chinese have no idea of an abstract set of laws that apply fairly and equally to everyone; instead they use 'who is being hurt?' question to decide right or wrong. Before you cry 'corruption,' apply this question.

CHAPTER TEN

Becoming A Good Barbarian

Are all Chinese the same? I use the term 'Chinese Asian' to describe all Chinese, and argue throughout that 'Chinese do X.' Are these generalizations fair? Are Chinese raised on Taiwan the same as those who hale from China, those born and bred in Singapore the same as those who call Hong Kong home? Are city Chinese the same as country Chinese, university educated Chinese different from those with high school or less? Is there a difference between Chinese educated overseas from those who went to school inside Chinese Asia? Is it reasonable to lump fashionable Shanghai city dwellers with Shenzhen factory workers, Singapore knowledge workers with Taipei taxi drivers? Is it *ever* fair to say, 'all Chinese do X?' Is 'Chinese Asia' even a place?

All good questions. When talking about what people do, or why they do it, there are no absolutes, no way correctly to say 'all X people do Y.' People are too complicated for such a simple description. Moreover, what you see depends on what you look at. If you want to prove that Chinese are not all the same just look at the parade on any crowded Chinese sidewalk, or travel from city to countryside; viewed by outside appearance it is clear not all Chinese are the same. Compare Chinese professionals to taxi drivers, and it is obvious each have different social habits, manners and lifestyles. They are different.

What about the differences between China, HK, Singapore and Taiwan Chinese? Anyone with more than a passing familiarity with two or more of these regions is quick to say that there are differences between the types. I agree; there are huge differences.

Nevertheless, it again depends on what you look at, what you compare. No matter which China you are in you flag down a taxi —sorry for all the taxi references—the same way: you extend an arm horizontally and wave your hand up and down (like waving goodbye in the West). Does this then mean that all Chinese are the same? No. What you see depends on what you look at.

What am I looking at when I write, 'all Chinese tend to…?' I look at the philosophic roots of Chinese culture, the common center inside each Chinese heart. Certainly, Chinese have diverged from this center, but not as much as you would think; after all less than 100 years ago all Chinese were the same (very minor differences at most between China and Hong Kong, Taiwan and Singapore). I argue that harmony and stability are still the overarching Chinese goals, even if the different Chinas live these goals to different degrees.[82] These common root goals lead to similar concepts of politeness, morality, values, and, especially, communication. A Hong Kong punk rocker, a China factory worker, a Taiwan engineer and a Singapore executive all have common standards of polite behavior, a common moral code and use common Rules of Communication. All Chinese are different, true, but equally true they are all the same. It depends on what you look at.

Has China Changed? Have The Chinese Changed?

The first time I visited Shanghai (1985) there were more bicycles than I'd ever seen before, ten abreast filling the entire road. I was trapped once, unable to figure out how to shift 'lanes' so I could turn right. I was scared. On a recent trip (2005) my Chinese friends convinced me to cross a street between intersections, cars filling the road. I hesitated and ended trapped in the middle, cars on each side roaring past. I was scared. Twenty years on, and Shanghai traffic is still frightening.

Does this mean that China *has* changed, from bicycles to cars, or *hasn't* changed, roads still full of madly rushing vehicles? It could mean both, depending on what you are looking at. As such, my traffic story is an apt metaphor for China today; much has changed but much has stayed the same. Let me deal with the changes first.

Changes in Chinese Asia

Traffic is a good place to start. In my twenty plus years working in Chinese Asia, vehicle traffic has exploded in each of the Chinas, bicycle to motorcycle to car to fancy car to SUV (parking spots have not kept up, but that is another issue). Twenty years ago the farther you went from Taipei the fewer cars and trucks you saw, replaced by human porters, bicycles, animal powered and other types of (often strange) motorized vehicles. The same is true today leaving any large coastal Chinese city: the countryside is a much different place than the city.

Buildings also changed, radically. Chinese cities used to be low-rise, houses surrounded by walls topped with broken glass and four-story walkup apartment buildings: there were few tall buildings, and eight stories was tall! Chinese cities today compete over who has the highest, shiniest, most avant-garde skyline. The first time I walked the Bund in Shanghai, Pudong across the river was nothing, a poor, somewhat squalid-looking area. There certainly was no reason to go there. Pudong today is, well, new, spectacular, an amazing destination in itself.

Restaurants are different as well. In the 80s I looked forward to trips to Hong Kong, a chance to eat real Western (pub) food, bangers and mash at *Ned Kelly's Last Stand*. Outside of Hong Kong and Singapore there was no real Western food: all you found in China or Taiwan were, ah, unique versions of Western dishes.[83] Then came the MacDonald's revolution.

Not of fast food—Macdonald's is slow compared to Chinese vendor fast food—or the introduction of Western restaurants, KFC, Burger King and other, real-food places, Italian, Greek and Thai. Macdonald's caused a revolution of manners, of standing politely in line for food, clearing the table and putting away your dirty dishes, not using the dishes as an ashtray or putting cigarettes out on the floor, no spitting. In less than one generation MacDonald's and (7/11 convenience stores) changed the Chinese.

Perhaps the most revealing change is in family size. While the government forces families to adopt a one-child policy in China, family size has dropped dramatically in Taiwan, Hong Kong and Singapore (Japan and Korea as well). Ancestor worship, where

every family must have a male child to pray to and honor ances-
tors, is older than Confucius. One generation ago, couples used to
keep having children until they had a son. Today a growing number of couples have one child, and if it is a female, that's okay.

Continuity in Chinese Asia

For every area of change, you can find an area of continuity.
To continue from above, falling Chinese birthrates does not mean
Chinese no longer respect the family. Far from it: in a time of fast-
paced change, the family is a key area of refuge, a place where the
timeless flow of Chinese life continues unchanged. Males still go
before females, and the father-patriarch's word is still law.

Another key area of continuity is the importance of *guanxi* in
doing business (and in life); mutually shared obligations and preserving relationships are still key goals. Chinese still see themselves as members of a guanxi group or clique, fragmenting Chinese society into small, zero-sum groups. Associated with the importance of guanxi is the fact that Chinese still hold the 'relationships are more important than law' attitude in business, making
'marry your business partner' more important than 'follow the
contract.' No different from a millennia ago.

Chinese also hold to the hierarchical nature of relationships
(business and social), meaning the top-down nature of decision
making something Confucius would recognize and approve of.
Two effects of this top-down emphasis are passivity and stifled
initiative, again just as things always were. Then there is the education system (formal and informal): while the curriculum has
changed (science instead of poetry) the rote-memorization way
Chinese educate children is unchanged from Tang Dynasty times.
Children are told what to learn and what the right answers are;
there is no room for (or desire for) developing individual opinions,
or for teaching debate and discussion skills. The key (but not only)
effect of the ongoing traditional education system is stifled crea-
tivity, a problem discussed (but not solved) by modern Chinese
leaders like Lee Kwan Yu, the fabled father of Singapore. Finally,
Chinese still teach and use their age-old Rules of Communication,
even when using English and communicating with Westerners.

It is possible to divide the Chinese changes into two types, avalanche and glacier change.

Is Chinese Asia Changing?	
Avalanche Changes	Glacier Changes
eating habits and diet	education system
clothes	importance of guanxi in business
buildings	respect for authority and hierarchy
transportation	importance of family
one-child families	Rules of Communication
women in workforce	'marriage' business relations

Table 20: Is Chinese Asia Changing?

Modern China: Change Or Continuity

Have Chinese changed? Yes. Have Chinese stayed the same? Yes. If both are true, which is the most important? The areas of continuity (or very slow change) are. Do a quick analysis of the two types of change. Which has the greater effects? Avalanches move quickly and are very dramatic, but their changes don't last, trees grow back and roads get fixed. Avalanches cause just surface changes, dramatic but superficial.

Chinese are group-oriented people and everything important revolves around the individual's responsibilities and actions towards the group. Avalanche changes involve only the individual however, not to the individual vis-à-vis the group. Changing dress and eating habits, buying a first car and moving to a new apartment are all individual choices; even the choice to have only one child involves only two people, the parents. Avalanche changes are like changes of fashion, each year something new.

Most political and economic changes of the last few decades are avalanches. Passing laws and economic directives are surface changes only, quick and easy words that may or may not signal actual changes in Chinese behavior. It is takes little time or effort to announce sweeping new laws, anti-counterfeiting say (a topical example), but is difficult and time consuming to enforce the law and stop counterfeiters. The Chinese government can trumpet the change—counterfeiting is illegal!—but the situation on the ground does not change. When counterfeiting actually stops the change will have huge and lasting effects—like a glacier—but until then a new law is just an avalanche of meaningless words.

A glacier moves very slowly and changes the landscape in fundamental ways. Glacier changes in a culture and a society are no less slow and difficult to make. It is fair to say that the Chinese are changing in the above-listed glacier areas, but change is slow and difficult, hard to see. A key reason for the slow speed is that glacier changes have nothing to do with fashion, involve nothing so simple as passing a law or erecting a building. To mix metaphors for a moment, if avalanche changes are of the skin and clothing, a glacier changes bone, muscle and organs. Glacier changes are fundamental, changes of what it means to *be Chinese*, of what Chinese are. Attributes and beliefs take millennia to form; expecting them to change quickly is not reasonable.[84]

Which type of Chinese changes, avalanche or glacier, are most important to Westerners? Avalanche changes affect your lifestyle in China, giving you nicer places to live and eat, and are creating new markets for Western goods and services, but are not as crucial to success as glacier changes. Until glacier changes occur, until business depends on performance and not guanxi, until Chinese schools teach students to think instead of memorize, Westerners of today and tomorrow will continue to face the same problems faced by Westerners of the 18th and 19th centuries.

I expect superficial change to continue its rapid pace, making China a new and different-looking place each time you visit. I also expect the Chinese to resist fundamental change, meaning Chinese on the inside will change slowly, evolution, not revolution. Chinese have little experience in making fundamental changes, and I expect them to resist basic changes as much as possible. My personal key indicator of change is the Chinese education system. If, and only if, Chinese schools begin to emphasize individual development, discussion and debate, and begin to reward ideas and arguments over memory and obedience, will I think the Chinese glacier is really about to move. Think decades, not years.

Not *My* Chinese

"Not my Chinese. They are different." I have lost count of how many times I have heard this sentiment over the last 15 years. Usually from Westerners new or relatively new to Chinese Asia, ones with only few wrinkles on their China hand. Their sentiment is understandable, on a couple of levels. One reason is that making critical statements about another culture is 'bad' in Western society today, thought arrogant and unfeeling, and anyone who makes such statements is politically incorrect. Sigh. A quick story.

Hired by a large American bank to improve cooperation between senior level Chinese and Westerners, I led a class containing both groups. Just a couple of hours into the all-day class a Westerner complained that what I was saying about the Chinese was wrong, that "our Chinese are not like that." I looked to the Chinese for support—all I was saying was what many hundreds of Chinese had heard and agreed to before—but received none. No Chinese was about to criticize their boss or criticize Chinese culture in front of Westerners. The more I tried to explain the deeper I dug the hole I was in, making it a long day. When I mentioned to the Westerner that he had only been in Chinese Asia for two months and still had much to discover, he self-righteously told me, "I don't have to be here for long to recognize racist statements when I hear them." It was a *very* long day.[85]

It is human nature to want to think the best of those you work with, doubly so when you are in new and strange surroundings and success depends on new coworkers. Westerners are mostly optimistic people, and feel uncomfortable when told they are up against an unmovable object, the Chinese glacier. Adding to this attitude or impression are the many surface similarities between New York and Nanjing, Toronto and Taipei, especially to those without much international experience.

The skyline is tall and dramatic, the streets full of nice restaurants, department stores and clubs, and there seems to be a Starbucks and/or MacDonald's on every corner. The wide streets are jammed with shiny new cars, including more-than-normal numbers of luxury models. The people on the streets and in the office are well dressed in Western fashion, no Mao jackets. The Chinese that Westerners tend to have contact with, higher-level officials, direct reports and hotel/club managers say, all speak English. It is only a short trip from these impressions to the idea that Chinese and Westerners are basically the same, so can be treated in the same way.

Good, Bad and Ugly Westerners

There are three basic types of Westerners in Chinese Asia: well, four actually. They are the Good, two types of Bad (romantic and naïve), and of course, the Ugly. In table form they are:

Good, Bad And Ugly Westerners	
Ugly	Romantic
believes there is only one "right" way, their way	believes it's impossible to understand the Chinese (not just the language)
tries to make the Chinese adapt to his or her (Western) "right" way	tries to give whatever the Chinese ask for (one-way compromise)
Naïve	Good
believes it is possible *fully* to understand and to master Chinese "rules"	believes that different cultures do things in different ways, and that it's possible to gain a workable understanding of Chinese culture
tries to beat the Chinese at their own game, to "out-Chinese-the-Chinese." This *never* works.	tries to identify key issues and concentrates on them, while accepting that other non-key issues can't be changed.

Table 21: Good, Bad And Ugly Westerners

Starting from the worst, the Ugly Westerner is someone who sees Chinese Asia as just a colorful variation of his/her home country. As one German pointed out to me, "Business is business; Chinese want to make money, just like we do. Besides language there are no real differences between us." A common addition to this is, "Chinese now work for [company name] and that means they have to do things the same way we do them."

Moving to Bad Westerners, the first is Romantic. Most Westerners are somewhat romantic about China at the start; perhaps no other country or culture fires the Western imagination more than the Celestial Kingdom.[86] No other culture is so different from Western culture, or so complicated. Romantic Westerners give up trying to understand Chinese culture rules, on one hand thinking them impossible to figure out, on the other thinking that the best results come from giving the Chinese exactly what they want, in the way and manner they want.

The alternate Bad Westerner is Naïve. These Westerners diligently study Chinese language, culture and history. In command of the subject and feeling themselves China 'experts,' Naïve Westerners try to use Chinese ways to get what they want, try in essence to out Chinese the Chinese.

Ugly and Bad don't work. Chinese will work for or with Ugly Westerners for just two reasons, they have no choice or they somehow receive larger-than-normal benefit. Neither are good reasons. Moreover, offices run by Ugly Westerners usually have high turnover rates and, as the best people tend to leave first, those who remain are largely unmotivated and unhappy. Romantic Westerners end up giving in and giving in, not realizing that as long as they keep giving in the Chinese will (understandably) keep taking. Romantic Westerners are what Chinese history has prepared Chinese to expect, barbarians who recognize and respect the superiority of Chinese ways.

What about Westerners who learn Chinese ways, become fluent in Chinese language and customs? Shouldn't they have an advantage? You would think so, and often they do. Equally as often though, such Sinophile Westerners forget who they are and who the home team is, and try to play the game entirely by Chinese rules. The problem is that while they do know many Chinese rules, the Chinese always know more, and are far better at 'being Chinese' than the Westerners are.

As I don't want to discourage people from learning Chinese language or customs, let me explain the Naïve Westerner problem a little more. A good friend did all the homework and became fluent—better than me—in Chinese, plus studied many Chinese customs, traditions and such. Over the phone he was Chinese. His problem? He stopped being a results-oriented Westerner and tried being a rules-following Chinese, tried to be Chinese in negotiating, managing and building business relationships. Using Chinese techniques caused him no end of trouble.

One Chinese technique for motivating staff is *Kill a Chicken to Warn a Monkey*. A boss or manager singles out one employee and, in front of other staff, gets angry at him or her. Staff know the boss is not just angry at the unlucky one being berated, but is angry with all staff: the real message is 'work harder … or else.' I have seen this technique used in a Chinese office, read about and discussed it with Chinese, and explain it in classes for Westerners. I would never dream, however, of trying it in real life; I just know I would somehow do it wrong, and would achieve the wrong result.

It is a Chinese technique, and staff expect it from a Chinese manager, not Western. Naïve Westerners (like my friend) forget this.

The truth is, no matter how many Chinese techniques you master, no matter how 'Chinese' you become, the Chinese know more techniques and are better at being 'Chinese' than you will ever be. They are the home team, and the home team always has the advantage. Don't try to be Chinese. That's naïve. Be Western. Be cute.

Become A Cute Barbarian

Being a Good Westerner starts by understanding what the Chinese expect and want from you. Chinese don't expect you to be Chinese! A non-Chinese can never be Chinese. As discussed in an earlier chapter, Chinese see themselves as inheritors of the Middle Kingdom. If Chinese are in the middle, what is the outside, the top and bottom? The top is heaven, an ill-defined place where Gods reside. The bottom? Barbarians. By definition *everyone* who is not Chinese, you, me and all other Westerners, are barbarians.

Don't like being called a barbarian? Try to get over it; the Chinese do not mean anything truly bad by it, just that you are not Chinese. Being a barbarian can actually be quite useful. Your goal is not overcoming being a barbarian, it is becoming a sensitive, sophisticated, even a cute barbarian.

Chinese measure civilized behavior by how close you follow Chinese norms. If you try to do things in a Chinese way you are cultured and respectful, a good barbarian. The Chinese don't expect you to be perfect though, able to do things the Chinese way without any mistakes whatsoever. Mistakes are inevitable; how you deal with your mistakes is what is important. This is where 'cute' comes in.

'Cute' does not mean child-and-puppy cute nor Hello Kitty / Snoopy / Cabbage Patch doll cute. I mean adult cute, namely the ability to laugh at yourself and your mistakes, and to make the Chinese smile while doing so. Not all people have enough inner confidence to laugh at themselves and their mistakes, but it sure helps in Chinese Asia. Don't take yourself too seriously. A good place to be cute is while eating. Find the humor in your attempts to eat sea slug with chopsticks, a task difficult for even Chinese. Go ahead and make a funny bad face after your attempt to eat 'stinky tofu,' try to show off by picking up two peanuts at once with chopsticks, not as difficult as it sounds (three at once is the true test). Ask questions, make faces, all is good so long as you try. Don't judge, complain or ask for a fork!

A Good Westerner

You don't have to be cute, not everyone can do it, but you do have to be respectful, and everyone can do that. A Good Westerner accepts that the Chinese do things in different ways, and that success comes from adapting to these ways, not by being Ugly and acting as if the differences don't exist. Moreover, a Good Westerner is sensitive to the fact that he or she is in Chinese Asia making Chinese money. It is their game and their rules.

Put the shoe on another foot: what would you expect if Chinese came to your hometown to do business? Would you expect the Chinese to learn a little of the local language? Expect them to follow normal business practices, say to follow the law or to come to meetings on time? I think most Westerners would: I know I would expect this, and more. Westerners are good hosts, yet still expect guests to follow some basic rules and customs. When in Rome do as the Romans do sums up how we feel guests should act when away from home. It should apply to how Westerners act while in Chinese Asia, but often doesn't.

The first part of being a Good Westerner is acknowledging that *you* are in *their* country, and it is your job to adapt to Chinese ways, not their job to adapt to Western. Again, the Chinese don't expect you to be perfect ... but they do expect you to try! Just one short example, speaking Chinese.

Learning Chinese to the point of fluency is hard, and takes a real commitment of time and effort. Naturally the Chinese would like Westerners to be fluent in Mandarin (Cantonese, Taiwanese, whatever), but they certainly don't expect it. Chinese know how difficult their language is (their mastery of it just another example of their great abilities). What Chinese do expect is that Westerners try to speak some Chinese.

Most Chinese know Western long-term residents who speak almost no Chinese. I know some too, their language skills limited to the basics: *Left Turn, Right Turn, Stop, Thank You* and *Give Me Another Beer*, all spoken in fractured, pidgin style. It is embarrassing to watch. Such an obvious lack of respect is harmful to success, even if the Chinese never mention it. Think about it: would you expect a long-term Chinese resident of Germany to speak more than a few lines of bad German, a French resident to speak basic French, a US resident to speak passable English? Imagine attending a meeting in your hometown with a Chinese who had lived there for ten years, only to discover he could not speak any of your language. Imagine if he expected you to speak Chinese! You would be unhappy to say the least, and would think (if not say), 'you are here, so adapt to our ways.' Chinese expect this from you.

The same is true for actions, building relationships, solving problems, planning, communicating, managing and motivating. Chinese have their own ways, and a Good Westerner does his/her best to know and use them. Will you ever know all Chinese customs or ways? No, not a chance. So what? Even Chinese don't know all Chinese customs. You can know the key customs and ways, however, and can use them. While not easy exactly, it is also not that difficult. You **can** do it.

If you know how to make a best friend at home, if you know how to make a marriage work, you know how to build relationships and succeed in Chinese Asia. There is no magic pill to swallow, no surefire simple method to learn. Chinese are just people, with all the same desires, feelings and emotions as you. Yes, they do things differently than you, often much different, but so does your spouse. You must compromise, but to compromise you must respect the Chinese ways, must think of them as legitimate. Chinese do things the way they do because to them they are the right things to do: they don't do them just to drive you crazy.

The key to success is understanding *why* Chinese do things as they do and what Chinese expectations are, then adapting your ways to match Chinese expectations. The first step is acquiring market knowledge, the second is marketing your actions and message. Don't expect the Chinese to adapt to your ways: never forget that you are in *their* country making *their* money. That being said, Chinese don't expect you to become Chinese, they simply expect you to be a Good Westerner, one sensitive to Chinese ways. Finally, you are a results-oriented Westerner; instead of looking at how Chinese do things you should focus on what you need to do to achieve the results you seek.

Living With Frustration

Working and living in Chinese Asia can be frustrating, and keeping frustration bottled up inside can stop you from being a Good Westerner. I have two pieces of advice. First, always keep aspirin in your purse or briefcase to deal with Chinese-inspired headaches; this will make it much easier for you to be pleasant and patient. Next, take up a sport like golf, tennis or handball, something where you can hit a ball as hard as you can; this will help prevent frustrations from building up and making it harder for you to be pleasant and patient.

After a long day in the Chinese trenches I often head to a driving range. I don't look where my first twenty shots go; head down, I picture the source of my frustration and grunt, 'Mr. Huang, Mr. Huang' with every shot. My frustrations are soon gone and I am warmed up, a perfect time to try to cure my slice. This works for me, and is far healthier than keeping it all bottled up inside, punching a wall or emptying the hotel mini-bar.

Themes and Lessons

Becoming a Good Westerners depends on two key points. First, you must understand the true nature of the Chinese environment, the nature of the people and the systems. Second, you must learn to be a sensitive barbarian; even better is if you can learn how to be 'cute.'

1. Chinese Asia is changing very rapidly, but there are two types of changes, and they are not equally important.
2. The changes most Westerners pay attention to are the visible, surface changes.
3. The visible changes are dramatic: tall, beautiful buildings; fashions; transportation; new laws; and people speaking English.
4. The changes Westerners do not see are the invisible, 'inside' changes.
5. The invisible changes are happening very slowly: role of relationships (guanxi) in doing business; education system; Rules of Communication; respect for the family and for authority; and a wait-to-be-told attitude.

6. The slow, invisible changes are far more important to doing business with Chinese than the fast-moving visible changes. Pay attention to the former or you will be fooled by the latter.
7. Be loyal to the Chinese you know, but also be realistic.
8. There are different types of Westerners, the Good, the Bad and the Ugly.
9. A Good Westerner is one who never forgets he or she is in Chinese Asia making Chinese money, so should adapt to Chinese ways, not ask the Chinese to adapt to Western ways. The Good Westerner does not try to become Chinese, but seeks to be a sensitive, polite Westerner.
10. Being 'cute' comes from laughing at yourself. Don't take yourself too seriously!

If you wish to be happy for an hour,
get drunk.

If you wish to be happy for three days,
get married.

If you wish to be happy for eight days,
kill your pig and eat it.

If you wish to be happy forever,
learn to fish.

Chinese proverb

Communication Principles

1. the goal of communication is complete and clear transfer of message from the sender to the receiver
2. the audience is more important than the speaker
3. communication success is measured by how much of the speaker's message is transferred clearly and completely to the audience
4. the audience determines what is polite, not the speaker

Greg's Tips

1. Two objections usually means disagreement.
2. Answers to Yes/No questions come from the story, not as one-word answers.
3. Do it *their* way to get *your* result: accept *how* it is done if you get *what* you want.
4. Irrelevant answers are relevant if they are negative; an irrelevant negative answer usually means No.
5. If a Chinese says anything other than Yes, he or she likely means No
6. An invitation can (not will) be offered as an optimistic, positive statement set in the future. Look for this in new relationships.
7. Listen to everything you hear as if every word has meaning.
8. In spoken communication, make your points one at a time.
9. If you want to know what a Chinese thinks, you can't say what you think first.
10. If things are not said in the right way, Chinese will stop listening to what you say.
11. Motivate by using a public secret: public (everyone knows it happens); secret (no one sees it happen).
12. Give orders or jobs one a time, not in sequence.

Rules To Live By

1. the Chinese expect you to follow their Rules
2. always be polite
3. never raise your voice, and NEVER YELL
4. never criticize someone in front of a group
5. if you must say something negative, always begin with a compliment (even if you don't mean it and have to lie)
6. never expect an honest answer or a frank opinion when in a group situation
7. never give your opinion first if you want to find out someone else's true opinion
8. try to avoid giving jobs with different finishing times
9. every word a Chinese says has meaning
10. silence does not mean "yes" or agreement
11. smiling does not mean agreement or happiness
12. never assume that because a Chinese doesn't ask a question he therefore understands what you've said
13. raising an objection usually means disagreement
14. never criticize anything about the country or culture
15. always be patient
16. when in doubt, smile

Endnotes

[1] Okay, the headache starts. How to write Chinese in English letters is a mess in Chinese Asia, Taiwan especially. While I think China's *pin yin* system makes the most sense, I don't change words already well known (like Chiang Kai-Shek) but written in a different system.

[2] the University of Victoria and the University of British Columbia, both in BC, Canada

[3] Please, no arguments from Taiwan about people on Taiwan being Taiwanese, not Chinese. Give me a break. The entire Taiwanese or Chinese issue in Taiwan and China is about politics and economics, and has nothing to do with culture (except the petty stubbornness both sides show). When my independence-minded friends in Taiwan are ready to say that Confucius is not the founder of their 'Taiwanese' culture (and can tell me who is!) I will start thinking of them as Taiwanese, not Chinese ... maybe. To my Chinese friends, please, I am NOT advocating Taiwan independence! Mentioning that something exists is not the same as arguing for it.

[4] By Chinese Asia I mean China, Taiwan Hong Kong, Singapore and large overseas Chinese communities in S. E. Asia and elsewhere. These countries and cultures are not identical, granted, but all share the same fundamental culture and, for the purposes of this book, can be treated as identical. All have identical Rules of Communication, education systems and *guanxi* business cultures.

[5] I had help. The client suing me was a Western firm, not Chinese; if Chinese I would have lost, for sure. I also had inside information about the client's case from one of their Chinese employees, my main contact at the client. I had helped his son enter a Western university (writing the entire application) and he was repaying me, a favor given for a favor received. *Guanxi*, the un-relationship relationship. See Chapter 5 for more information about how *guanxi* works. Needless to say, I was plenty relieved when I won.

[6] Chinese Asia has changed since, and Chinese New Year is now one of the busiest shopping times of the year, but my story happened long ago, before McDonalds.

[7] One of my favorite brand names of all time, I suspect Long Life dates from the 50s when cigarette ads featured doctors. While long life (長壽) is a very popular saying in many contexts in Chinese Asia, only the Chinese could continue to market cigarettes using that name: Long Life cigarettes are sold by the Taiwan government. Political correctness is creeping into Chinese Asia though, and I suspect Long Life will soon become something bland, Long Taste perhaps. This happened some years back to "Darkie Toothpaste" which became "Darlie" (still with smiling blackface logo though).

[8] For the record I am still friends with James. I showed embarrassment and confusion, and apologized openly, and he gave me another chance. There is a lesson here.

[9] No slight intended. I speak what I call 'Engese,' English Chinese.

[10] If you can't wait, go to Chapter 7 for the end of the story.

[11] Used to learning English (more than Westerners are to learning Chinese), many Chinese will do further language study: go to a class, learn more vocabulary or buy a book on English idioms. It helps, but does not solve the problem.

[12] This is my first wife. I preserve marital harmony by restricting 'wife examples' to her.

[13] This includes internal as well as external customers. If not familiar with business process terms, just think of 'person' or 'friend' whenever you read 'customer.'

[14] This is a story in itself. The short version is that unlike rich Chinese men (who often have more than one wife), I married, divorced then remarried. A chance to learn the Chinese marriage laws going and coming.

[15] I teach both Chinese and Westerners, in English and Mandarin as needed. I've taught numerous business-type classes, Quality Management, Situational Leadership, Presentation Strategies, Performance Management and Business Process Improvement as examples, but now teach programs of my own design. For Chinese I offer my 3-day *Logical Thinking and Communication* and 1-day *Working With Westerners/In A Multinational*; for Westerners my 1-day *Wearing Chinese Glasses: How (Not) to Go Broke in Chinese Asia*. See *treasuremountain.com* for more details.

[16] Chinese inventions were numerous and dramatic. Three famous inventions are gunpowder, the compass and the stern post rudder. Each of these inventions were gladly borrowed by the West and then used to shape the course of Western history. The same is not true in China; these inventions were not used, and did not change Chinese history. Chinese invented gunpowder but not guns, the compass but almost-never went traveling, and, with the brilliant exception of Zheng He's seven voyages during the Ming Dynasty, never used the sternpost rudder to explore the oceans. Chinese believed they were the "Middle Kingdom," the bridge between heaven and earth, and already had the best, the perfect society, thus had very little desire to try to change what they were already doing, or to learn about the outside world.

[17] I admit this analysis pays short shrift to African and Central/South American civilizations. Grand these civilizations may be though, they had little effect upon the development or growth of Western or world history.

[18] The Chinese rewrote much of Indian Buddhism to make it match Confucian norms, i.e., it was only accepted when it enhanced previous Chinese beliefs, not when it—as it did in its original state—challenged them.

[19] I refuse to be dragged into the 'traditional vs. simplified Chinese characters' and the 'which alphabet system to write characters is best' wars. No hero though, I split the difference, using China's *pin yin* alphabetic system for everything except some more traditionally-spelled people and places. Why? Because I think it is more accurate. I like traditional characters (used everywhere but China). Why? I learned traditional, not simplified, characters, and because many lose their beauty and eloquence if simplified.

[20] Don't worry about being a 'barbarian.' As explained in later chapters, being a barbarian is very useful in dealing with the Chinese. Your goal should not be to stop being a barbarian—futile—but to become a respectful or 'cute' barbarian.

[21] Until the *pinyin* system was adopted (see above footnote), *Qin* was spelled *Chin*. Short of just the final 'a,' this is where the name 'China' came from.

[22] For an excellent account of the role of wall-building in general and the creation of the 'Great Wall' of today, and what it all says about Chinese thinking about how to keep the outside out, I recommend, *The Great Wall: China Against the World, 1000 BC - 2000 AD*, Julia Lovell, Grove Press, 2006

[23] The most famous was Daoism (often Taoism) of Lao Zi (Lao Tzu) and the Dao De Jing (Tao). See Chapter 5 for more.

[24] Confucianism is discussed in more detail in Chapter 5

[25] I oversimplify, but ask academics and China Hands to see my point here, that this is how the Qian Long emperor and the educated class saw China's place in the world. Their perception was the Chinese reality they based their decisions on.

[26] Just an aside to show how advanced China was, even in shipbuilding. In 1492 Columbus led a 3-ship fleet to America. His largest ship, the Santa Maria, was 60 feet long. Between 1405 and 1433, decades before Columbus, Zheng He led seven epic voyages to as far away as Africa. Zheng He's flagship was 440 feet long, just one of his 317-ship fleet (and 27,000 men)! This one Chinese fleet probably surpassed the combined European fleets of the day. Problem was, it was the only significant Chinese fleet, ever, and was ordered destroyed by the emperor after completing the seventh voyage.

[27] China's had three main ways of dealing with barbarians wanting to trade/visit China. First were the caravan traders in the Northwest, the China end of the Silk Road. This area was of immense strategic importance—invaders normally came from this direction—and trade and contact was strictly regulated. Trade was controlled by the Li Fan Yuan (Office of Border Affairs), who designated which Chinese these traders could deal with. Trade could only happen how these Chinese officials wanted and when they wanted it. An Arab caravan leader could not find his own customers or suppliers, decide prices or even goods: he did what he was told, period.

The next group of barbarians was the missionaries. As they didn't want to trade per se, the Chinese considered dealing with missionaries as affecting Chinese prestige, not national interests, thus needed to be controlled by officials sensitive to the emperor's prerogatives. Thus the missionaries were not controlled by the Li Fan Yuan but by the imperial household, the vast bureaucracy that surrounded the emperor. Regulating missionaries was just a small part of the imperial household's job, with much more important duties being currency and food reserves, the imperial estates and lands, collecting salt taxes and preserving the secret of manufacturing silk and porcelain. Nonetheless, the imperial household still found time to strictly regulate the missionaries: who they could see, where they could live and what they could wear.

Then there was the Tributary System, China's tried-and-true way of dealing with the cultures and peoples that most closely orbited the Chinese star, Korea, Japan, Vietnam and S.E Asia. These were the cultures that had borrowed the most from China; their language, traditions, systems and beliefs all were homegrown variations of the Chinese originals.

The Tributary System was based on both fact and fiction. Basically it worked like this, that if a culture would make public acknowledgement of Chinese supremacy, say by bowing to the Emperor (doing the ritual *kow tow*) and using subservient language in diplomatic communications, they would be allowed to trade with China. Crucial was that all the right actions and forms were followed so to maintain the appearance of accepting Chinese cultural hegemony; that this was often fiction, and both sides knew it, was less important than maintaining appearances. Trade and good relations with China were so important that if it took a little playacting at being humble to make Chinese feel better, well that was okay.

Each year delegations from the almost-Chinese countries would come to China, bearing presents and, following the rules and acting as supplicants, would show public fealty and subservience to the emperor and to China. In return the Ministry of Rituals, the Chinese officials in charge of the Tributary System, would grant rights to trade. Not trade as these smaller countries wanted though, not free trade, but trade as determined by the Ministry: trade was held on a fixed schedule, with fixed goods at a fixed volume, all sold through fixed agents, with traders living only at a fixed address.

[28] From Jonathan D. Spence, *The Search For Modern China*, W.W. Norton & Company, New York, 1990, pg. 129. If you only read one book on China's transformation from ancient regime to modern nation, read this book. Read his other books too.

---

[29] Including notables like William Jardine, founder of Jardine Matheson, reputedly the Noble House in James Clavell's popular novels of the period, *Taipan* and *The Noble House*. Years ago at Jardine headquarters in Hong Kong I mentioned to a very-British director that Jardine Matheson had been involved in the opium war. "Involved," he thundered, "we started it!" He was quite proud of that.

[30] Spence, ibid., pg. 154.

[31] This actually shows a crucial difference between Chinese and Western attitudes towards authority. To *kow tow* you must get on hands and knees and bang your forehead on the ground. This shows that you give in totally to the wishes of the authority (be they lord, boss etc.). Think about it. With hands, knees and forehead on the ground you are utterly defenseless, you have no way to protect yourself.

What about in the West? We go down on one knee then slightly bow our head. Can we protect ourselves in this position? Damn right we can! If we see the Lord about to hurt us, it is up quick on our feet with sword in hand ready to fight back.

The Chinese believe a person should give in 100% to authority, be it teacher, parent, boss or bureaucrat, whereas in the West we believe in giving in only partially to authority, that even if a person is an authority figure it does not mean he/she controls us. While this attitude is somewhat eroding in modern times, it is the source of the Imperial Nature that government figures, teachers and bosses show when dealing with commoners, like us.

[32] Here I court trouble. After a fairly-long web search it appears that the copyright for "Situational Leadership" is owned by the Center for Leadership Studies, Inc., a firm headed by Dr. Paul Hersey. When I taught Situational Leadership I always thought it was written by Dr. Hersey and Ken Blanshard (from "One Minute Manager" fame). Whoever owns the rights to it, Situational Leadership is one of the most useful principles I've taught in classes throughout Chinese Asia. Taught properly it—unlike most Western training programs—is not burdened by Western cultural concepts and thus is readily understood by Chinese.

[33] The Ugly Westerner. See Chapter 10 for more on Good, Bad and Ugly Westerners.

[34] I pay attention to the personal part of our communication, not like a common Western attitude of seeing the personal parts as just window-dressing before the main event, business. Paying attention means buying into the importance of the personal in business-to-business relations.

[35] The concept of Selling vs. Marketing is useful in a many areas, not just cross-culture. A common business example would be the problems sales and finance staffs often have over credit applications. Reaching agreement or compromise is difficult because each side *sells* their arguments instead of marketing them: sales starts with the idea that increasing sales is most important, therefore … and finance starts with the idea that protecting company is most important, therefore … reaching common ground is difficult.

If your success depends in any way of gaining cooperation, support or help from other people, the more you are willing to adjust to their needs the easier it will be for them to give you the cooperation or help you seek. *Give other people what they need in order to get what you need.* This principle applies to business in your home town and life inside your home as much as it does with working with the Chinese. If life as well as business is about satisfying needs, thinking about how satisfying other peoples' needs will help you satisfy your own needs is the easiest path to success. Certainly much easier than selling, trying to make people want to help you satisfy your needs by paying attention to your needs, not theirs. Being selfish to gain cooperation doesn't seem to make sense.

[36] I started to wonder about this after a comment made by an IBM HR manager during a discussion we were having about how Chinese expressing negative feelings; "But Greg, you have to realize that Chinese also have a hard time expressing compliments. We don't have much experience doing it." After that I started to ask more questions, especially to my first wife (a teacher), her parents (both teachers) and her teacher friends. All told me they focused on teaching through punishing (though that isn't what they called it), an answer I've since heard many times when I've asked Chinese students about their education experiences. I also discovered that a focus on punishment applies equally well to the Chinese way of raising children, a subject that often causes arguments with my wife as we raise our daughter. My wife says I am too lenient, too quick to praise and compliment. I disagree, and add she only seems to focus on what our daughter does wrong. We probably are both right.

For an academic look at this point see M.H. Bond, *Beyond The Chinese Face: Insights From Psychology*, Oxford University Press, Hong Kong, 1991 and Bond, ed., *The Psychology of the Chinese People*, Oxford University Press, Hong Kong, 1986.

[37] Please, take a breath. I am not saying that discovering knowledge is the only important thing in Western culture! One of the defining characteristics about Western culture is diversity, that we accept many different views and beliefs as legitimate, even if we don't personally believe in them. (In large part such acceptance is due to our underlying goal of discovering knowledge.) I fully recognize that I have given short shrift to spirituality, and that the lessons taught by scripture (no matter the book) are crucial to both individual and societal development. Yet I stand behind my conviction that religion is not the foundation of Western culture, just a crucial modifying aspect of it.

[38] I apologize to my professors and serious students of philosophy. But my words are not wrong I think, just few.

[39] I'm not saying only Westerners contribute to scientific progress, but … divide the number of Nobel Prizes by culture and it is clear that Western culture dominates at least this measure.

[40] The end of history idea comes from an article titled *The End of History?* by Francis Fukuyama, published in the journal The National Interest, Summer, 1989. In it Fukuyama argues that the Western history has been directional, i.e., has been moving towards something, and that the end of the Cold War and the demise of the Soviet Union marked the end of the struggle between communism (Marx) and liberal democracy (Hegel), with the latter winning out. Fukuyama did not say that 'events' would stop, or that peace and goodwill to all would reign, but that actions and efforts would now be focused on making the end work rather than deciding which end we should have.

[41] Yes, of course there are other reasons for mistakes, but almost all are opportunities as well. If a person makes a mistake because he/she has too much work to do, or my directions were not clear (just two examples), then I now have a chance to fix the problem, say by reducing the work or giving clearer directions. In fact the only time a mistake is not a learning opportunity is when a person makes a mistake on purpose, and that is a very rare case. Even mistakes made by sloppiness or not paying attention point towards something that needs to be fixed or a person that needs to be taught.

[42] While team goals and achievements are important and talked about, most performance appraisals are of what one person did, not what the team did. Further, it is numbers, things can be counted, that are normally measured, not 'soft' things like how one gets along with coworkers or how well one communicates. This is a failing of the way performance management is undertaken in most organizations, but that is a subject for another book.

[43] Dating the beginning of the Zhou Dynasty is uncertain. Different dates have been proposed by different historians, though most are within the hundred years between the 12th and the 11th Century BC. Also, many historians break the Zhou into two dynasties, the Western Zhou from beginning to 771BC, and the Eastern Zhou from 770 BC to 221 BC. I leave the exact dates to others; whenever it started or is divided, the Zhou Dynasty lasted a very long time.

[44] Well, not exactly. Confucius is like Socrates: we don't know what either of them really said or wrote, only what others said they said or wrote. For Socrates it was Plato who saved his words for posterity; for Confucius it was his grandson who dutifully wrote down what he claimed he heard the Great Sage say.

[45] The only real philosophical threat to Confucius after 204 BC was *Laozi* and *Taoism* (Daoism). Yet, as the common saying has it, "Chinese are Confucianist during the day, while they are Daoists at night." Confucian thought and rules were used to govern, while Daoist ideas were used after work when mandarins drank and wrote poetry.

[46] I can't recall who was killed, and have no patience to reread the book to find out.

[47] There are a whole series of 'comic book classics,' serious cartoon (an oxymoron I admit) versions of the most important philosophers, Confucius, Mencius and Laozi, the celebrated military thinker Sunzi's *Art of War* as well as classic novels like *Romance Of The Three Kingdoms* and *Dream Of The Red Chamber*. Far more readable than the complete texts, they include the key principles and thoughts. If you can't find them on a shelf you could try chinasprout.com.

[48] Translation is never an exact science, especially when translating specific terms like *guanxi* into English and initiative into Chinese. As these ideas or practices don't exist in the respective cultures, translating the terms is prone to error and misunderstanding.

[49] The majority of my findings are from Taiwan, but I expect similar findings in China as well.

[50] The new generation of Chinese entrepreneurs is trying to change this, but even when a boss wants staff to show initiative, his desires don't go very deep inside the company.

[51] For example, my nephew just started university to become an architect, a total surprise to him and the whole family. He wasn't even sure what an architect was or did. He now thinks being an architect is cool. If only he had a talent for drawing.

[52] This is probably why I have always enjoyed working with the Dutch. I (almost) always know where I stand, quickly and clearly. That said, I have had the good fortune to work with people from almost every Western country and have no likes or dislikes: good people come in all flavors, colors and sexes.

[53] Not that we always (or often?) achieve this wonderful state of clarity. Instructions don't make sense, objectives are not clear, rules are fuzzy, all forcing us to guess, all a big obstacle to our goal: do the right thing/achieve the right result. Every wrong guess adds cost, be it time, money or lost opportunity, an enormous hidden drag on economies everywhere. When I read of high school and university students unable to write clearly, I don't worry about losing our next Shakespeare or Bob Dylan Thomas—poetic license allows for guessing and ambiguity—I worry about all the waste that misunderstanding and bad guesses create. We have an obligation to do the most we can with the fewest resources used; such efficiency depends on being clear from the start.

One more point. Yes, I know that some goals depend upon not being clear, sales and politics come to mind. Yet think about it: both sales and politics often depend upon misdirection and, ah, allowing people to hear what they want to hear. Both professions try to lead people to a predetermined conclusion: buy this, you can't trust him, vote for me. These forms get lots of publicity and attention but actually are just a very small part of the communication universe we live in. On most planets it pays (or is cheaper) to be clear. Moreover, we still measure communication success by whether the audience receives the intended message.

[54] Robert III, Henry M., Evans, William J., et al, editors., *Robert's Rules Of Order*, 10th Edition. Harper and Collins, 2000 (originally published in 1896). Every smooth-running meeting owes a debt to General Henry M. Robert for his classic on how to debate and discuss in a productive and fair manner. Without fair rules that apply to everyone there is no progress, or at least no friendly progress.

[55] This was a Chinese-controlled company, not foreign-invested or -controlled. I owned only 49% of the shares. It was the simplest of all corporations to create.

[56] I don't know how to collect an accurate total of the added costs caused by misunderstandings. If I extrapolate from my own experiences, building my own business, leading numerous projects and listening to hundreds of stories, I would guess somewhere north of 10% of the total contract or project cost. Further, once trust is lost or even questioned (because of appearing two-faced say) it can never be totally regained, which in turn adds huge costs (of wasted time if nothing else) to all transactions.

[57] Chinese language is littered with these colorful sayings, usually 4 characters long, that communicate a big message. You know you are close to being fluent when you can spend a day speaking Chinese without being confused by one of them.

[58] Other than Mozart of course, for I've heard some believe more Mozart = better milk.

[59] see Dale Carnegie, *How To Win Friends and Influence People*, Simon and Schuster, NY, NY, 1936, 1982. While not all of the advice and techniques in this book work in Chinese Asia, the overall idea that you make a friend by showing interest in his/her life does.

[60] Though not as much as the Japanese do. By some measures the most literate nation on Earth (total publications divided by population), the Japanese love to write about how unique the Japanese are. By this measure, the Chinese are far more modest.

[61] I am not arguing for the ends justifying the means! Of course you do not do things you think are morally wrong, and you don't break the law, theirs or yours. But, there is a LOT of wiggle room once you move away from the extremes.

[62] This description of how communication works, as well as many other themes and issues in the book, is geared towards business communication. The principles and lessons work equally as well in personal communication, though maybe a touch softer.

[63] Yes, some will argue that saying *I'm not sure* or *I have no feelings about it* are also relevant, but ... okay, I'll say they are. Yet neither is very useful in a business context, the thrust of this book.

[64] Please, don't get angry. I am NOT saying that Chinese are stupid, or that they don't have ANY concept of relevance! Far from it. In respect of the former, I find Chinese to be very smart, just poorly educated. Relevance, indeed logic itself, is something everyone must learn; no one is born with logic. Learning logic is a hard, painful process. Westerners learn it throughout childhood, answering those damn *why* questions from parents, enduring debates and class discussions at school, answering those damn *why* questions on exams.

[65] This is where my company name, Treasure Mountain Consulting, comes from. As I developed my new business plan (which I still follow), I needed a name. Thinking I would choose a better or 'real' name down the road, I used the words on the bus stop outside my front door, 寶山 (Treasure Mountain) as my company name. It stuck.

[66] Don't laugh. I drove taxi for 5 years to put myself through university, and there is no end to the drama customers force drivers and taxi companies to experience.

[67] *Big Nose* is one of the nicknames Chinese give to Westerners; not really disparaging or insulting, and our noses do tend to be larger.

[68] Search done at 08:22 on August 4, 2006. A Yahoo search returned only 21,500,000 hits!

[69] Many Westerners also seek individual results rather than group or meeting results. Sigh. A focus on group results is the ideal, an ideal not met in too many companies.

[70] My wife and I use "white face black face" here in Canada; one time we use it is with inconvenient invitations. I'll ask my wife, "white or black?" If she answers "white" then we blame our 'apologies' on my schedule; if she says "black" then she's the reason we can't attend. We share being black, trying to ensure we both end up a similar grey.

[71] My continental European friends would call it an Anglo-Saxon (read American and English) idea, not a Western idea.

[72] Even more than sports, think of the celebrity culture in the West, the Top Ten shows on TV and people being famous for just being famous. The West is, if not obsessed by 'best' then at least entranced by the whole idea of No. 1 and 'best.' To paraphrase Andy Warhol slightly, Westerners all want, or accept, our personal "15 minutes of fame."

[73] Empowerment is one of the most misused and dangerous management techniques in Chinese Asia. I am all for the goal of empowerment, granting people ownership of their work lets call it, but only when people are ready to take such responsibility. Many of the empowerment efforts I've seen remind me of giving a driver's license to a person just because they reach 16, not because they have either the ability to drive or the mindset to drive safely.

[74] Don't reward nor punish in public; both are good times for a public secret.

[75] I spent over 15 years consulting on productivity improvement-type projects, from Quality Management to Business Process Improvement/Reengineering to Performance Management to Balanced Scorecard.

[76] My 50th birthday present to myself was giving up project management to focus on my true love, cross-culture teaching and writing. Leading projects day-to-day is hard, a job for the younger generation.

[77] The company operations all were ISO 900X certified, though that did not mean much in real-world operations. The use and abuse of ISO certification is a subject worth its own book.

[78] See Chapter Five.

[79] Lawless in the sense of no system of clear, neutral laws applied equally, not of a society rife with crime and chaos (another book).

[80] Please, as said earlier in the book, I am NOT SAYING that Chinese are stupid or anything similar! In fact, I believe the opposite; I believe Chinese are very intelligent and (especially the younger generations) intellectually curious. The problem is with how Chinese are educated. No one is born with logic; we all must learn it, always a difficult, painful process. Nowhere in Chinese education, at home, school or work, are Chinese taught logical skills.

[81] You can only use the lure of a future good deal to solve the current bad deal when you have a long-standing relationship ... but if you had such a good, long-term relationship, a problem like this probably would not happen.

[82] I put vibrant and loud Taiwan and Hong Kong on one side, and conformist and quiet China and Singapore on the other. Again this is a generalization, and exceptions not only exist, there is a loud and vibrant wave marching inland in China.

[83] My favorite (except for the food!) was "Burger Queen," a burger place that definitely missed its King.

[84] The most telling example of mistaking glacier for avalanche changes was from Mao Zedong, when he wrote:

Apart from their other characteristics, the outstanding thing about China's 600 million people is that they are "poor and blank." This may seem a bad thing, but in reality it is a good thing. Poverty gives rise to the desire for change, the desire for action and the desire for revolution. On a blank sheet of paper free from any mark, the freshest and most beautiful pictures can be painted. Mao Zedong (1893-1976), "Introducing a Co-operative" (April 15, 1958). Quoted in *Quotations from Chairman Mao Tse-Tung* (1967).

Mao's point was that because China's vast peasantry was devoid of culture the Chinese Communist Party could impose communist ideals and beliefs—all the baggage associated with becoming a "socialist man"—upon them. Mao was proved wrong, and beyond lip-service and vocabulary, it is hard to see any lasting effects of the "most beautiful pictures" the CCP tried to paint on the supposedly blank Chinese canvas. The reality was (is) that the Chinese people, in city and country, hold tight to a rich and varied culture, deeply-held beliefs that will take a large, persistent glacier many decades if not centuries to change. Yes, in that time they will begin to watch TV, drive cars and change how they dress, but these are surface, avalanche-type changes, not quite the same changes Mao had in mind.

[85] A follow-up: this bank closed its doors a couple of years later, in part because of antiquated banking laws certainly, but also (so I was told) because of poor working relations between Westerners and Chinese, and because of poor staff performance. The Westerners had tried to create a Western bank, hoping that the changes to the system would change the Chinese, thus lead to profits. This is backwards ... but I never got the chance to tell them that.

[86] The best book on this subject is Jonathan D. Spence, *The Chan's Great Continent: China In Western Minds*, New York, W.M. Norton, 1998. The back cover reads, "China has transfixed the West since the earliest contacts between the civilizations." From Romans to Napoleon to Western executives wanting into the supposed 'billion aspirin a day' market, China lures people into its orbit. It lured me.

LaVergne, TN USA
24 February 2011
217852LV00005B/183/A